Anti-Judaism and
Christian Orthodoxy

Anti-Judaism and Christian Orthodoxy

Ephrem's Hymns in Fourth-Century Syria

ℭℭℭ

Christine Shepardson

The Catholic University of America Press

Washington, D.C.

Copyright © 2008
The Catholic University of America Press
All rights reserved

The paper used in this publication meets the minimum requirements of
American National Standards for Information Science—Permanence of
Paper for Printed Library Materials, ANSI z39.48-1984.

∞

LIBRARY OF CONGRESS CATALOGING-IN-PUBLICATION DATA
Shepardson, Christine C., 1972–
Anti-Judaism and Christian orthodoxy : Ephrem's hymns in fourth-
century Syria / Christine Shepardson.
p. cm. — (North American Patristics Society patristic
monograph series ; v. 20)
Includes bibliographical references and index.
ISBN 978-0-8132-1536-5 (cloth : alk. paper)   1. Ephraem, Syrus, Saint,
303–373   2. Hymns, Syriac—History and criticism.   3. Christianity
and antisemitism.   4. Judaism (Christian theology)—History of
doctrines—Early church, ca. 30–600.   I. Title.   II. Series.
BR65.E636S54 2008
270.2092—dc22   2008006257

In memory of my grandmothers,
Barbara Carran and Sarah Shepardson

Contents

Acknowledgments

It is my great pleasure to acknowledge the many people who have made this project possible, and first among them are my two exceptional dissertation advisors, to whom I am extremely grateful: Elizabeth A. Clark, an inspirational model of scholarly excellence and a compassionate mentor; and Lucas Van Rompay, whose deep knowledge of Syriac language, literature, and history—along with his kindness and generosity—ensured that I could fully pursue my interest in early Syriac Christianity. Without them, this book would not exist.

I first encountered Ephrem's writings in a graduate class at Duke University, where his mixture of beautiful poetry and biting polemic and his unfamiliar Syrian context piqued my curiosity. I became interested in early Christian anti-Judaism through undergraduate work at Swarthmore College with Amy-Jill Levine and Jacqueline Pastis and explored the topic in more depth through graduate work at Boston University with Paula Fredriksen, whose mentoring friendship remains invaluable to me. While I was at Duke University, in addition to Elizabeth Clark and Lucas Van Rompay, I had the good fortune to work with Bart D. Ehrman, Dale B. Marin, Eric M. Meyers, and Orval Wintermute, who continue to teach and encourage me as they did throughout my graduate education. My thanks to them, and to the other scholars and friends who offered feedback on earlier written and oral versions of this project: Lewis Ayres, Catherine M. Chin, L. Stephanie Cobb, Garry J. Crites, George Demacopoulos, Sidney H. Griffith, Susan Ashbrook Harvey, Andrew S. Jacobs, Lawrence Lazarus, Pamela Mullins, Michael P. Penn, Gil Renberg, Jeremy Schott, Melissa Solomon, Caroline T. Schroeder, and Christopher Whitsett. More recently Derek Krueger, Michael Kulikowski, Philip Rousseau, and the members of the faculty seminar on "The Mediterranean World in Late Antiquity" at the University of Tennessee have also given me helpful feedback. I sincerely thank series editor Philip Rousseau for his help through the manuscript review process, Susan E. Bond for her sharp editing skills, press director David McGonagle, and managing editor Theresa Walker for overseeing the book's production. The Lindsay Young Library Endowment at the University of Tennessee made it possible to acquire necessary library resources to finish this project. Any errors that remain are, of course, entirely my own.

I deeply appreciate all my friends and family who have seen me through this long process. In particular, I thank my parents, Carl and Marjorie Shepardson, for their lifelong encouragement; my brother, Randy Shepardson, for keeping me thinking; and Claudine Nagel for her loving support. This book is dedicated to the memory of my grandmothers, Barbara Carran (1921–1983) and Sarah (Sally) Shepardson (1921–2000), two extraordinary women whose graduate educations paved the way for my own.

Earlier versions of some portions of this book have appeared previously. See Christine Shepardson, "Anti-Jewish Rhetoric and Intra-Christian Conflict in the Sermons of Ephrem Syrus," in *Studia Patristica,* vol. 35, XIII International Conference on Patristic Studies (Louvain: Peeters, 2001), 502–507; "'Exchanging Reed for Reed': Mapping Contemporary Heretics onto Biblical Jews in Ephrem's *Hymns on Faith,*" *Hugoye: Journal of Syriac Studies* 5, no. 1 (2002); "Defining the Boundaries of Orthodoxy: Eunomius in the Anti-Jewish Polemic of His Cappadocian Opponents," *Church History* 76, no. 4 (2007): 699–723; and "Syria, Syriac, Syrian: Negotiating East and West in Late Antiquity," in *Blackwell Companion to Late Antiquity,* ed. Philip Rousseau (Blackwell, forthcoming, 2008).

Abbreviations

The following abbreviations are used in this work. Abbreviations of academic journals that are not listed below follow the standards of the *Journal of Biblical Literature*.

Ephrem's Writings

Comm. Diat.	Commentary on the Diatessaron. Ed. Leloir.
Comm. Exod.	Commentary on Exodus. CSCO 152–153, SS 71–72.
Comm. Gen.	Commentary on Genesis. CSCO 152–153, SS 71–72.
CH	Hymns against Heresies. CSCO 169–170, SS 76–77.
CJ	Hymns against Julian. CSCO 174–175, SS 78–79.
Eccl.	Hymns on the Church. CSCO 198–199, SS 84–85.
Cruc.	Hymns on the Crucifixion. CSCO 248–249, SS 108–109.
HdF	Hymns on Faith. CSCO 154–155, SS 73–74.
Ieiun.	Hymns on Fasting. CSCO 246–247, SS 106–107.
Nat.	Hymns on the Nativity. CSCO 186–187, SS 82–83.
CNis.	Hymns on Nisibis. CSCO 218–219, SS 92–93; CSCO 240–241, SS 102–103.
HdP	Hymns on Paradise. CSCO 174–175, SS 78–79.
Res.	Hymns on the Resurrection. CSCO 248–249, SS 108–109.
Azym.	Hymns on Unleavened Bread. CSCO 248–249, SS 108–109.
Virg.	Hymns on Virginity. CSCO 223–224, SS 94–95.
Pr. Ref.	Prose Refutations. Ed. Mitchell.
de Dom. nos.	Sermon on Our Lord. CSCO 270–271, SS 116–117.
SdF	Sermons on Faith. CSCO 212–213, SS 88–89.

Journals and Series

ANF	The Ante-Nicene Fathers. New York: Charles Scribner's Sons, 1886– .
CSCO	Corpus scriptorum christianorum orientalium. Louvain: Secretariat of the CSCO, 1903– .
FC	The Fathers of the Church: A New Translation. Washington, D.C.: The Catholic University of America Press, 1947– .
GCS	Griechischen Christlichen Schriftsteller. Leipzig: J. C. Hinrichs, 1899– .
JSOR	Journal of the Society of Oriental Research.
LCL	Loeb Classical Library. Cambridge, Mass.: Harvard University Press, 1912–.
NPNF	The Nicene and Post-Nicene Fathers of the Christian Church. New York: Christian Literature Compay, 1892– .
OC	Oriens Christianus.
OCA	Orientalia Christiana Analecta.
OCP	Orientalia Christiana Periodica.
PdO	Parôle de l'Orient.
PG	Patrologia Graeca. Ed. J.-P. Migne. Paris: Migne, 1857–1866.
PS	Patrologia Syriaca. Ed. R. Graffin et al. Paris: Frimin-Didot et socii, 1894–1926.
SC	Sources chrétiennes. Paris: Éditions du Cerf, 1943– .
TU	Texte und Untersuchungen zur Geschichte der altchristlichen Literatur. Berlin: Academy Press, 1883– .

Anti-Judaism and
Christian Orthodoxy

CHAPTER ONE

ဢၢ

Syria and the Politics of Christian Orthodoxy

One spring in Mesopotamia as Passover and Easter approached, Ephrem's fourth-century church resounded with the anti-Jewish refrain from another of his Syriac hymns: "Glory be to Christ through whose body the unleavened bread of the [Jewish] People became obsolete, together with the [Jewish] People itself!"[1] Ephrem's renowned choir of Christian women sang to his congregation, warning of the danger that he perceived in the unleavened bread of the Jewish Passover: "The evil [Jewish] People that wants our death, enticing, gives us death in food."[2] Again, after each verse, came the reverberating rhythm of the hymn's insistent, alliterative refrain (shubḥâ la-mshiḥâ da-byad pagreh bṭel paṭṭir ᶜammâ ᶜammeh d-ᶜammâ). Through their own voices, Ephrem, Christian deacon and poet, charged his church members to "loathe" and "flee from" the unleavened bread.[3] In this overlapping liturgical season, he recalled a murderous history of "the [Jewish] People" who "killed the Son" and whose hands were "defiled with the blood of the prophets."[4] With an allusion to Matthew 27: 25, the choir warned, "Do not take, my brothers, that unleavened bread from the [Jewish] People whose hands are covered with blood. . . . For that blood for which they cried out that it might be upon them is mixed in their festivals and in their Sabbath."[5] The

---

1. Ephrem, *Azym.* 19. All translations from these hymns are from the Syriac text in Edmund Beck, ed., *Des Heiligen Ephraem des Syrers Paschahymnen*, CSCO 248, SS 108 (Louvain, 1964). I profusely thank Lucas Van Rompay for helping me learn to read Ephrem's Syriac poetry.

2. Ephrem, *Azym.* 19.5.   3. Ephrem, *Azym.* 19.11–12.

4. Ephrem, *Azym.* 19.19, 21.   5. Ephrem, *Azym.* 19.16, 25.

hymn's anti-Jewish rhetoric peaked in the final polemical verses: "The People that does not eat from a pig is a pig that wallows in much blood. Flee and distance yourself from [the People]! Look, it shakes itself off! Do not let the sprinkling of the blood contaminate you!"[6]

Through this hymn and others like it, Ephrem (ca. 306–373) taught his congregation to distinguish "Jewish" from "Christian" behavior, and claimed that God loved only Christians and rejected the "obsolete" Jews.[7] Others of Ephrem's hymns similarly denounced "Arian" Christians as dangerous heretics who imitated the blind, rejected, murderous Jewish people. Ephrem's congregants thus left his church services each week prepared to see a world that mirrored the ideals of the Council of Nicaea (325 CE), which ostensibly established Christian orthodoxy for the Roman Empire by rejecting "Arian" teachings and forbidding Christians to celebrate during the Jewish Passover. Through his hymns, Ephrem trained his church attendees to think of Christians and Jews as binary opposites, to shun the Passover festival, and to fear contemporary Jews and "Arian" heretics, who should be clearly distinct from "true" Christians. Ephrem's worldview reflects the "orthodoxy" of the Council of Nicaea. The liturgical rhetoric of his hymns, however, suggests that the local religious boundaries in eastern Syria were not so clearly defined. His pleas that his church congregants not partake of the unleavened bread and his suggestions that there were some in his audience persuaded by "Arian" theology imply that Ephrem struggled through his hymns to call into existence a *new* Syriac Christianity, one that better reflected the outcome of the Council of Nicaea that he understood to define Christian orthodoxy.

Ephrem's poetry participated in empire-wide conversations on the relationship between Judaism and Christianity, the definition of Christian orthodoxy, and the theological and political controversies that followed the Council of Nicaea. His writings are, however, strikingly absent from scholarly

---

6. Ephrem, *Azym.* 19.27–28.

7. Scholars debate how best to translate the Syriac word *madrâshê*, which I translate here as "hymns." In his article "Sind Ephraems Madrâshê Hymnen?" Michael Lattke notes that "hymn" does not sufficiently capture the rich nuances of the Syriac genre of madrâshê, which also served an important teaching function in the liturgy (*OC* 73 [1989]: 38–43). The present examination of the anti-Jewish language of Ephrem's madrâshê rests upon the assumption that these texts were pedagogical tools that Ephrem expected would teach his audience not only about Scripture, but also about their community. As the genre of Ephrem's texts is not here under discussion, I will continue to translate the Syriac genre as "hymns," with the understanding that this word signifies the richer Syriac term.

conversations on these topics.[8] From late antiquity to the present, eastern Roman Syria has conjured up exotic, "oriental" images for western writers.[9] For those accustomed to the known classics of the Greek East and the Latin West, the Syriac writer Ephrem has remained an obscure figure, shrouded behind the impenetrable veil of a language that never became a sine qua non of western erudition. Although eastern Syria has stood at the margins of western scholarship on early Christianity, Ephrem's Syriac texts demonstrate his passionate participation in the imperial theological struggles of the fourth century, as well as his relation to his Greek-speaking contemporary Athanasius. The violent anti-Judaism within Ephrem's hymns represents his calculated effort to leave his Syrian congregation with no alternative but to conform to the imperial orthodoxy of the Council of Nicaea.

The politically embroiled and sharply divided Council of Nicaea provided a turbulent beginning to Christianity's imperial struggle for self-definition. Questions of ultimate truth aside, those who could legally claim the title of Christian "orthodoxy" were those whose teachings had the backing of the emperor's legal and military authority. Despite the concrete decisions of the Council of Nicaea, though, the decades that followed witnessed an ongoing battle for authority between those pro-Nicene Christians who supported its outcome and those "Arian" Christians who did not. In their attempts to invalidate their opponents' claims to orthodoxy and equate their own views with the ideal Christianity, pro-Nicene leaders such as Ephrem conflated their fourth-century "Arian" Christian opponents with the stereotypical "Jew," by the fourth century so clearly and conveniently not Christian. Far from a random association, there is a distinct theological connection between Judaism and "Arian" Christianity in that some pro-Nicene leaders such as Athanasius argued that both groups similarly subordinate the Son to God the Father. Comparison will show, however, that for all his similarities to Athanasius

8. Until Edmund Beck's edition and translation project in the middle of the twentieth century, the majority of Ephrem's works were available only in uncritical Syriac editions, mostly with Latin translations. This, in itself, is one reason that Ephrem's works have not played a larger role in western histories until very recently.

9. Edward Said began a critical discussion of this with his book *Orientalism* (New York: Pantheon Books, 1978). See also Benjamin Isaac, "Orientals and Jews in the Historia Augusta: Fourth-Century Prejudice and Stereotypes," in *The Near East under Roman Rule,* ed. Benjamin Isaac (New York: Brill, 1998), 268–82; Benjamin Isaac, *The Invention of Racism in Classical Antiquity* (Princeton: Princeton University Press, 2004), 335–51. Isaac's use of the word "racism" is problematic in the context of late antiquity, but these articles cite a variety of significant late ancient stereotypes of Syrians.

in some respects, Ephrem highlights his Christian opponents' Pharisee-like searching instead of elaborating at length on the "Jewish" details of "Arian" teachings about the Son in the ways that Athanasius did.

In the face of somewhat permeable local Syrian boundaries between church and synagogue, Ephrem's sharp anti-Jewish rhetoric helped to call into existence clear Nicene borders around Syriac Christianity, cutting off from that community (in the very act of defining it) both Judaizers (whose behavior was "too" Jewish) and "Arians" (with a subordinationist theology).[10] Refusing to doubt, even in the face of imperial opposition, that Nicene Christianity was the only true Christianity, and that Christian orthodoxy should be synonymous with the Roman Empire, Ephrem spread his message about the new Nicene boundaries of Roman Christianity through his Syriac liturgical writings. Ephrem's highly nuanced rhetoric illuminates the complex ways in which both Syriac and Greek authors employed anti-Jewish language in the fourth-century conflicts that consumed Roman Christianity.

Defining Christianity against Heretics and Jews

By the fourth century, Christianity already had a long history of denouncing allegedly false Christian teachers and also Jews as threats to "true" Christians.[11] Even so, scholars of late antiquity have long recognized that from the perspective of historical scholarship claims of truth and orthodoxy are relative.[12] Just as the proto-orthodox Christian leader Irenaeus upbraided second-century gnostic teachers for misinterpreting Scripture and warned his

10. While these terms receive further treatment below, they point to some of the complications surrounding naming and identification that this project and Ephrem's writings address. In the fourth-century Roman Empire, a wide variety of competing communities took for themselves the name "Christian" and denied that name to their opponents. In such a context, whether one was "Christian," "Arian," "orthodox," "heretical," or "too Jewish" depended on which of many possible definitions of "Christian" were being used. Thus, "Judaizers" and "Arians" here represent categories constructed by pro-Nicene Christians to define other Christians whose beliefs and behavior differed from their own in particular ways.

11. The following chapter will provide a more detailed account of this earlier history of Christian anti-Judaism.

12. See particularly the formative work of Walter Bauer, *Orthodoxy and Heresy in Earliest Christianity*, trans. Philadelphia Seminar on Christian Origins (Mifflintown, Pa.: Sigler Press, 1996); Original German version, *Rechtgläubigkeit und Ketzerei im ältesten Christentum* (Tübingen: Mohr, 1934).

audience against being persuaded by gnostic interpretations,[13] so too the second-century gnostic teacher Ptolemy instructed his reader against the inaccurate scriptural interpretations and teachings of his proto-orthodox opponents.[14] While modern historians may grant equal weight to each of these claims, early Christian writers themselves engaged in an aggressive struggle to construct and preserve their conception of Christian orthodoxy. With the political triumph—at least momentarily—of Athanasius's supporters at the imperially convened Council of Nicaea, a Christian orthodoxy nominally emerged with the political support to enforce its doctrine and practices. In light of this outcome, earlier proto-orthodox authors appeared to narrate the natural and necessary progression of Christianity in the face of divisive heresies. Such writers as Irenaeus and Tertullian attempted to naturalize and enforce a particular version of Christian "orthodoxy," providing models for later authors. Even though Ephrem wrote after the Council of Nicaea, he too denounced his opponents and promoted his views in a context in which there were still competing claims of Christian orthodoxy.

Not only arguments against heresies, but also early Christian attacks on Jews, Judaism, and Judaizing proved influential on fourth-century writers. In the years after Jesus' death, his first followers struggled to interpret the relationship of their Jewish messiah to other forms of first-century Judaism. The one-time Pharisee Paul of Tarsus describes his disagreement with other apostles about whether or not Gentiles needed to follow the law of Moses in order to join the Jesus movement.[15] Later Christian texts reflect the continuation of this debate, with authors portraying Jews and Judaism in a wide variety of negative ways.[16] Christians adopted the Jewish Scriptures and reinterpreted them, proclaiming that Jesus had fulfilled their prophecies. In order to differentiate themselves from Jews, authors such as Tertullian, Justin Martyr, Melito of Sardis, and the author of the *Epistle of Barnabas* compiled accusations and faults of Jews and Judaism, arguing that the Jews had misinterpreted these Scriptures and rejected the God who had given them. Over time these collective descriptions supported strong negative Christian stereo-

---

13. Irenaeus, *Against the Heresies*. Compare also the writings of other early heresiologists, such as Tertullian and Hippolytus.

14. Ptolemy, *Letter to Flora*. Compare also the Coptic *Apocalypse of Peter.*

15. Gal 2.

16. See, for example, passages from the New Testament Gospels; the *Epistle of Barnabas;* Justin Martyr, *Dialogue with Trypho;* Melito, *Peri Pascha;* and the Gospel of Peter.

types of Jews and Judaism. Such anti-Jewish Christian writings provide the background for Ephrem's anti-Jewish polemic. They also allowed Ephrem to use the familiar figure of "the Jew" more broadly as an anti-type of an orthodox Christian.

Ephrem, Empire, and Fourth-Century Christian Controversy

Ephrem's anti-Jewish writings emerged in the context of the complex Trinitarian controversy that consumed Roman Christianity during the fourth century. As Christianity gained political support across the empire, political and religious leaders battled to define and legitimate one version of Christianity as orthodoxy. In the inflamed rhetoric of the disputants, this struggle crystallized into a disagreement over the definition of the nature of the Son, the Second Person of the Trinity.[17] In the course of the fourth century, Nicene Christians' opponents changed from the followers of Arius, to Aetius, to Eunomius. Yet throughout, writers such as Ephrem who claimed the validity of the first Council of Nicaea leveled accusations that included anti-Jewish rhetoric against these so-called Arian opponents.[18]

This intra-Christian conflict, which began as a local disagreement in Alexandria between Arius and the Alexandrian bishop Alexander, soon affected

17. Unfortunately, repeating the theological vocabulary of these early authors necessarily perpetuates their masculine language for the divine, particularly in their descriptions of God the Father and the Second Person of the Trinity as the Son. Modern feminist theologians have long challenged this vocabulary for contemporary Christianity. See, for example, the early groundbreaking work by Mary Daly, *Beyond God the Father: Toward a Philosophy of Women's Liberation* (Boston: Beacon Press, 1973). See also the more recent discussion of this vocabulary in its early Christian context in Virginia Burrus, *"Begotten, Not Made": Conceiving Manhood in Late Antiquity* (Stanford: Stanford University Press, 2000).

18. The use of the term "Arian" can be misleading, since it has been used in scholarship to refer to a wide range of movements and beliefs, which themselves are not synonymous with the teachings of Arius. See, for example, Joseph T. Lienhard, "The 'Arian' Controversy: Some Categories Reconsidered," *TS* 48 (1987): 415–37; Michael Slusser, "Traditional Views of Late Arianism," in *Arianism after Arius*, eds. Michel R. Barnes and Daniel H. Williams (Edinburgh: T&T Clark, 1993), 3–30; and in the same volume, Rebecca Lyman, "A Topography of Heresy: Mapping the Rhetorical Creation of Arianism," 45–62. Beck used the term "Arians" to describe the subordinationist views of Ephrem's Christian opponents in his *Sermons on Faith*, since the conflict was a problem of the definition of God and the createdness of the Son (Edmund Beck, *Ephraems Reden über den Glauben* [Rome: Orbis Catholicus, 1953]). Compare also the arguments in Edmund Beck, *Die Theologie des heilige Ephraem in seinen Hymnen über den Glauben* (Rome: Orbis Catholicus, 1949); Edmund Beck, *Ephräms Trinitätslehre im Bild von Sonne/Feuer, Licht und Wärme*, CSCO 425, Sub. 62 (Louvain: Peeters, 1981); and the discussion in Ayres, *Nicaea*, 229–35.

religious and political ties across the empire. Arius accused Alexander, and his assistant Athanasius, of teaching that there were "two Unbegottens" within the Godhead—one unbegotten Father and one unbegotten Son—thereby threatening Christian monotheism and approaching dangerously near the Sabellian "heresy," which did not distinguish clearly enough among the three Persons.[19] If the Father and the Son were of exactly the same substance, each one unbegotten, then, Arius argued, Christians would have two gods and not one, a theology that Christian Scripture clearly rejected. Arius's opponents, on the other hand, accused him of degrading the Son to the status of (mere) creature through his claim, "there was when he [the Son] was not."[20] If there was a time when the Son was not—in other words, if the Son were the Father's first creation, rather than unbegotton like the Father—then, Athanasius argued, the Son was not fully God and therefore could not effect salvation for humanity, another of the Father's creations.

In 325 CE Constantine, sole emperor of the Roman Empire since 324, called a council of bishops at Nicaea in order to settle, among other things, this dispute about the nature of God's Son. Ephrem's bishop, Jacob of Nisbis, attended this council, and Ephrem spent the rest of his life advocating for its outcomes. Although Athanasius's supporters prevailed at this Council, it proved to be only the beginning of this imperial controversy. In the following decades Christian leaders continued to debate the language of Trinitarian orthodoxy, and political leaders continued to influence the outcome by giving their support to one side or another of the conflict.[21]

Emperors' participation in this struggle heightened its significance for Christian leaders such as Ephrem. For much of Ephrem's adulthood, for example, the emperor who controlled Syria rejected the Council of Nicaea whose "orthodoxy" Ephrem upheld. The far-reaching impact of this dispute became particularly pronounced with the involvement of Julius, Bishop of Rome. Although Athanasius had been exiled from his see in Alexandria in 335 amid the general support for Arius in the eastern empire, Athanasius gained the favor of Julius and other western bishops. The debate over Christian doctrine soon became a matter that involved the Roman emperors as well, with

19. See Arius, *Ep. Ad Alex.* (compare Eusebius of Nicomedia, *Ep. Ad Paulin.* 3).

20. See Athanasius's accusation in *Ar.* 1.10, 11, 22; *Decr.* 18; *Ep. Afr.* 6.

21. The continuation of this debate is clear from the numerous councils at which church leaders debated these issues in the following decades, as well as from Athanasius's repeated exiles from and recalls to his position as Bishop of Alexandria.

complex political repercussions as the Roman Empire fell under the control of emperors of differing religious sympathies. After Constantine's death in 337, imperial control was split among his sons, and pro-Nicene Christians experienced different fortunes in different parts of the empire. Specifically, Constans, who ruled the western half of the empire, supported Athanasius, while his brother Constantius ruled the eastern half in which Ephrem lived and supported Athanasius's "Arian" opponents. Constantius gained control of the entire empire upon Constans's death in 350, and political favor (as shown in official legislation, episcopal appointments, decrees of exile) moved further away from the position defined at Nicaea. Following Constantius's death in 361, Julian "the Apostate" became sole ruler of the empire. Although Julian is perhaps best known for his anti-Christian stance and his support of traditional Roman religious practices, he nonetheless recalled several pro-Nicene bishops from exile, ostensibly in order to foment further discord within the already fractious Christian community. The rule of Julian's successor, Jovian, was fleeting (363–364), and in 364 Valens, who supported subordinationist Christian teachings, took control of the eastern empire. Within this context, pro-Nicene Christians such as Athanasius and Ephrem had good reason to fear that their "heretical" opponents could "win" and their rhetoric against them became increasingly sharp.

Despite the complexity of this intra-Christian controversy, by the 340s Athanasius had begun to portray the struggle as a clear debate between (pro-Nicene) "Christians" and (heretical) "Arians," a group that Athanasius insistently calls into existence *as* a coherent group through his writings. In and out of exile, Athanasius remained a key figure throughout the fourth century as, acerbically attacking Arius and "Arians," he worked to distill what was eventually to be seen by his supporters as a sharp either "orthodox" or "Arian" dichotomy within Christianity. His rhetoric was so persuasive that in the following decades Ephrem and other supporters of Nicaea aggressively continued to press any Christian opponents who subordinated the Son to the Father into the category of "Arian," despite the new variations in their teachings. As such, Aetius and Eunomius both found themselves described in the writings of pro-Nicene Christian leaders as "Arians," and their subordinationist teachings subjected them to similar anti-Jewish accusations.

In the fourth-century Roman Empire, a legal differentiation between "heresy" and Christian "orthodoxy" became a matter of imperial politics. Long after the Council of Nicaea, charges of "heresy" and claims of "orthodoxy" echoed around the empire as Christian leaders continually vied for the support of successive emperors in the East and the West; their personal fates and the Christian messages that they preached were inexorably bound up with the changing political scene. In this world of political and ecclesiastical turmoil, it could help your claims to "orthodoxy" to prove definitively the unorthodoxy of your opponents.

Toward this end, pro-Nicene Christians made effective use of the charge of Judaizing. From at least the time of Paul, Jesus' followers were forced to consider the complex question of where Jesus' teachings and followers stood in relation to "Jews" and to Jewish law.[22] In the long and difficult process of self-definition that followed, those who came to be called "Christians" developed a variety of accusations, explanations, and reinterpretations that helped them to claim Jews' history, Scripture, and divine covenant while at the same time denouncing Jews who did not recognize Jesus as the Messiah. In the process of constructing definable (and therefore defensible) boundaries between "Christians" and "Jews," Christian *adversus Iudaeos* and *verus Israel* literature portrayed Judaism as the antithesis of Christianity, a dangerous but clear "other" against the ideal Christian "self."[23] It is perhaps not surprising, then, that it is the trope of "the Jew," the quintessential "other" to Christianity, that Christian leaders such as Ephrem used in their rhetorical attempts to distance their "Arian" opponents from claims to "Christianity."

Ephrem's Life, Writings, and Context

Despite Ephrem's active engagement in imperial conversations on "orthodoxy" and "heresy" as well as the shocking virulence of his anti-Jewish rhetoric, both topics that have attracted much scholarly inquiry in recent decades, the details of his life and the content of his numerous texts remain relatively unfamiliar to western readers, even scholars of late antiquity. Ephrem was born around 306 CE in or near Nisibis, a small but politically significant town,

22. See, for example, Gal 2.

23. See the recent work done in an effort to nuance these discussions, and to challenge any too simple distinctions made between "Jews" and "Christians" in this early period: Daniel Boyarin, *Border Lines: The Partition of Judaeo-Christianity* (Philadelphia: University of Pennsylvania Press, 2004); Charlotte Fonrobert, "The *Didascalia Apostolorum:* A Mishnah for the Disciples of Jesus," *JECS* 9, no. 4 (2001): 483–509; Judith Lieu, *Neither Jew Nor Greek? Constructing Early Christianity* (New York: T&T Clark, 2002); and Adam Becker and Annette Yoshiko Reed, *The Ways that Never Parted: Jews and Christians in Late Antiquity and the Early Middle Ages* (Tübingen: Mohr Siebeck, 2003).

then on the eastern border of Roman Syria, that was on the great Silk Route that connected the Roman Empire with lands to its east.[24] Based on scanty references in Ephrem's own writings, modern scholars argue that Ephrem was most likely raised by a Christian family, and so learned about Christianity at an early age.[25] As a young man in Nisibis, Ephrem came under the tutelage of Jacob, who was bishop of Nisibis from 308/9–338, and who participated in the Council of Nicaea in 325.[26] It appears that Ephrem's position under Jacob was as a deacon and an interpreter for the church in Nisibis.[27] After

24. See Sozomen, HE 3.16. Scholars do not know the precise year of Ephrem's birth, but use the year 306 as a plausible estimate. As McVey notes, later vitae of Ephrem do exist, but are not as trustworthy as the passing remarks about his life in his own writings and in the writings of early Greek writers such as Palladius, Sozomen, and Theodoret (Kathleen McVey, "Introduction," in Ephrem the Syrian: Hymns, ed. and trans. Kathleen McVey [New York: Paulist Press, 1989], 5). Others have already presented cogent introductions to Ephrem's life and context. See, for example, Edmund Beck, Ephräm des Syrers Psychologie und Erkenntnislehre, CSCO 419, Sub. 58 (Louvain: Peeters, 1980); André de Halleux, "Saint Ephrem le Syrien," Revue théologique de Louvain 14 (1983): 328–55; Sidney Griffith, "Ephraem, the Deacon of Edessa, and the Church of the Empire," in Diakonia: Studies in Honor of Robert T. Meyer, eds. Thomas Halton and Joseph Williman (Washington, D.C.: The Catholic University of America Press, 1986), 22–52; McVey, "Introduction," 3–48; Sebastian Brock, "Introduction," in St. Ephrem the Syrian: Hymns on Paradise (Crestwood, N.Y.: St. Vladimir's Seminary Press, 1990), 7–75; Sebastian Brock, The Luminous Eye: The Spiritual World Vision of Saint Ephrem the Syrian (Kalamazoo, Mich.: Cistercian Publications, 1992); Edward Mathews and Joseph Amar, "General Introduction," FC 91 (Washington, D.C.: The Catholic University of America Press, 1994); Sidney Griffith, "Faith Adoring the Mystery": Reading the Bible with Ephrem the Syrian (Milwaukee: Marquette University Press, 1997). See also B. Outtier, "Saint Éphrem d'après ses biographies et ses oeuvres," PdO 4 (1973): 11–33; Joseph Amar, "The Syriac Vita Tradition of Ephrem the Syrian," (Ph.D. diss., The Catholic University of America, 1988); Edward Mathews, "The Vita Tradition of Ephrem the Syrian, the Deacon of Edessa," Diakonia 22 (1988–89): 15–42; Sebastian Brock, "St. Ephrem in the Eyes of Later Syriac Liturgical Tradition," Hugoye: Journal of Syriac Studies 2, no. 1 (1999) [online journal], available from http://syrcom.cua.edu/hugoye/Vol2No1/HV2N1Brock.html (accessed 1/18/03).

25. This is the current scholarly consensus, based primarily on vague allusions in Ephrem's own writings, despite later hagiographic traditions that Ephrem's father was a pagan priest. See Ephrem, CH 26.10 and Virg. 37.10.

26. For Jacob's presence at the council, see E. Honigmann, "Liste originale des Pères de Nicée," Byzantion 14 (1939): 17–76; and more recently, M.-L. Chaumont, La christianisation de l'empire iranien des origines aux grandes persécutions du IVᵉ siècle, CSCO 499, Sub. 80 (Louvain: Peeters, 1988), 147–51. For information about Jacob, see Ephrem, CNis. 13–21 (esp. 14); and Jean-Maurice Fiey, Nisibe: Métropole syriaque orientale et ses suffragants des origines à nos jours, CSCO 388, Sub. 54 (Louvain, 1977), 21–26; Jean-Maurice Fiey, "Les évêques de Nisibe au temps de saint Éphrem," PdO 4 (1973): 123–36. Later tradition alleges that Ephrem joined Jacob at the Council of Nicaea.

27. Jerome describes Ephrem as a deacon in de vir. ill. 115, as does Sozomen, HE 3.16, which also includes a later tradition, perhaps an effort to explain why Ephrem remained a deacon, that Ephrem thwarted an attempt to ordain him bishop. Scholars base Ephrem's position as an interpreter on a later Syriac biography of Ephrem (Addai Sher, "Mar Barhadbeshabba ʿArbaya: Cause de la fondation des écoles," PO 4, no. 4 [1908]: 327–397). Jacob of Sarug also identifies

Jacob, Ephrem was a deacon under the subsequent Nisibene bishops Babu (ca. 338–350), Vologeses (ca. 350–361), and Abraham (ca. 361 through the Romans' loss of Nisibis in 363), and he mentions these leaders in his writings.[28] Ephrem's hymns filled the Nisibene church, his homilies and commentaries explained the Scriptures, and he directed the choir of women who sang his hymns, whose fame was recorded by Greek authors within years of his death.[29] Although he remained a deacon, there is no doubt that he significantly shaped the Christianity of eastern Syria.

Ephrem was a prolific writer; he composed hundreds of hymns as well as a variety of verse homilies and prose works.[30] The majority of Ephrem's extant writings are hymns, or madrâshê, poetic metered verses with a refrain that would have been repeated after each stanza.[31] Critical appraisal by mod-

---

Ephrem as a teacher (see Joseph Amar, "A Metrical Homily on the Holy Mar Ephrem by Mar Jacob of Sarug: Critical Edition of the Syriac Text, Translation and Introduction," *PO* 47, no. 1 [1995]). As McVey notes, later authors would look back to Ephrem's position as "interpreter" for Nisibis as the beginning of the so-called "School of Nisibis" (McVey, "Introduction," 10). The issues surrounding the histories of Christian schools in Nisibis and Edessa form a complex topic in their own right and are not the focus of this present study. See Adam Becker, *The Fear of God and the Beginning of Wisdom: The School of Nisibis and Christian Scholastic Culture in Late Antique Mesopotamia* (Philadelphia: University of Pennsylvania Press, 2006).

28. See Ephrem, *CNis.* 13–21. See also Fiey, "Les évêques"; Fiey, *Nisibe*, 21–38; Brock, "Introduction," 10; David Bundy, "Bishop Vologese and the Persian Siege of Nisibis in 359 CE: A Study in Ephrem's *Memre on Nicomedia*," *Encounter* 63, no. 1–2 (2002): 55–63. Archaeological evidence also testifies to the episcopacy of Vologeses in the form of a baptistry from 359/360 that mentions him by name (G. Bell, *The Churches and Monasteries of the Tur ʿAbdin* [London: Pindar Press, 1982], 142–45, plates 70–83). It is worthwhile to note that this fourth-century Nisibene inscription is in Greek, not Syriac.

29. Tradition follows Jacob of Sarug's above-mentioned homily on Ephrem, which claims that Ephrem conducted choirs of women who sang his hymns. See also Michael Lattke, "Sind Ephraems Madrâshê Hymnen?" *OC* 73 (1989): 38–43; Susan Ashbrook Harvey, "Spoken Words, Voiced Silence: Biblical Women in Syriac Tradition," *JECS* 9, no. 1 (2001): 105–31; Susan Ashbrook Harvey, "Revisiting the Daughters of the Covenant: Women's Choirs and Sacred Song in Ancient Syriac Christianity," *Hugoye: Journal of Syriac Studies* 8, no. 3 (2005).

30. Not all scholars have appreciated Ephrem's legendary verbosity. Burkitt once wrote, "What has given S. Ephraim his magnificent reputation it is hard to say . . . It is a weary task, gleaning the grains of wheat among the chaff. Ephraim is extraordinarily prolix, he repeats himself again, and for all the immense mass of material there seems very little to take hold of. His style is as allusive and unnatural as if the thought was really deep and subtle, and yet when the thought is unraveled it is generally commonplace" (F. C. Burkitt, *Early Eastern Christianity* [London: John Murray, 1904], 95–96).

31. See Harvey, "Spoken Words," 107–8. See these discussions of the meter and history of Syriac poetry: de Halleux, "Ephrem," 336–38; Brock "Introduction," 36–39; Edmund Beck, "Ephräm des Syrers Hymnik," in *Liturgie und Dichtung* (St. Ottilien: EOS Press, 1983), 345–79; Michael Lattke, 38–43; A. S. Rodrigues Pereira, *Studies in Aramaic Poetry (c. 100 B.C.E.–c. 600 C.E.)* (Assen, The Netherlands: Van Gorcum, 1997), 110–13.

ern scholars once claimed that Ephrem's poetry "shows little profundity or originality of thought, and his metaphors are laboured. His poems are turgid, humourless, and repetitive."[32] More frequent in recent scholarship on Ephrem, however, are the expressions of effusive admiration for the nuance and beautiful metaphors of his poems, such as the identification of Ephrem as "the greatest poet in the Syriac language" and of his poetry as "mature and sophisticated in form and content."[33] There is no doubt that Ephrem's poems are masterful and frequently beautiful expressions of the Syriac language. In addition to their melodic poetry, the liturgical and lyrical nature of his hymns would have insured their persistent repetition in the ears of his audience.[34] Early references to the widespread proliferation and translation of Ephrem's writings attest to the initial popularity of his texts, and many of his writings survive in early manuscripts from the sixth century. As with many authors in antiquity, however, the popularity of Ephrem's name also attracted a number of texts that were falsely attributed to him.[35] While I have made brief references to Ephrem's *Prose Refutations*,[36] *Commentary on Genesis, Commentary on Exodus,* and *Commentary on the Diatessaron*,[37] I have focused pri-

32. J. B. Segal, *Edessa, "The Blessed City"* (New York: Oxford University Press, 1970), 89. Compare also Burkitt, *Early*, 99. The numerous works of Sebastian Brock and Sidney Griffith represent the much more flattering views of Ephrem's poetry (compare also, Robert Murray, *Symbols of Church and Kingdom: A Study in Early Syriac Tradition,* ed. J. H. Crehan [Cambridge: Cambridge University Press, 1975], which has also been reprinted by Gorgias Press, 2004).

33. Pereira, *Aramaic Poetry,* 110. Compare the much-cited quotation from Robert Murray that describes Ephrem as "the greatest poet of the patristic age and, perhaps, the only theologian-poet to rank beside Dante" (Murray, *Symbols,* 31 [cf. Murray, "Ephrem Syrus," *Catholic Dictionary of Theology,* vol. 2 (New York: Nelson, 1967), 220–23]).

34. For a recent discussion of Ephrem's hymnody, see Harvey, "Revisiting."

35. Brock notes, "Anonymous and spurious works . . . have a strong tendency to become attached to famous names, and it is now known that a large number of works attributed to St. Ephrem are certainly not by him, and nowhere does this apply so much as to the body of writings in Greek and Latin which are transmitted under his name" ("Introduction," 34). See also Brock, "Eyes of Later"; Brock, "The Transmission of Ephrem's Madrashe in the Syriac Liturgical Tradition," *Studia Patristica* 33 (1997): 490–505; and Ephrem Lash, "The Greek Writings attributed to Saint Ephrem the Syrian," in *Abba: The Tradition of Orthodoxy in the West,* eds. John Behr, Andrew Louth, and Dimitri Conomos (Crestwood, N.Y.: St. Vladimir's Seminary Press, 2003), 81–98. I have relied on Brock's categorization of Ephrem's works as genuine, questionable, or spurious ("Introduction," 230–33), and have used the works that he defines as genuine for this project.

36. This study does not focus on Ephrem's *Prose Refutations,* largely because of their primary emphasis on denouncing the teachings of Mani, Marcion, and Bardaisan instead of Jews, Judaizers, or Christians with a subordinationist theology. Nonetheless, these refutations do contain some anti-Jewish language and in a future study it would be interesting to use them to place Ephrem's anti-Judaism into the context of his arguments against Mani, Marcion, and Bardaisan.

37. These three commentaries attributed to Ephrem generally have a different rhetorical

marily on his *Homily on Our Lord, Hymns against Heresies, Hymns against Julian, Hymns on the Church, Hymns on the Crucifixion, Hymns on Faith, Hymns on Fasting, Hymns on the Nativity, Hymns on Nisibis, Hymns on Paradise, Hymns on the Resurrection, Hymns on Unleavened Bread, Hymns on Virginity,* and *Sermons on Faith.*[38] Unfortunately, scholars have not been able to date many of Ephrem's texts with much specificity, with the exception of his *Hymns against Julian,* which discuss the events of 363, and his *Hymns on Nicomedia,* which date to the earthquake in 359.[39] His *Hymns on Faith* and the later of his *Hymns on Nisibis* appear to be from his time in Edessa after 363, and his *Sermons on Faith* and hymns 1–21 of his *Hymns on Nisibis* from before 363.[40]

---

relation to Judaism than do his sermons and hymns, and contain significantly less anti-Jewish rhetoric. For example, Ephrem's presentation of the creation of the golden calf (Exodus 32) in his *Commentary on Exodus* is without the pointed anti-Judaism that he connects with this passage in his other writings. Likewise, his *Commentary on the Diatessaron* glosses over the reference to the Jews as children of the devil (John 8:44) with scarcely a comment, while he makes use of this passage extensively elsewhere in his anti-Jewish hymns (*Comm. Diat.* 16.26; compare also his treatment of John 11:8 in *Comm. Diat.* 17.1). Some of these commentaries even echo Jewish exegetical traditions. Sten Hidal argues that these similarities with Jewish commentaries reflect a shared context (*Interpretatio Syriaca: Die Kommentare des Heiligen Ephräm des Syrers zu Genesis und Exodus mit besonderer Berücksichtigung ihrer auslegungsgeschichtlichen Stellung,* Coniectanea Biblica, Old Testament Series, 6 [Sweden: Lund, 1974]). Lucas Van Rompay and Tryggve Kronholm, however, argue that Ephrem and his audience may have been more directly familiar with these Jewish textual traditions (see Lucas Van Rompay, "Antiochene Biblical Interpretation: Greek and Syriac," in *The Book of Genesis in Jewish and Oriental Christian Interpretation,* eds. Judith Frishman and Lucas Van Rompay [Louvain: Peeters, 1997], 103–23; Tryggve Kronholm, *Motifs from Genesis 1–11 in the Genuine Hymns of Ephrem the Syrian, with particular reference to the influence of Jewish exegetical tradition,* Coniectanea Biblica, Old Testament Series 11 [Uppsala: Lund, 1978]). For further discussion, contrast Paul Feghali, "Influence des targums sur la pensée exégétique d'Ephrem?" in *IV Symposium Syriacum 1984,* eds. H. J. W. Drijvers et al. (Rome, 1987), 71–82; Michael Weitzman, *The Syriac Version of the Old Testament: An Introduction* [New York: Cambridge University, 1999]). These scholarly works also participate in the controversy over the authorship of these commentaries, which is open to some discussion. The rhetoric in Ephrem's commentaries with respect to Jews deserves a full study in its own right, but these texts do not appear frequently in this study on Ephrem's negative treatment of the Jews and his use of that negative image against Christian opponents.

38. There is also a hymn explicitly devoted to denouncing the Jews that has been falsely attributed to Ephrem (Sermon 3 in Edmund Beck, ed., *Des Heiligen Ephraem des Syrers Sermones II,* CSCO 311, SS 134 (Louvain, 1970). This hymn is worthy of analysis for its own (acerbic) anti-Judaism, though as a pseudonymous text it is not the subject of this current study. Ephrem's *Hymns on Nicomedia* survive in Armenian, but do not add significantly to this particular study.

39. See also Bundy, "Bishop Vologese."

40. See de Halleux, "Ephrem," 338. Beck claims that Ephrem's *Hymns on Faith* are from his Edessene period because he includes the person of the Holy Spirit, which Beck claims Ephrem does not include in his *Sermons on Faith* from the earlier Nisibene period (Edmund Beck, *Des Heiligen Ephraem des Syrers Hymnen de Fide,* CSCO 155, SS 74 [Louvain, 1955], i). This conclusion is complicated somewhat by the recognition that while the second of these sermons does

Stories about Ephrem's life circulated widely around the Roman Empire in a variety of languages. Within a few years of Ephrem's death, Epiphanius of Salamis referred to him in his Greek *Panarion*.[41] Only nineteen years after Ephrem's death, Jerome named him in his book *On Illustrious Men*, demonstrating that Ephrem's fame had already spread across linguistic differences and geographical distances.[42] Likewise, in the early fifth century Palladius mentioned Ephrem's help in a famine in Edessa shortly before his death.[43] Sozomen also devoted a section to Ephrem, extolling his erudition.[44] In addition, several later vitae also survive, some even attributed to Ephrem himself.[45] These later stories include fictional tales that Ephrem accompanied Jacob to the Council of Nicaea, and that he later traveled to Cappadocia and visited Basil of Caesarea as well as to Egypt to visit the Coptic monk Bishoi.[46] While there are not many events in Ephrem's life that we know with any certainty, we do know of one specific event that had a significant impact on his life. In 363, with the fateful death of the emperor Julian while he was on campaign in Persia, his successor Jovian ceded Roman Nisibis to the Per-

conspicuously lack any mention of the Holy Spirit in its discussion of the Father and the Son (e.g., *SdF* 2.1–32), Sermon 4 contains a significant discourse on the Father, Son, and Holy Spirit (e.g., *SdF* 4.29–45, 129–143, 159–207). These sermons do still appear to be earlier than his *Hymns on Faith*, though the dating of all of these writings is as yet rather uncertain. For a recent examination of this, see Lewis Ayres, *Nicaea and its Legacy: An Approach to Fourth-Century Trinitarian Theology* (New York: Oxford University Press, 2004), 229–35.

41. Epiphanius, *Panarion* 51.22.7.

42. Jerome, *de vir. ill.* 115. See also Sebastian Brock, "The Changing Faces of St. Ephrem as Read in the West," in *Abba: The Tradition of Orthodoxy in the West*, eds. John Behr, Andrew Louth, and Dimitri Conomos (Crestwood, N.Y.: St. Vladimir's Seminary Press, 2003), 65–80.

43. Palladius, *Lausiac History* 40.

44. Sozomen, *HE* 3.16. Compare also Theodoret, *HE* 4.29. For a recent survey of these traditions and scholarship on them, see Brock, "Eyes of Later." Arthur Vööbus also addressed this topic, but his work is less critical than more recent scholarship (Arthur Vööbus, *Literary Critical and Historical Studies in Ephrem the Syrian* [Stockholm: ETSE, 1958]).

45. For a survey of these vitae, see Amar, "Vita"; Mathews, "Vita"; Brock, "Introduction," 21–22; Brock, "Eyes of Later."

46. See Amar, "Vita"; Mathews, "Vita"; Brock, "Introduction," 21–22; Brock, "Eyes of Later." Sozomen also records that Basil admired Ephrem (*HE* 3.16). For a critique of the possibility of Ephrem visiting Basil, see O. Rousseau, "La rencontre de S. Ephrem et de S. Basile," *L'Orient Syrien* 2 (1957): 261–84, and 3 (1958): 73–90. Brock notes, however, that this unhistorical narrative does point to an actual theological similarity between Ephrem and Basil (as well as Gregory of Nazianzus and Gregory of Nyssa); a similarity that I discuss in more detail in chapter 5 (Brock, "Introduction," 21). See also the following two articles by David Taylor: "Basil of Caesarea's Contacts with Syriac-speaking Christians," in *Studia Patristica* XXXII, ed. E. A. Livingstone (Louvain: Peeters, 1997), 204–10; "St. Ephraim's Influence on the Greeks," *Hugoye: Journal of Syriac Studies* 1, no. 2 (1998) [online journal], available from http://syrcom.cua.edu/hugoye/Vol1No2/HV1N2Taylor.html (accessed 5/2/05).

sians as part of the peace treaty. Ammianus Marcellinus records that before the town was handed over to the Persians, the inhabitants of the city were allowed to evacuate.[47] Ephrem was one of the Christian refugees who left Nisibis around this time, and nearing the age of sixty he traveled approximately one hundred miles west to the city of Edessa, where he joined the Edessene Christian community under the authority of Bishop Barsai (361–371).[48] Ephrem lived the remaining ten years of his life actively supporting Nicene Christianity in Edessa until his death in 373, shortly before the death in 378 of the Emperor Valens, whose theology Ephrem so stridently opposed.[49]

Aside from the details of Ephrem's own life, the wide variety of religions in eastern Syria as well as the region's unstable political ties complicate the context in which Ephrem wrote, and form an important backdrop to interpreting his rhetoric. Ephrem's home of Nisibis had become a Roman *colonia* in 194, though as a politically significant border town it was the victim of multiple sieges, including several Persian sieges by Shapur II during Ephrem's lifetime.[50] Julian's death in 363 certainly did not mark the first time that Nisibis changed hands from one political power to another, but until that time the city had been under Roman control for several generations. It is not surprising, then, that Ephrem also looked to Christian leaders in the Roman Empire to define his Christian community within the limits of Nicene "orthodoxy."

By the third century, Ephrem's later home Edessa also had newly solidified ties with the Roman Empire.[51] After the end of Seleucid control in the

47. Ammianus Marcellinus, *Res Gestae* 25.8–9. Since soon after the death of Constantine in 337, the Persian king Shapur II waged war against Rome. Apparently many Christians refused to pay the heavy taxes that Shapur ordered for financing this campaign, and as a result there was Persian persecution of Christians until Shapur's death in 379. Given this situation, it is not surprising that many Roman Christians chose to leave Nisibis when it was ceded to Persian control. See T. D. Barnes, "Constantine and the Christians of Persian," *JRS* 75 (1985): 126–36; McVey, "Introduction," 12–17. Compare also Sebastian Brock, "Christians in the Sasanian Empire: A Case of Divided Loyalties," in *Religion and National Identity,* ed. Stuart Mews (Oxford: Basil Blackwell, 1982), 1–19.

48. See Griffith, *Faith,* 8; Griffith, "Deacon," 25. See also de Halleux, "Ephrem," 331; Griffith, "Ephraem the Syrian's Hymns 'Against Julian': Meditations on History and Imperial Power," *VC* 41 (1987): 238–66.

49. For the date of Ephrem's death, see *The Chronicle of Edessa.*

50. See Segal, *Edessa,* 14; M. Maróth, "Le siège de Nisibe en 350 ap. J.-Ch. d'après des sources syriennes," *Acta Antiqua Academiae Scientiarum Hungaricae* 27 (1979): 239–43; Brock, "Introduction," 10; McVey, "Introduction," 12–23. Ephrem wrote about these sieges in his *Hymns on Nisibis.* See also David Bundy, "Bishop Vologese," 55–63.

51. For the history of Edessa, see Segal's monumental work on this topic (Segal, *Edessa*). See also, Fergus Millar, *The Roman Near East, 31 B.C.–A.D. 337* (Cambridge, Mass.: Harvard Univer-

region in the second century BCE, local kings ruled Edessa under loose Parthian control.[52] By 166 CE, after ongoing power struggles between the Romans and Parthians for control of the city, the local ruler became officially tied to the Roman emperor through a treaty.[53] Nonetheless, despite occasional skirmishes with Rome, particularly under Trajan, and a few brief hiatuses between Edessene kings, the dynasty continued to rule until 213/14 when Caracalla deposed king Abgar IX and declared Edessa a Roman *colonia*.[54] Although nominal kings continued in Edessa, by sometime in the 240s the Edessene monarchy had completely ended and the city remained under Roman control.[55] Shifting between Parthian and Roman leaders, while maintaining a local kingship, Edessa had a complex history as a multilingual center of cultural exchange that continued long after the end of the kingship. Although Syriac was the predominant language under the kings and through Ephrem's time, Latin Edessene names, local inscriptions in various languages, and Edessene coins in Syriac and Greek, show that by the fourth century Edessa had been strongly influenced culturally and linguistically by the Greek- and Latin-speaking empire to its west.[56]

As both Nisibis and Edessa were important cities on the major trade routes that connected the Roman Empire with India and China; people and ideas, in a variety of languages, flowed through the cities freely.[57] Within this tumultuous political context and bustling route of commerce, eastern Syria boasted a wide variety of religious expression. Here the second- and third-century teachings of Marcion, Mani, and Bardaisan flourished, as even the later fourth-century writings of Ephrem show.[58] Likewise, traditional "pagan" practices in

---

sity Press, 1993); Steven Ross, *Roman Edessa: Politics and Culture on the Eastern Fringes of the Roman Empire, 114–242 C.E.* (New York: Routledge, 2001); and Bas ter Haar Romeny, "Hypothesis on the Development of Judaism and Christianity in Syria in the Period after 70 C.E.," in *Matthew and the Didache: Two Documents from the Same Jewish-Christian Milieu?* ed. Huub van de Sandt (Minneapolis: Fortress Press, 2005), 13–33.

52. Segal, *Edessa*, 9.

53. Segal, *Edessa*, 12–13. In the late second century, Abgar VIII (Abgar the Great) even adopted the Latin names Lucius Aelius Aurelius Septimius, demonstrating his allegiance to Roman forces under Septimius Severus; and Abgar's son, Abgar IX, also added the name Severus to his own (Segal, *Edessa*, 14).

54. Segal, *Edessa*, 9–15.   55. Segal, *Edessa*, 110.

56. See Segal, *Edessa*, 16–17, 27, 29, 30.

57. McVey notes that the population of Nisibis "was a conglomeration of Arameans, Arabs, Greeks, Jews, Parthians, Romans, and Iranians" (McVey, "Introduction," 5). See Amir Harrak, "Trade Routes and the Christianization of the Near East," *Journal of the Canadian Society for Syriac Studies* 2 (2002): 46–61.

58. Arguments against these three leaders permeate Ephrem's writings. See especially his

various forms continued to be a visible presence through the fourth century.[59] In particular, *The Syrian Goddess,* attributed to Lucian of Samosata, describes the cult of the goddess Atargatis in nearby Hieropolis, and the *Teaching of Addai* notes the many pagan temples (especially to Bêl and Nebo) in Edessa.[60] Worship of these deities continued to thrive in Edessa at least until the strict fifth-century leadership of Bishop Rabbula.[61] Along with this rich mixture of pagans and all those competing for the name "Christian," including particularly in the fourth century the "Arian" Christians whose subordinationist theology drew Ephrem's anger, eastern Syria also had a significant population of Jews in Nisibis and Edessa during Ephrem's lifetime.[62] In both

---

Prose Refutations and his *Hymns against Heresies.* Early Syriac texts witness to a multitude of religious affiliations, so that Walter Bauer concluded that "the earliest history of Christendom in Edessa had been determined by the names of Marcion, Bar Daisan, and Mani" (Bauer, *Orthodoxy and Heresy,* 16). Bauer notes Ephrem's complaint that "orthodox" Christians were called "Palûtians" after their bishop Palût, since the name "Christian" already belonged to others in the city (Ephrem, *CH* 22.5–6; Bauer [1996], 21–24). See David Bundy, "Marcion and the Marcionites in Early Syriac Apologetics," *Le Muséon: Revues d'Études Orientales* 101 (1998): 21–32; Edmund Beck, *Ephräms Polemik gegen Mani und die Manichäer im Rahmen der zeitgenössischen griechischen Polemik und der des Augustinus,* CSCO 391, Sub. 55 (Louvain, 1978). The chapters below will also discuss the fourth-century "Arian" Christianity that Ephrem confronted.

59. For a detailed introduction to these practices, see H. J. W. Drijvers's works: *Cults and Beliefs at Edessa* (Leiden: Brill, 1980); "The Persistence of Pagan Cults and Practices in Christian Syria," in *East of Byzantium: Syria and Armenia in the Formative Period,* eds. Nina Garsoïan, Thomas Mathews and Robert Thompson (Washington, D.C.: Dumbarton Oaks, 1982), 35–43.

60. See *The Syrian Goddess (De Dea Syria) Attributed to Lucian,* eds. and trans. H. W. Attridge and R. A. Oden, Society of Biblical Literature Texts and Translations, IX (Missoula, Mont.: SBL, 1976); and *The Teaching of Addai,* ed. and trans. George Howard (Chico, Calif.: Scholars Press, 1981).

61. See, for example, Rabbula, *Canons* 55, in which he forbids those in his audience to castrate themselves, a practice that was important in the Syrian cult of Atargatis. Legend also claims that Rabbula aggressively attacked pagan temples (see G. G. Blum, *Rabbula von Edessa: Der Christ, der Bischof, der Theologe,* CSCO, Sub. 34 [Louvain, 1969], 30–32; R. Doran, *Stewards of the Poor: The Man of God, Rabbula, and Hiba in Fifth-Century Edessa,* Cistercian Studies 208 [Kalamazoo: Cistercian Publications, 2006]; and the *Life of Rabbula,* Acta Martyrum et Sanctorum, vol. 4, ed. P. Bedjan [Paris: Harrassowitz, 1894], 407–9). See also Ephrem's fourth-century treatises against paganism (for example, *Hymns against Heresies*).

62. For Nisibis, there is evidence from rabbinic sources. See, for example, Jacob Neusner's discussions about the "academy of R. Judah b. Bathyra II at Nisibis" (*A History of the Jews in Babylonia* I [Leiden: Brill, 1965], 149) and about Judah b. Bathyra II's "relationship with the *archisynagogus* of Nisibis" (*History* I, 124n; Lam. Rabbah 3.17). Jean-Maurice Fiey also notes that much later in Nisibis's history there were three synagogues in the city, one of which was named for Judah b. Bathyra, showing that the association of this rabbinic name with Nisibis continued (*Nisibe,* 101). See also Yer. Talmud Yevamoth 12.1; Bab. Talmud Yevamoth 102a; Bab. Talmud Pesahim 3b; Bab. Talmud Sanhedrin 32b. Finally, Josephus suggests that Nisibis was a local Jewish center, in that the local Temple tax was collected in Nisibis from the surrounding area before it was sent on to Jerusalem. See Josephus, *Antiquities* 18.9.1. Josephus also writes that in the first century Jews from southern Mesopotamia fled to Nehardea and Nisibis and found safety

towns in which he lived, therefore, Ephrem would have encountered pagans, Jews and various types of Christians. Within this complex context on the geographical periphery of the Roman Empire, Ephrem was far from isolated, but rather lived in constant contact with travelers from the west as well as the east.[63] From his insults of the Jews as murderous, ignorant, putrid, and blind, to his warnings to his Christian audience to flee from Christian heretics and Jews, Ephrem's writings reflect the intense competitions of this intricate imperial context.

Given the numerous religious leaders competing for congregants in eastern Syria, it is not surprising that Ephrem's texts so frequently criticize other groups in the process of promoting his own Christianity. His numerous texts cover a vast variety of topics, from his irenic series of hymns about paradise, to his learned commentaries on Scripture, to his poetic praises for virginity. Even his polemical writings themselves cover a wide array of topics, from Judaism, to the followers of Mani, Marcion, and Bardaisan, to his Christian opponents who call God's Son a mere creature. As the focus of this book is particularly Ephrem's anti-Jewish rhetoric, it should in no way be mistaken for a comprehensive survey of Ephrem or his writings; it should supplement

---

there partly due to the large size of the Jewish population in these cities (*Antiquities* 18.9.9).

For Edessa there is archaeological as well as literary evidence of local Judaism in late antiquity. See H. Pognon, *Inscriptions sémitiques de la Syrie, de la Mésopotamie et de la région de Mossoul* (Paris: Imprimerie Nationale, 1907), 78ff.; J. B. Segal, "The Jews of North Mesopotamia," in *Sepher Segal*, eds. J. M. Grintz and J. Liver (Jerusalem: Kiryat Sepher, 1964), 40; Segal, *Edessa*, 42; Han J. W. Drijvers, "Jews and Christians at Edessa," *JJS* 36, no. 1 (1985): 90. These inscriptions, three in Hebrew and one in Greek and a separate menorah, are located in Kirk Magara, "the Forty Caves," one of several ancient burial sites around Edessa. This evidence corroborates earlier assumptions about Judaism in Edessa during the time of early Christianity, assumptions that had largely been based on later Syriac literature such as the *Teaching of Addai*. See Eusebius, *HE* 1.13; *Teaching of Addai* 5 (all references to the *Teaching of Addai* are to the page numbers of the Syriac text in *The Teaching of Addai*, ed. and trans. George Howard [Chico, Calif.: Scholars Press, 1981]). For the date of the *Teaching of Addai*, see Sebastian Brock, "Eusebius and Syriac Christianity," in *Eusebius, Christianity, and Judaism*, eds. Attridge and Hatra (Detroit, Mich.: Wayne State University, 1991), 212–34. Also relevant is the story of the conversion to Judaism of Queen Helena of Adiabene and her son Izates. See Josephus, *Antiquities* 20.2–4. Compare also Neusner, *History* I, 58–64. For Talmudic references to the financial support that Helena, Izates, and Izates' brother Monobazes II gave to the Jews in Jerusalem after their conversion, see Neusner, *History* I, 60; Tosefta Sukkah 1; Yoma 3.10; Tosefta Peah 4; Pal. Talmud Peah 1, 1; and Bab. Talmud Baba Bathra 11a.

For a fuller discussion of the evidence, see Jacob Neusner, *A History of the Jews in Babylonia* I (Leiden: Brill, 1965); and Christine Shepardson, "In the Service of Orthodoxy: Anti-Jewish Language and Intra-Christian Conflict in the Writings of Ephrem the Syrian" (Ph.D. diss., Duke University, 2003).

63. For a discussion of Ephrem's relation to Greek language and culture, see chapter 2.

but not supplant the centuries of earlier scholarship that lauds the rich beauty of his poetry and honors his position as a saint. As with earlier scholarship on figures such as Augustine of Hippo and John Chrysostom, however, sainthood sometimes brings with it an initial scholarly reticence to address some of the more difficult aspects of the early Christian's writing, including the anti-Jewish rhetoric. These less comfortable facets of early Christian leaders, too, form an important part of their writings as well as their legacy. So it is for Ephrem. While his shrill anti-Jewish language remains a piercing note amid other aspects of his poetry, it nonetheless represents a significant part of his world and one important theme within many, although not all, of his writings. More fully addressing Ephrem's anti-Judaism can begin to bring it forth from the deep shadows into which earlier readers have relegated it, helping to place Ephrem more completely within his fourth-century Roman Christian world.

The following chapters examine Ephrem's rhetoric within his context in order to address more fully the politics behind his anti-Jewish language as well as the effects that such liturgical writings could have had in fourth-century Syria. They begin with an examination (chapter two) of Ephrem's anti-Judaizing rhetoric. Ephrem's extensive anti-Jewish language suggests that some church congregants interacted with "Jews" and the local synagogue in ways that challenged Ephrem's efforts to promote Nicene Christianity. The conflict between Judaizing behavior and the Nicene model of Christian orthodoxy, along with Ephrem's insistence that Nicene Christianity should be the orthodoxy of the empire, makes his anti-Judaizing language particularly vivid and anticipates the more nuanced interpretations of his anti-Jewish rhetoric.

Ephrem manipulates his rhetoric in order not only to criticize contemporary Jewish and Judaizing behaviors, but in fact to reify a coherent Jewish "other" that no longer relies on a local Jewish community but rather is steeped in the language (and authority) of Christian Scripture (chapter three). Using the stories preserved in Scripture, Ephrem weaves a scriptural narrative that praises "Christians" and denigrates "Jews," even as the history itself defines those categories and new social boundaries around the religious communities of Ephrem's fourth-century context. Pinpointing two critical moments— the worship of the golden calf and the crucifixion of Jesus—Ephrem traces two historical lineages: a Christian history that embodies God's promise, and a negative history pertaining to Jews, whom Ephrem describes as dangerous and rejected by God. Again, however, this rhetoric is in the service of his ultimate goal of fostering a pro-Nicene Christian Empire. By producing a description of Jews that depends primarily on scriptural verses, Ephrem creates a template of "the Jews" that he can easily apply to the "Arian" Christians whom he compares to "the Jews." Ephrem offers his audience a worldview in which rhetorical insult and historical narrative meet. Throughout history, Ephrem suggests, there have been two types of people—those who follow God (Christians) and those who reject God (Jews). Ephrem pleads with his audience to flee from the contemporary "Jewish" threats to the safety of (Nicene) Christianity.

Within this framework, Ephrem's anti-Jewish rhetoric encourages his church audience to conform to his model of Christian orthodoxy, rejecting Judaizing in their behavior, and also "Arian" Christianity, which he conflates with Judaism, in their beliefs (chapter four). Ephrem portrays Christianity in Nisibis and Edessa as threatened both by Jews and by Christians who theologically subordinate the Son to the Father, and he uses sharp anti-Jewish rhetoric to invalidate both positions. In contrast to traditional interpretations, Ephrem directed much of his anti-Jewish language against heretical Christians in addition to Jews and Judaizers. Ephrem's engagement with the "Arian" controversy demonstrates his full participation in broader fourth-century imperial and intra-Christian discussions. Investigating similar rhetoric in the Greek writings of Athanasius of Alexandria (and briefly Basil of Caesarea, Gregory of Nazianzus, and Gregory of Nyssa) continues to bridge the perceived gap between Greek and Syriac Christianity. Not only does Ephrem's language have much in common with that of Athanasius, but the comparison outlines more clearly the role that anti-Jewish language played in this fourth-century Trinitarian controversy.

This study challenges earlier academic assumptions about Syriac Christianity, Ephrem's anti-Jewish language, and the so-called Arian controversy. In the face of somewhat permeable boundaries between church- and synagogue-attendees, Ephrem deploys sharp anti-Jewish rhetoric to delineate clear borders around Christianity, cutting out both Judaizers and "Arian" Christians. Through his rhetorical narrative, Ephrem presents his audience with a picture of clearly bounded religious alternatives that belies the apparent fluidity that other descriptions of his context suggest. Ephrem's use of anti-Jewish language in the "Arian" controversy thus demonstrates his relation to his Greek-speaking neighbors, while also providing significant new insight into the complexities of how pro-Nicene leaders constructed Christian "orthodoxy" within the religious conflicts of the fourth-century Roman Empire.

CHAPTER TWO

ΩΏ

Defending Nicaea against
Jews and Judaizers

In the turbulent Christian controversies of the fourth century, church leaders engaged in the struggle to convert congregants as well as emperors to their views of Christian orthodoxy. While scholars of late antiquity have long scoured early Greek and Latin sources for information about this fourth-century religious and political struggle, Ephrem's Syriac texts, which also provide significant insight into the controversy, have not yet been part of the major academic discussions concerning it.[1] Nestled within Ephrem's po-

1. There are, of course, some notable exceptions, most recently Lewis Ayres, *Nicaea and its Legacy: An Approach to Fourth-Century Trinitarian Theology* (New York: Oxford University Press, 2004). See also the foundational earlier work of Sidney Griffith: "Ephraem, the Deacon of Edessa, and the Church of the Empire," in *Diakonia: Studies in Honor of Robert T. Meyer*, eds. Thomas Halton and Joseph Williman (Washington, D.C.: The Catholic University of America Press, 1986), 22–52; "The Marks of the 'True Church' according to Ephraem's *Hymns against Heresies*," in *After Bardaisan: Studies on Continuity and Change in Syriac Christianity in Honour of Professor Han J. W. Drijvers*, eds. G. J. Reinink and A. C. Klugkist, *Orientalia Lovaniensia Analecta* 89 (Louvain: Peeters, 1999), 125–40; "Setting Right the Church of Syria: Saint Ephraem's *Hymns against Heresies*," in *The Limits of Ancient Christianity: Essays on Late Antique Thought and Culture in Honor of R. A. Markus*, eds. William Klingshirn and Mark Vessey (Ann Arbor: University of Michigan Press, 1999), 97–114. See also Edmund Beck, *Die Theologie des heilige Ephraem in seinen Hymnen über den Glauben* (Rome: Pontifical Institute, 1949), 62–80; Edmund Beck, *Ephraems Reden über den Glauben* (Rome: Orbis Catholicus, 1953), 111–18; Peter Bruns, "Arius hellenizans?—Ephräm der Syrer und die neoarianischen Kontroversen seiner Zeit," *Zeitschrift für Kirchengeschichte* 101 (1990): 21–57; Paul Russell, *St. Ephraem the Syrian and St. Gregory the Theologian Confront the Arians* (Kerala, India: St. Ephrem Ecumenical Research Institute, 1994); Paul Russell, "An Anti-Neo-Arian Interpolation in Ephraem of Nisibis' Hymn 46 *On Faith*," in *Studia Patristica XXXIII*, ed. Elizabeth Livingstone (Louvain: Peeters, 1997), 568–72; Sebastian Brock, *From Ephrem to Romanos: Interactions between Syriac and Greek in Late Antiquity* (Brookfield, Vt.: Ashgate Press, 1999). While these works note Ephrem's participation in imperial Christian controversy, however, they do not focus on his anti-Jewish rhetoric and its role in this struggle.

etry is a persistent interest in establishing Nicene Christianity as the religious orthodoxy of the Roman Empire.[2] In that effort, anti-Jewish language plays a critical role in Ephrem's writings, against both Judaizing Christians and "Arian" Christians, in helping him establish the boundaries of (Nicene) Christianity that his liturgical texts try to enforce. Although not Ephrem's only target, Jews and Judaizers were certainly one significant object of Ephrem's sharp anti-Jewish rhetoric.

Christian Anti-Jewish Language

Despite the preponderance of vitriolic anti-Judaism within Ephrem's writings, few scholars note its presence, let alone discuss its implications.[3] Scholars have traditionally read Ephrem's anti-Jewish language as describing only contemporary Jews and Judaism, and as detailing hostile interactions between Jews and Ephrem's Christian audience.[4] This monotone reading of

2. See particularly Sidney Griffith's observations ("Deacon," 22–52).

3. See Darling, "Church"; Kazan (1962, 1963); Kathleen McVey, "The Anti-Judaic Polemic of Ephrem Syrus' Hymns on the Nativity," in *Of Scribes and Scrolls: Studies on the Hebrew Bible, Intertestamental Judaism, and Christian Origins*, eds. Harold W. Attridge, John J. Collins, and Thomas H. Tobin (New York: University Press of America, 1990), 229–40; Andy P. Hayman, "The Image of the Jew in the Syriac Anti-Jewish Polemical Literature," in *"To See Ourselves as Others See Us": Christians, Jews, "Others" in Late Antiquity*, eds. Jacob Neusner and Ernest S. Frerichs (Chico, Calif.: Scholars Press, 1985), 423–41; Dominique Cerbelaud, "L'antijudaïsme dans les hymnes *de Pascha* d'Éphrem le Syrien," *PdO* 20 (1995): 201–7; Benin, "Commandments," 135–56; P. J. Botha, "The Poetic Face of Rhetoric: Ephrem's polemics against the Jews and heretics in *Contra Haereses* xxv," *Acta Patristica et Byzantina* 2 (1991): 16–81; H. Botha, "A Poetic Analysis of Ephrem the Syrian's Hymn de Azymis XIII," *Acta Patristica et Byzantina* 14 (2003): 21–38; Karl Kuhlmann, "The Harp out of Tune: The Anti-Judaism/Anti-Semitism of St. Ephrem," *The Harp: A Review of Syriac and Oriental Studies* 17 (2004): 177–83; Andreas Heinz, "Antijudaismus in der christlichen Liturgie? Das Beispiel der Syrischen Kirchen in der 'Grossen Woche,'" in *Syriaca II: Beiträge zum 3.deutschen Syrologen-Symposium in Vierzehnheilegen 2002*, Studien zur Orientalischen Kirchengeschichte 33, ed. Martin Tamcke (Münster: LIT Press, 2004), 307–25.

4. See, for example, Edmund Beck, *Ephraems Reden*, 118–19; Stanley Kazan, "Isaac of Antioch's Homily against the Jews, Continued," *OrChr* 47 (1963): 89–90; Stephen D. Benin, "Commandments, Covenants and the Jews in Aphrahat, Ephrem and Jacob of Sarug," in *Approaches to Judaism in Medieval Times*, ed. David R. Blumenthal (Chico, Calif.: Scholars Press, 1984), 143. One exception to this opinion is S. Krauss's early work ("The Jews in the Works of the Church Fathers," *JQR* 6 [1894]: 82–99), which maintained that Ephrem's anti-Jewish polemic was a theological response and that Ephrem hardly ever came into contact with any Jews, an argument that was denounced by Kazan, "Isaac" (1963), 92. More recent scholarship has begun to temper Kazan's very trusting read by at least recognizing the anti-Arian focus of many of Ephrem's writings. See, for example, Han J. W. Drijvers, "Jews and Christians at Edessa," *JJS* 36, no. 1 (1985): 97–98; Sidney Griffith, "Deacon," 22–52; Robin A. Darling, "The 'Church from the Nations' in the Exegesis of Ephrem," eds. H. J. W. Drijvers et al., *IV Symposium Syriacum, 1984* (Rome: Pontifical Institute, 1987), 120. See particularly the recent discussion in Bas ter Haar

Ephrem's rhetoric overlooks the evidence that not all of his anti-Jewish language addresses most pressingly a Jewish threat, or even Christians in his audience who allegedly Judaize by participating in Jewish festivals and traditions.[5] There is no doubt, however, that at least some of Ephrem's language does relate to Christian-Jewish interactions, and reflects his concern that Judaizing behavior such as participating in Passover celebrations is inconsistent with the decrees of the Council of Nicaea. Before we can examine the non-Jewish threat, therefore, we must first understand the role that anti-Jewish rhetoric played in early Christian history and in Ephrem's specific context, as it reveals one way in which Ephrem worked to shape his local Syriac Christianity to fit the mold of Nicene Christianity.[6]

Ephrem's anti-Jewish language participates in a long history of Christian anti-Jewish rhetoric that had already clearly established itself in the Roman Empire by the fourth century.[7] With the rise of Christianity, new and signifi-

---

Romeny, "Hypothesis on the Development of Judaism and Christianity in Syria in the Period after 70 C.E.," in *Matthew and the Didache: Two Documents from the Same Jewish-Christian Milieu?* ed. Huub van de Sandt (Minneapolis: Fortress Press, 2005), 13–33.

5. This restates the standard problematic reading of Ephrem's texts. These problems extend also to scholars' uncritical use of "Jewish," as in "Jewish festivals," and "Christian," as in "Judaizing Christian," to describe what is a less clear-cut situation in fourth-century Syria. It is not clear if Ephrem's Judaizers would define themselves as "Christians," or understand that as antithetical to being "Jews." What is more clear is that Ephrem makes that claim about them in his writings. See also John Gager, *The Origins of Anti-Semitism* (New York: Oxford University Press, 1983), 117–33; Wolfram Kinzig, "'Non-Separation': Closeness and Cooperation between Jews and Christians in the Fourth Century," *VC* 45 (1991): 27–53; John Gager, "Jews, Christians and the Dangerous Ones in Between," in *Interpretation in Religion*, eds. S. Biderman and B. A. Scharfstein (Leiden: Brill, 1992), 249–57; Reuven Kimelman, "Identifying Jews and Christians in Roman Syria-Palestine," in *Galilee through the Centuries: Confluences of Cultures*, ed. Eric Meyers (Winona Lake, Ind.: Eisenbrauns, 1999), 301–33.

6. Ephrem understood Nicene Christianity to be the destined Christianity of the Roman Empire even when the Roman emperors were themselves supporters of a more subordinationist form of Christianity. See the discussion in the following chapters, as well as Sidney Griffith, "Deacon," 22–52; Sidney Griffith, "Setting Right"; Sidney Griffith, "The Marks of the 'True Church'"; Russell, *Arians*, 4.

7. The numerous studies of anti-Judaism in late antiquity largely focus on Greek- and Latin-speaking authors. See, for example, Marcel Simon, *Verus Israel: Etude sur les relations entre Chrétiens et Juifs dans l'Empire Romain (135–425)* (Paris: Editions de Boccard, 1948); Robert Wilde, *Treatment of the Jews in the Greek Christian Writers of the First Three Centuries* (Washington, D.C.: The Catholic University of America Press, 1949); Rosemary Radford Ruether, *Faith and Fratricide: The Theological Roots of Anti-Semitism* (New York: Seabury, 1974); Menahem Stern, ed., *Greek and Latin Authors on Jews and Judaism*, 3 vols. (Jerusalem: Israel Academy of Sciences, 1974–1984); J. Alvarez, "Apostolic Writings and the Roots of Anti-Semitism," *Studia Patristica* 13 (1975): 69–76; Alan Davies, ed., *Anti-Semitism and the Foundations of Christianity* (New York: Paulist Press, 1979); K. Frank, *Adversus Judaeos in der Alten Kirke: Die Juden als Minderheit in der Geschichte* (Munich, 1981); H. Schreckenberg, *Die christlichen Adversus-Judaeos-Texte und ihr*

cantly different issues began to complicate the character of the pre-Christian
anti-Judaism that had existed in the Roman Empire.[8] Since Christianity presented itself as the fulfillment of promises made to the Jews, early Chris-

---

literarisches und historisches Umfeld (1.–11. Jh.) (Frankfurt: Peter Lang, 1982); Gager, *Origins;* Peter Richardson, David Granskou, and Stephen Wilson, eds., *Anti-Judaism in Early Christianity,*
vols. 1–2 (Waterloo, Ontario: Wilfrid Laurier University, 1986); Robert MacLennan, "Four Christian Writers on Jews and Judaism in the Second Century," in *From Ancient Israel to Modern Judaism,* vol. 1, ed. Jacob Neusner (Atlanta: Scholars Press, 1989), 187–202; Miriam S. Taylor, *Anti-Judaism and Early Christian Identity: A Critique of the Scholarly Consensus* (Leiden: Brill, 1995); Judith
M. Lieu, *Image and Reality: The Jews in the World of the Christians in the Second Century* (Edinburgh: T&T Clark, 1996); Ora Limor and Guy G. Stroumsa, eds., *Contra Iudaeos: Ancient and
Medieval Polemics between Christians and Jews,* Texts and Studies in Medieval and Early Modern
Judaism, vol. 10 (Tübingen: Mohr Paul Siebeck, 1996); Peter Schäfer, *Judeophobia: Attitudes to-
ward the Jews in the Ancient World* (Cambridge, Mass.: Harvard University Press, 1997). Robert
Wilken has produced a noteworthy study on the anti-Jewish discourses by John Chrysostom,
but although Chrysostom lived in Roman Syria, he too wrote in Greek (Robert L. Wilken, *John
Chrysostom and the Jews* [Berkeley: University of California Press, 1983]). See also G. Richter,
"Über die älteste Auseinandersetzung der syrischen Christen mit den Juden," *ZNW* 35 (1936):
101–14; Fred Allen Grissom, "Chrysostom and the Jews: Studies in Jewish-Christian Relations
in Fourth-Century Antioch" (Ph.D. diss., Southern Baptist Theological Seminary, 1978); Wayne
Meeks and Robert Wilken, *Jews and Christians in Antioch in the First Four Centuries of the Common
Era* (Missoula, Mont.: Scholars Press, 1978); Paul W. Harkins, "Introduction" FC 68, xxi–lxii;
Pieter van der Horst, "Jews and Christians in Antioch at the End of the Fourth Century," in
Christian-Jewish Relations through the Centuries, eds. Stanley Porter and Brook Pearson (Sheffield:
Sheffield Academic Press, 2000), 228–38.

   One notable exception to the sole focus on Greek and Latin anti-Jewish language is the
work that has been done on the Syriac writings of Aphrahat. See, for example, F. Gavin,
"Aphraates and the Jews," *JSOR* 7 (1923): 95–166; Lukyn Williams, *Adversus Judaeos: A Bird's-eye
View of Christian Apologiae until the Renaissance* (Cambridge: Cambridge University Press, 1935),
95–102; Stanley Kazan's four-part article, "Isaac of Antioch's Homily against the Jews," *OrChr*
45 (1961): 30–53, 46 (1962): 87–98, 47 (1963): 88–97, 49 (1965): 57–78; Jacob Neusner, *Aphrahat and
Judaism: The Christian-Jewish Argument in Fourth-Century Iran* (Leiden: Brill, 1971); J. G. Snaith,
"Aphrahat and the Jews," in *Interpreting the Hebrew Bible: Essays in the Honor of E. I. J. Rosenthal,*
eds. J. A. Emerton and S. E. Reif (Cambridge: Cambridge University Press, 1982), 236–50; Benin,
"Commandments," 135–56; Gager, *Origins,* 122–23; Andy P. Hayman, "The Image of the Jew in
the Syriac Anti-Jewish Polemical Literature," in *"To See Ourselves as Others See Us": Christians,
Jews, "Others" in Late Antiquity,* eds. Jacob Neusner and Ernest S. Frerichs (Chico, Calif.: Scholars Press, 1985), 423–41; Naomi Koltun-Fromm, "Jewish-Christian Polemics in Fourth-Century
Persian Mesopotamia: A Reconstructed Conversation" (Ph.D. diss., Stanford University, 1993);
Naomi Koltun-Fromm, "A Jewish-Christian Conversation in Fourth-Century Persian Mesopotamia," *JJS* 47 (1996): 45–63; Adam Becker, "Anti-Judaism and Care for the Poor in Aphrahat's *Demonstration 20," JECS* 10, no. 3 (2002): 305–27. See also S. Krauss, "The Jews."

   8. See Stern, *Greek and Latin.* The beginnings of Christian anti-Judaism are a matter of some
debate, specifically the question of whether (and to what extent) it is the perpetuation of earlier Greek and Roman polemic. See, for example, J. Sevenster, *The Roots of Pagan Anti-Semitism
in the Ancient World* (Leiden: Brill, 1975); John Meagher, "As the Twig Was Bent: Antisemitism
in Greco-Roman and Earliest Christian Times," in *Antisemitism and the Foundations of Christianity,* ed. Alan Davies (New York: Paulist Press, 1979), 1–26; Gager *(Origins),* 35–112; Schäfer, *Judeophobia.*

tians understood themselves to inherit the Jews' covenant as God's chosen people.[9] As a result, from the very beginning those who claimed Jesus to be the Messiah struggled against Jews who did not accept him as theirs, and who thereby threatened to discredit both the Messiah and his followers.[10] Furthermore, those who came to be called Christians accused those who remained "Jews" not only of rejecting their Messiah, but even of being responsible for his death.[11] These early accusations took place in a world in which Jews were a small but generally respected minority within the Roman Empire, while Christians faced periodic persecutions, both local and imperial, because of the perceived novelty of their teachings and the possible threat that they posed to imperial authority.[12] Thus, the earliest Christian anti-Judaism originated in a context of self-definition in an effort to win the title of God's chosen people away from those who already had it. As Christian-

9. These claims can be seen as early as Paul's writings. See, for example, Rom 9–11, in which he claims that Gentiles who follow Christ have been grafted onto the tree of Israel. (Note that in this passage, however, he reminds his audience that even though some Jews may have fallen away from the covenant, they are still able to be grafted back onto the tree.) There is a wealth of scholarship on this topic. See, for example, Karl Ludwig Schmidt, *Die Judenfrage im Lichte der Kapitel 9–11 des Römerbriefes* (Zürich: Evangelical Press, 1947); Johannes Munck, *Christus und Israel: Eine auslegung von Röm. 9–11* (Aarhus: University Press, 1956); Christian Müller, *Gottes Gerechtigkeit und Gottes Volk: Eine Untersuchung zu Römer 9–11* (Göttingen: Vandenhoeck & Ruprecht, 1964); Paul E. Dinter, "The remnant of Israel and the stone of stumbling in Zion according to Paul (Romans 9–11)" (Ph.D. diss., Union Theological Seminary, 1980); James Aageson, "Paul's Use of Scripture: A Comparative Study of Biblical Interpretation in Early Palestinian Judaism and the New Testament, with Special Reference to Romans 9–11" (Ph.D. diss., University of Oxford, 1983); Hans Hübner, *Gottes Ich und Israel: Zum Schriftgebrauch des Paulus in Römer 9–11* (Göttingen: Vandenhoeck & Ruprecht, 1984); Hans-Martin Lübking, *Paulus und Israel im Römerbrief: Eine Untersuchung zu Römer 9–11* (New York: Peter Lang, 1986); Johann Kim, *God, Israel, and the Gentiles: Rhetoric and Situation in Romans 9–11* (Atlanta: SBL, 2000). See also John Gager, *Reinventing Paul* (New York: Oxford University Press, 2000).

10. This struggle appears already in canonical depictions (see John 5:16–18, 7:1, 9:22, 16:1–3; Acts 7: 21–22).

11. Although the canonical Gospels recognize that it was the Roman officials who condemned Jesus to death (Matt 27; Mark 15; Luke 23; John 18), they already accuse the Jewish leaders of orchestrating the trial and of forcing Pilate to kill Jesus (see, for example, John 18:29–31).

12. A number of explicit early Christian *apologiae* survive, and still more early Christian writings contain an apologetic motif with respect to traditional Roman society. See, for example, Justin Martyr, *First Apology* and *Second Apology;* Athenagoras, *Plea Regarding the Christians; Epistle to Diognetus;* Origen, *Against Celsus.* See also Henry Chadwick, *Early Christian Thought and the Classical Tradition* (Oxford: Clarendon Press, 1966); Johannes Geffcken, *Zwei griechische Apologeten* (New York: Georg Olms Press, 1970); L. W. Barnard, *Athenagoras: A Study in Second Century Christian Apologetic* (Paris: Beauchesne, 1972); George Kennedy, *Classical Rhetoric and Its Christian and Secular Tradition* (Chapel Hill: University of North Carolina Press, 1980); Robert Grant, "Forms and Occasions of the Greek Apologists," *Studi e Materiali di Storia delle Religioni* 52 (1986): 213–26; Robert Grant, *Greek Apologists of the Second Century* (Philadelphia: Westminster, 1988); Aryeh Kofsky, *Eusebius of Caesarea against Paganism* (Boston: Brill, 2000).

ity spread, however, the context of Christian anti-Jewish language, and its effects, quickly began to change.

The New Testament records some of the earliest writings by Jesus' followers about their difficulties with Jews who did not believe that Jesus was the Messiah.[13] The books canonized in the New Testament contain descriptions, such as Matthew 27, that have perpetuated negative and harmful portrayals of Jews and Judaism for almost two thousand years.[14] The Gospel of John is particularly anti-Jewish in its language and tone, combining the more common Gospel accusations that Jewish leaders argued with Jesus and were responsible for his death with accusations such as that the Jews are children of the devil.[15] These biblical texts not only reflect the language of early Chris-

13. Although Ephrem was familiar with Tatian's Diatessaron, he knew other Gospel traditions as well. Kuriakose Valanolickal has concluded, "With regard to the question of the text(s) of the Syriac Gospels used by Aphrahat and Ephrem, the result of our research . . . indicates their probable dependence on both the Diatessaron and on a form of Old Syriac" (*The Use of the Gospel Parables in the Writings of Aphrahat and Ephrem,* Studies in the Religion and History of Early Christianity 2 [New York: Peter Lang, 1996], 361). For a discussion of Ephrem and the Diatessaron, including the authenticity of the *Commentary on the Diatessaron* that has been attributed to him, see Louis Leloir, ed. and trans., *Saint Ephrem, Commentaire de l'Evangile concordant: Texte syriaque* (Louvain: Peeters, 1990); Carmel McCarthy, *St. Ephrem's Commentary on Tatian's Diatessaron: An English Translation of Chester Beatty Syriac MS 709* (Oxford: Oxford University Press, 1993); Valovanolickal, *Gospel Parables;* Michael Weitzman, *The Syriac Version of the Old Testament: An Introduction* (New York: Cambridge University Press, 1999); and particularly two recent works by Christian Lange: "A View on the Integrity of the Syriac Commentary on the Diatessaron," *Journal of Eastern Christian Studies* 56 (2004): 129–44; and *The Portrayal of Christ in the Syriac Commentary on the Diatessaron,* CSCO 616, Subsidia 118 (Louvain: Peeters, 2005). See also Sebastian Brock, *The Bible in the Syriac Tradition* (Kerala, India: St. Ephrem Ecumenical Research Institute, 1989).

14. See, for example, Douglas Hare, "The Rejection of the Jews in the Synoptic Gospels and Acts," in *Anti-Semitism and the Foundations of Christianity,* ed. Alan Davies (New York: Paulist Press, 1979), 27–47; Wayne Meeks, "Breaking Away: Three New Testament Pictures of Christianity's Separation from the Jewish Communities," in *"To See Ourselves as Others See Us,"* eds. Jacob Neusner and Ernest S. Frerichs (Chico, Calif.: Scholars Press, 1985), 93–115; and in the same volume, Sean Freyne, "Vilifying the Other and Defining the Self: Matthew's and John's Anti-Jewish Polemic in Focus," 117–43.

15. John 8:44. Of all the canonical Gospels, John contains some of the sharpest anti-Jewish language and distinguishes more clearly between Jesus (and his followers) and "the Jews" who sought to kill him and did not believe in him (e.g., John 5:18, 7:1, 8:34–59). There is a vast amount of literature on the Gospel of John, and on its anti-Jewish language. See, for example, Raymond Brown, *The Gospel According to John,* vol. 1 (New York: Doubleday Press, 1966); Robert Fortna, *The Gospel of Signs: A Reconstruction of the Narrative Source Underlying the Fourth Gospel* (London: Cambridge University Press, 1970); Ruether, *Faith and Fratricide,* 111–16; Wayne Meeks, "'Am I a Jew?' Johannine Christianity and Judaism," in *Christianity, Judaism and Other Greco-Roman Cults,* vol. 1, ed. Jacob Neusner (Leiden: Brill, 1975), 163–86; Severino Pancaro, *The Law in the Fourth Gospel* (Leiden: Brill, 1975); Louis Martyn, "Glimpses into the History of the Johannine Community," in *The Gospel of John in Christian History: Essays for Interpreters*

tian communities, but their canonization ensured the perpetuation of that language. Primary among these earliest claims is that the Jews, as a people, harassed, rejected, and eventually killed their own Messiah.[16] In the second century, Melito of Sardis elevated this last charge in his *Peri Pascha* when he accused Israel of killing not just their Messiah, but even God, a charge that Ephrem also makes in his fourth-century hymns.[17]

The New Testament also contains texts, such as the Epistle to the Hebrews, that explain the supersessionist nature of Christian teachings, that Jesus' teachings enlighten what was earlier in shadow and only partially understood.[18] This doctrine of supersession, the idea that with the Messiah's advent new divine promises and rules replaced the old (Jewish) ones, and a new Christian people replaced God's former (Jewish) people, led some early Christians such as Justin Martyr to define themselves as "true Israel," *verus Israel,* the rightful inheritors of God's divine covenant with the people Israel.[19] In his second-century text *Dialogue with Trypho, a Jew,* Justin Martyr explains to his fictitious conversation partner, Trypho, how it is that Christians

---

(New York: Paulist Press, 1978), 90–121; J. Townsend, "The Gospel of John and the Jews: The Story of a Religious Divorce," in *Anti-Semitism and the Foundations of Christianity*, ed. Alan Davies (New York: Paulist Press, 1979), 72–97; Urban von Wahlde, "The Terms for Religious Authorities in the Fourth Gospel: A Key to Literary Strata?" *JBL* 98, no. 2 (1979): 231–53; Freyne, "Vilifying," 93–116; Meeks, "Breaking Away," 93–116; J. Ashton, "The Identity and Function of the '*Judaioi*' in the Fourth Gospel," *NovT* 27, no. 1 (1985): 40–75; Moody Smith, "Judaism and the Gospel of John," in *Jews and Christians: Exploring the Past, Present, and Future*, ed. J. Charlesworth (New York: Crossroad Press, 1990), 76–96; John Christopher Thomas, "The Fourth Gospel and Rabbinic Judaism," *ZNW* 82 (1991): 159–82; Robert Kysar, "Anti-Semitism and the Gospel of John," in *Anti-Semitism and Early Christianity: Issues of Polemic and Faith*, eds. Craig Evans and Donald Hanger (Minneapolis: Fortress Press, 1993); Urban von Wahlde, "The Gospel of John and the Presentation of Jews and Judaism," in *Within Context: Essays on Jews and Judaism in the New Testament*, eds. David Efroymson et al. (Collegeville, Minn.: Liturgical Press, 1993), 67–84.

16. These accusations are found throughout the canonical Gospels. See, for example, Matt 9:34; 10:17–18; 12:1–3, 14 (cf. Mark 2:23–24, Luke 6:1–2); 15:1–2 (cf. Mark 7:1–2); John 7:1; 18:29–31.

17. Melito of Sardis, *Peri Pascha* 96 (cf. Ephrem, *SdF* 3.359 and *Ieiun.* 5.6; Eusebius of Caesarea, *VC* 3.24; Grg. Naz. *Or.* 5). See also E. Werner, "Melito of Sardes: The First Poet of Deicide," *HUCA* 37 (1966): 191–210; S. G. Hall, "Melito in Light of the Passover Haggadah," *JTS* 22 (1971): 29–46; K. Noakes, "Melito of Sardis and the Jews," *Studia Patristica* 13, no. 2 (1975): 244–49; Stephen Wilson, "Melito and Israel," in *Anti-Judaism in Early Christianity*, vol. 2, ed. Stephen Wilson (Waterloo, Ontario: Wilfrid Laurier University, 1986), 81–102; Robert MacLennan, *Early Christian Texts*, 89–116; Lieu, *Image*.

18. See Barnabas Linders, *The Theology of the Letter to the Hebrews* (Cambridge: Cambridge University Press, 1991); Stephen Wilson, "Supersession: Hebrews and *Barnabas*," in *Related Strangers: Jews and Christians, 70–170 C.E.* (Minneapolis: Fortress Press, 1995), 110–42.

19. See Simon, *Verus Israel*. Justin Martyr's *Dialogue with Trypho* is simply one example of this early Christian argument.

can claim the Jews' Scripture as their own and yet not follow the law as pre-scribed by God's commandments. He explains that the law was sufficient for its time, but that it predicted the coming of the Messiah and those predic-tions were fulfilled in Jesus.[20] After the Messiah came, Justin argues, the for-mer (Jewish) law was replaced by a new law, and the former (Jewish) peo-ple was replaced by a new (Gentile, Christian) people.[21] As such, according to Justin, who quotes Scripture copiously to support his views, the Jews and their law are outdated and Christians are now God's chosen people, *verus Is-rael*.[22] The anti-Jewish language in Ephrem's Syriac writings echoes this ear-lier Greek rhetoric.

The second-century *Epistle of Barnabas* takes this replacement argument to an extreme and claims that in fact the Jews were never the rightful inheri-tors of God's covenant, because at the very moment in which Moses received the covenant on Mt. Sinai, the Jews had already broken it through their cre-ation and worship of the golden calf at the foot of the mountain.[23] The *Epis-tle of Barnabas* twice describes God's giving of the covenant to Moses, and

---

20. These ideas are throughout Justin Martyr, *Dial.* On Justin and Judaism, see A. von Har-nack, "Judentum und Judenchristentum in Justin Dialog mit Trypho," *TU* 39 (1913): 47–98; See L. W. Barnard, "The Old Testament and Judaism in the Writings of Justin Martyr," *VT* 14 (1964): 395–406; L. W. Barnard, *Justin Martyr: His Life and Thought* (Cambridge: Cambridge University Press, 1966); B. Z. Bokser, "Justin Martyr and the Jews," *JQR* 64 (1973–74): 97–122, 204–11; P. J. Donahue, "Jewish Christian Controversy in the Second Century" (Ph.D. diss., Yale University, 1977); H. Remus, "Justin Martyr's Argument with Judaism," in *Anti-Judaism in Early Christian-ity*, vol. 2, ed. Stephen Wilson (Waterloo, Ontario: Wilfrid Laurier University, 1986), 59–80; Ma-cLennan, *Texts*, 49–88; Martin Hengel, "The Septuagint as a Collection of Writings Claimed by Christians: Justin and the Church Fathers before Origen," in *Jews and Christians: The Parting of the Ways*, ed. James Dunn (Grand Rapids: Eerdmans, 1992), 39–83; and in the same volume, Wil-liam Horbury, "Jewish-Christian Relations in Barnabas and Justin Martyr," 315–45; Stephen Wil-son, "Dialogue and Dispute: Justin," in *Related Strangers: Jews and Christians, 70–170 C.E.* (Min-neapolis: Fortress Press, 1995), 258–84; Graham Harvey, *The True Israel: Uses of the Names Jew, Hebrew and Israel in Ancient Jewish and Early Christian Literature* (New York: Brill, 1996), 253–354; Lieu, *Image*; Marc Hirshman, "The Exegetical Debate: Justin Martyr and the *Dialogue with Try-pho the Jew*," in *A Rivalry of Genius: Jewish and Christian Biblical Interpretation in Late Antiquity*, trans. Batya Stein (Albany: SUNY Press, 1996), 31–41; Tessa Rajak, "Talking at Trypho," in *Apol-ogetics in the Roman Empire*, eds. Mark Edwards et al. (Oxford: Oxford University Press, 2000), 59–80.

21. See, for example, Justin Martyr, *Dial.* 11, 12, 14, 34, 117, 118, 122.

22. See Justin Martyr, *Dial.* 125, 135.

23. *Ep. Barn.* 4, 14 (Ex 32). See, for example, S. Lowy, "The Confrontation of Judaism in the Epistle of Barnabas," *JJS* 11 (1960): 1–33; L. W. Barnard, "Is the Epistle of Barnabas a Paschal Homily?" *VC* 15 (1961): 8–22; MacLennan, *Texts*, 21–48; Horbury, "Jewish-Christian," 315–45; Har-vey, *True Israel*, 251–53. Some later texts, such as the *Didascalia* and some of Ephrem's writings, also reflect this narrative, as discussed in chapter 3.

both times highlights the error of the people who made the golden calf.[24] The epistle goes so far as to claim that God made a covenant with Moses, but the people were not worthy to receive it.[25] As a result, the epistle describes, God's covenant belongs not with Jews but with Christians.[26] Ephrem later offers a version of this argument in his own presentation of the significance of the golden calf incident in the history of the Jews.

Early Greek Christian texts further described Jews in a variety of negative ways, including the frequent stereotypes that they were blind and carnal, in contrast to the spiritual clarity of Christians.[27] The accusations that Jews were, to their detriment, focused on the flesh instead of the spirit was a recurring theme in early Christian writings that had a dual meaning: Christians accused Jews of mistakenly trying to please God through physical actions instead of spiritual faith, and many Christians also accused Jews of (mis)interpreting the Scriptures literally instead of spiritually, or allegorically.[28] In addition, early Christian writers claimed that Jews acted against God,[29] and did not recognize the Messiah when he came.[30] Texts such as these provide the background for Ephrem's fourth-century writings, which echo so many of these early accusations.

Judaizing and Fourth-Century
Christian Orthodoxy

With Constantine's support, in the early fourth century Christianity gained a political power that it had not previously had. As a result, anti-Jewish rhetoric that had begun as forceful statements of self-definition against a more respected and more integrated group quickly became the means as well as the

24. *Ep. Barn.* 4, 14.
25. *Ep. Barn.* 14.1, 4.
26. *Ep. Barn.* 4.8, 14.4 (cf. Justin Martyr, *Dial.* 12).
27. See, for example, Justin Martyr, *Dial.* 97, 112, 123; *Didascalia* 21, 26. See also Daniel Boyarin, *Carnal Israel: Reading Sex in Talmudic Culture* (Berkeley: University of California Press, 1993); David Brakke, "Jewish Flesh and Christian Spirit in Athanasius of Alexandria," *JECS* 9, no. 4 (2001): 453–81.
28. Justin Martyr, *Dial.* 12, 14, 16, 18, 44, 135; *Ep. Barn.* 10; Origen, *Comm. Jn.* 1.1, 1.9.
29. Origen, *C. Cels.* 1.15; *Didascalia* 21, 26.
30. Justin Martyr, *First Apol.* 36, 49; *Didascalia* 21, 26. See also the list of insults listed in Jean Juster, *Les juifs dans l'empire romain: Leur condition juridique, économique, et sociale,* vol. 1 (Paris: Paul Geuthner Library, 1914), 44–48; as well as G. Stanton, "Aspects of Early Christian-Jewish Polemic and Apologetic," *NTS* 31 (1985): 377–92.

justification for Christian persecution of Jews. It was in this fourth-century setting of newly Christian political power that Ephrem and his contemporaries wrote their anti-Jewish polemic. With the establishment of a politically dominant orthodoxy at the Council of Nicaea (325), Christian Judaizing, associated largely with the easternmost parts of the Roman Empire, became a problematic breach of that orthodoxy. Many of the early fourth-century discussions concerning Judaizing focus on holidays, particularly the overlapping traditions of Easter, Passover, and the Feast of Unleavened Bread.[31] The date of the Easter celebration, and its relation to Passover, was a highly charged issue, and many early Christian communities initially celebrated Easter on 14 Nisan, the day of the Passover celebration, and only later changed to the first Sunday after 14 Nisan.[32]

In his *Life of Constantine,* Eusebius of Caesarea recreates a letter that Constantine allegedly distributed after the Council of Nicaea.[33] In Eusebius's narration, this letter urges Christians around the empire to unite, and mentions particularly the importance of celebrating Easter on the same day, which must *not* be the day of the Jews' festival celebration.[34] This letter's negative descriptions of the Jews are consistent with Ephrem's hostile language, both driven by the urgency to make Judaism and its practices clearly unappealing and unacceptable to anyone claiming the name "Christian." Specifically, this letter claims that it is in the eastern parts of the empire that this would be a concern, whereas Christians in the other parts of the empire already follow the Easter practices specified at the Council of Nicaea.[35] The Council of

31. The problem of identifying the days of Jesus' death and resurrection goes back at least as far as the writing of the canonical Gospels, which disagree about whether Jesus' last supper on the evening before he was killed was a Passover meal (Matt 26, Mark 14, Luke 22), or whether he was killed on the day of the upcoming Passover meal (John 19).

32. See Wolfgang Huber, *Passa und Ostern: Untersuchungen zur Osterfeier der alten Kirche* (Berlin, 1969); Stephen Wilson, "Passover, Easter, and Anti-Judaism: Melito of Sardis and Others," in *"To See Ourselves as Others See Us": Christians, Jews, "Others" in Late Antiquity,* eds. Jacob Neusner and Ernest Frerichs (Chico, Calif.: Scholars Press, 1985), 337–55. See also J. Gribomont, "Le triomphe de Pâques d'après S. Ephrem," *PdO* 4 (1973): 147–89; J. Gribomont, "La tradition liturgique des Hymnes Pascales de Saint Ephrem," *PdO* 4 (1973): 191–246; Edmund Beck, "Das Bild vom Sauerteig bei Ephräm," *OC* 63 (1979): 1–19; Pierre Yousif, "Les controverses de S. Ephrem sur l'Eucharistie," *Euntes Docete* 33 (1980): 405–26; Pierre Yousif, "Le sacrifice et l'offrande chez Saint Ephrem de Nisibe," *PdO* 15 (1988–89): 21–40; Dominique Cerbelaud, "L'antijudaïsme dans les Hymnes de Pascha d'Ephrem le Syrien," *PdO* 20 (1995): 201–7.

33. Eusebius, *VC* 3.17–20.

34. Eusebius, *VC* 3.18. See also S. Bacchiocchi, *Anti-Judaism and the Origin of Sunday* (Rome, 1975), 86.

35. Eusebius, *VC* 3.19. For further evidence, see also the *Didascalia* 21 (and Rouwhorst, *Les*

Antioch (341 CE) also refers to this Nicene decision in the act of suggesting that church leaders in the East must do even more to make sure that their churches uphold this Nicene injunction.[36] Even as this later council acknowledges the decision at Nicaea that Eusebius describes, canon one implies that in 341 some eastern churches continued to celebrate Easter on 14 Nisan. As this council took place in Syria in the city of Antioch, there is little doubt that Ephrem would have been aware of its decrees. As the discussion below on his *Hymns on Unleavened Bread* shows, his hymns contain rhetoric that addresses precisely this issue with the same goal of making his Syrian congregation conform with the guidelines of Nicaea. Judging by the Council of Antioch and Ephrem's arguments in Hymn 19, Constantine's imperial command that "Christians" should not celebrate on 14 Nisan with the Jews was slow to take effect fully in parts of the eastern empire.

That Ephrem is intent on doing his part to enforce Nicene (and the later Council of Antioch's) injunctions against being too "Jewish" is perhaps nowhere more clear than in his *Hymns on Unleavened Bread*. In this series of hymns, Ephrem castigates members of his church audience for participating in a festival at the synagogue, and he struggles to draw clear lines between "Jews" and "Christians" and to identify proper "Christian" behavior, such that it coincides with the outcome of the Council of Nicaea.[37] In the process, Ephrem relies on vitriolic anti-Jewish language to persuade his audience of the validity of his claims.

A broad study of Ephrem's rhetoric must necessarily cover scattered phrases and metaphors from a large number of different texts. Nonetheless, in relying on excerpted phrases from numerous different texts written over the course of several decades in two different locations, such a study risks losing touch with Ephrem's hymns as a whole, as his audience would have heard and sung them. Number nineteen of Ephrem's *Hymns on Unleavened Bread* in-

---

hymnes pascales d'Ephrem de Nisibe: Analyse théologique et recherché sur l'évolution de la fête pascale chrétienne à Nisibe et à Edesse et dans quelques églises voisines au quatrième siècle, Supplement to *VC* 7, no. 1/2 [New York: Brill, 1989], 157–93); Aphrahat, *Dem.* 12; Ephrem, *Azym.;* John Chrysostom, *Discourses against Judaizing Christians* 3; Wilson, "Passover," 338–43; Rouwhorst, "Jewish Liturgical Traditions in Early Syriac Christianity," *VC* 51 (1997): 81–82.

36. *Canons of the Council of Antioch,* Canon 1. Compare also Canon 7 (8) of *The Apostolic Canons.*

37. Ephrem's rhetoric reflects Boyarin's observations regarding the imposition from above of clear borders onto what was on the ground a much more complex situation. See Daniel Boyarin, *Border Lines: The Partition of Judaeo-Christianity* (Philadelphia: University of Pennsylvania Press, 2004).

troduces how in this one hymn Ephrem attempts to enforce Nicene behavior for a church congregation that appears to have had more interaction with local Jews than Ephrem claims the Nicene decisions allow. In order to convey the urgency of his message, he uses different rhetorical tools to convey negative ideas about Jews and Judaism, and their relation to those in his audience, and to create a strong image of the depravity of contemporary Jews and the threat that they pose to his community. It is useful to keep in mind that the refrain of this hymn would have been repeated after each line:

Refrain: Glory be to Christ through whose body the unleavened bread of the People became obsolete, together with the People itself.

1. The lamb of Truth arose and broke his body for the innocent ones who ate the lamb of Passover.

2. The paschal lamb he slaughtered and ate, and he broke his body. He caused the shadow to pass over and he provided the Truth.

3. He had eaten the unleavened bread. Within the unleavened bread his body became for us the unleavened bread of Truth.

4. The symbol that ran from the days of Moses until there, was ended there.

5. But the evil People that wants our death, enticing, gives us death in food.

6. Desirable was the tree that Eve saw, and equally desirable is the unleavened bread.

7. From that desirable [tree], a manifest death; in the beautiful unleavened bread, a concealed death.

8. Although the dead lion was impure, its bitterness gave sweetness [Judges 14:8–9].

9. In the bitter lion, beautiful honey; in the sweet unleavened bread, the bitterness of death.

10. On account of its symbol, the angels yearned for that unleavened bread that Sara had baked [Genesis 18:1–15].

11. Loathe the unleavened bread, you, my brothers, in which the symbol of Iscariot dwells!

12. Moreover, flee, my brothers, from the unleavened bread because stench dwells within its purity.

13. For that putrid reputation that Moses described indeed dwells in the purity of that unleavened bread.

14. Garlic and onions the People had desired [Numbers 11:5]. Their unleavened bread itself stank, together with the eating of it.

15. From the impure ravens Elijah took loaves, because he knew that they were pure [1 Kings 17:6].[38]

16. Do not take, my brothers, that unleavened bread from the People whose hands are covered with blood,

17. Lest it cling to that unleavened bread from that filth that fills their hands.

18. Although flesh is pure, no one eats from that which was sacrificed [to idols], because it is unclean.

19. How impure therefore is that unleavened bread that the hands that killed the Son kneaded!

20. The hand that is defiled with the blood of animals, one is loathe to take food from that [hand].

21. Who would therefore take from that hand that is completely defiled with the blood of the prophets?

22. Let us not eat, my brothers, along with the drug of life the unleavened bread of the People as a deadly drug.[39]

23. For the blood of Christ mixes in and dwells in the unleavened bread of the People and in our [Eucharist] offering.

24. The one who received it in our [Eucharist] offering received the drug of life. The one who ate it with the People received a deadly drug.

25. For that blood for which they cried out that it might be upon them is mixed in their festivals and in their Sabbaths.

26. And whoever is joined together in their festivals, to that one the sprinkling of the blood also comes.

27. The People that does not eat from a pig is a pig that wallows in much blood.

28. Flee and distance yourself from [the People]! Look, it shakes itself off! Do not let the sprinkling of the blood contaminate you![40]

---

38. Compare also Ephrem, *Comm. Diat.* 7.13.

39. Compare Ignatius of Antioch's earlier language of the Eucharist as a life-giving drug in contrast to a deadly drug (*Ep. Trall.* 6, 11; *Ep. Eph.* 20). See also Sebastian Brock, *The Luminous Eye: The Spiritual World Vision of Saint Ephrem the Syrian* (Kalamazoo: Cistercian Publications, 1985), 99–103. Like the Greek *pharmakon*, the Syriac word for drug [*sammâ*] can be used either positively to mean "medicine" or negatively to mean "poison." In this hymn (and elsewhere), Ephrem takes advantage of this dual meaning to use the word positively in reference to the Christian Eucharist and negatively in reference to the unleavened bread of the Jews. Ephrem frequently employs the metaphor of a physician. See Brock, *Luminous*, 40, 99–103; Tryggve Kronholm, "Abraham, the Physician: The Image of Abraham the Patriarch in the Genuine Hymns of Ephraem Syrus," in *Solving Riddles and Untying Knots,* eds. Ziony Zevit et al. (Winona Lake, Ind.: Eisenbrauns, 1995), 107–15.

40. Ephrem, *Azym.* 19. All translations from these hymns are from the Syriac text in Edmund Beck, ed., *Des Heiligen Ephraem des Syrers Paschahymnen,* CSCO 248, SS 108 (Louvain, 1964).

In this hymn Ephrem touts some of the most vitriolic anti-Jewish imagery in his repertoire, combining the insulting images of the Jews as an evil and rejected people that stinks like garlic and onions with explicit warnings about the deadly threat that the Jews pose to those who would partake of the Christian Eucharist in his church. Ephrem here uses derogatory language to describe the Jews, and then places the Jews in sharp contrast to Christians. Jews eat unleavened bread, which is "a deadly drug," while Christians eat the Eucharist offering, which is the "drug of life"; the shadows have passed and (Christian) truth has arrived.

The final lines of this hymn reflect the vitriolic anti-Jewish language to which Ephrem sometimes resorts in his struggle to define Christianity and Judaism as distinct from one another and to persuade his audience that only Christianity is acceptable. In verses 25–28 Ephrem echoes the Jews' cry in Matthew 27:25 for Jesus' blood to be on them and on their children, and he warns his audience about the danger of the blood-contaminated Jews and their unleavened bread.[41] Here Ephrem combines New Testament "history" with the violent imagery of the blood-soaked hands of the Jews, sprayed by the blood of the sacrificed Christ.[42] For Ephrem, however, this is hardly only a literary creation, or even distant history. Just as Christ's blood is ever-present for Christians in the Eucharist, in the same way Ephrem claims Christ's blood forever contaminates the hands of the Jews and the unleavened bread that their hands knead. Ephrem tells his audience that the Jews

---

41. Ephrem, *Azym.* 19.25–28.

42. The relation between narrative and history is, of course, highly nuanced. The work of Hayden White has helped decades of scholars rethink this connection. See, for example, Hayden White, *Metahistory: The Historical Imagination in Nineteenth-Century Europe* (Baltimore: Johns Hopkins University Press, 1973); *Tropics of Discourse: Essays in Cultural Criticism* (Baltimore: Johns Hopkins University Press, 1978); *The Content of the Form: Narrative Discourse and Historical Representation* (Baltimore: Johns Hopkins University Press, 1987); *Figural Realism: Studies in the Mimesis Effect* (Baltimore: Johns Hopkins University Press, 1999). Likewise, more recent works have deepened this discussion, noting the ways in which authors construct contemporary history, and later historians in turn weave those histories into new narratives. See for example, works such as Michel de Certeau, *The Writing of History,* trans. Tom Conley (New York: Columbia University Press, 1988); Christopher Gill and T. P. Wiseman, eds., *Lies and Fiction in the Ancient World* (Austin: University of Texas Press, 1993); T. P. Wiseman, *Historiography and Imagination: Eight Essays on Roman Culture* (Exeter: University of Exeter Press, 1994); F. R. Ankersmit, *Historical Representation* (Stanford: Stanford University Press, 2001); T. P. Wiseman, *The Myths of Rome* (Exeter: University of Exeter Press, 2004); Gabrielle Spiegel, ed., *Practicing History: New Directions in Historical Writing after the Linguistic Turn* (New York: Routledge, 2005).

pose an immediate threat from which they must flee or risk being contaminated by the blood of the crucifixion.[43]

The anti-Jewish rhetoric of this hymn is particularly pointed, and undoubtedly reflects the complex liturgical season for which Ephrem wrote it,[44] as well as his intent to conform to the Nicene model for Christian orthodoxy. In this hymn, Ephrem implies that "Christians" are being enticed into "Jewish" festivals and practices. He writes, "the evil People that wants our death, enticing, gives us death in food,"[45] describing Jews luring his church audience to Jewish festivals. Similarly, Ephrem describes the unleavened bread as "desirable," "beautiful," and "sweet."[46] Scholars have used this rhetoric, along with his exhortation that his audience flee and distance themselves from the Jews, in order to support the notion of an active and successful Jewish proselytism that targeted and physically threatened a coherent group of Christians whom Ephrem represents in fourth-century Nisibis.[47] For example, in his introduction to the German translation of Ephrem's *Hymns on Unleavened Bread* Edmund Beck states that the last twelve of these hymns move to a polemic that is caused by Jewish propaganda.[48] Ephrem's language does suggest that there was some overlap in people and behaviors between those who attended Ephrem's church and those who participated in Jewish festivals, but given the history of complexity surrounding 14 Nisan celebrations, this is *not* most plausibly the result of proactive "Jewish propaganda."[49]

Ephrem frequently used anti-Jewish and anti-Judaizing rhetoric concurrently to insult Jews and to warn his audience of the danger that Jews, Judaism, and Judaizing allegedly pose. The assumption that Ephrem's language is a response to active Jewish proselytism is misleading in that Ephrem uses this rhetoric as a means of constructing a clear "Nicene" boundary that appears

---

43. It is interesting to note the language that Ephrem uses to distinguish the Christian Eucharist from the unleavened bread of the Jews, particularly in that both contain the blood of Christ, according to Ephrem, one as a drug that gives life and the other as a drug that kills. Like Ignatius of Antioch, Ephrem claims that for innocent Christians this blood is a redemptive "drug of life," and in the unleavened bread of the Jews, who are guilty of murder, Christ's blood becomes a "deadly drug."

44. See Andreas Heinz, "Antijudaismus," 307–25.

45. Ephrem, *Azym.* 19.5.   46. Ephrem, *Azym.* 19.6, 7, 9.

47. Ephrem, *Azym.* 19.28.

48. Beck writes, "Die folgenden Hymnen gehen zu einer offenen Polemik . . . , verursacht durch jüdische Propoganda" (Beck [CSCO 249, SS 109], I).

49. See Miriam Taylor's critique of jumping too easily to this conclusion on the basis of early Christian anti-Jewish rhetoric (Taylor, *Anti-Judaism*).

not yet to have existed along the lines that he wishes between local "Judaism" and "Christianity." Given that the Council of Nicaea attempted to institute a break from a tradition of some eastern Syrian Christians celebrating on 14 Nisan with the Jews, this would have come into sharp focus, accompanied by biting polemic, particularly around the Easter and Passover season.[50]

Boundary-Drawing against "Real" Jews

Ephrem's anti-Jewish rhetoric reflects his concern about the danger, not only at the time of Easter, of unclear boundaries between those who attended the synagogue and the church.[51] While the large majority of Ephrem's descriptions of Jews and Judaism echo Scripture, there are also many instances, in addition to *Hymns on Unleavened Bread* 19, in which his rhetoric suggests

---

50. Compare Melito of Sardis's *Peri Pascha* homily (see also Wilson, "Passover"). Scholars argue that Melito was a Quartodeciman.

51. The numerous anti-Jewish writings by early Christian authors have sparked a wealth of scholarship, not only detailing the language and accusations of these ancient authors, but also speculating on the relationship between their anti-Jewish rhetoric and the authors' own social and religious "realities." Andrew Jacobs offers a clear and cogent summary of this recent trend in scholarship to attempt to sift the "rhetorical" from the "real" in these early Christian anti-Jewish texts (Andrew S. Jacobs, "The Imperial Construction of the Jew in the Early Christian Holy Land" [Ph.D. diss., Duke University, 2001], 244–55). See also Jacobs' book *Remains of the Jews: The Holy Land and Christian Empire in Late Antiquity* (Stanford: Stanford University Press, 2004); Judith Lieu, "'The Parting of the Ways': Theological Construct or Historical Reality?" *JSNT* 56 (1994): 101–19. Marcel Simon *(Verus Israel)* believed that Jewish proselytism was widely practiced and wildly successful up through the fourth century, and that this proselytism posed a very real threat to early Christian communities; this success prompted the heated polemic found in early Christian (and Jewish) texts. This belief colored academic interpretations of early Christian anti-Judaism such as Ephrem's for decades. More recently, Miriam Taylor has critiqued Simon's position for his use of Christianizing categories in order to reconstruct Judaism in antiquity, and in thus perpetuating the very Christian anti-Judaism that he was studying. (Criticisms of Simon's work are throughout Taylor, *Anti-Judaism*.) Taylor argues that far from being taken literally, in fact the Christian anti-Judaism of the late ancient authors should be understood almost entirely as literary rhetoric without basis in reality (*Anti-Judaism*, 1–2, 166). Judith Lieu largely agrees with Taylor's conclusion, emphasizing the "rhetorical role" of anti-Jewish language rather than any historical "reality" that it represents (*Image and Reality*, 12–13). Andrew Jacobs has traced a pattern of change over time in his historiographical survey about the interpretation of early Christian anti-Jewish rhetoric ("Imperial," 244–55). Between the two extremes of "rhetoric" or "reality" Jacobs notes that there is also a growing academic plea for a middle ground that recognizes the rhetorical nature of the texts but in the process does not render useless our limited sources of information about Christian-Jewish interactions in antiquity (Jacobs, "Imperial," 251–52). See also James Carleton Paget, "Anti-Judaism and Early Christian Identity," *Zeitschrift für Antikes Christentum* 1 (1997): 195–225; Stephen Shoemaker, "'Let Us Go and Burn Her Body': The Image of the Jews in the Early Dormition Traditions," *CH* 68 (1999): 775–823.

that he is familiar with contemporary Jews and Jewish practices, and wishes to stop any local permeability between "Christianity" and "Judaism." Ephrem mentions contemporary Jewish fasts and festivals, prayer, Scripture reading practices, and synagogues.[52] He also refers to the destruction of the Temple in Jerusalem, as well as the failed attempt made under Julian during ·Ephrem's lifetime to rebuild the Temple. In addition, Ephrem notes about some contemporary Jewish festival practices that, according to Scripture, God required Jews only celebrate in Jerusalem at the Temple and that with the destruction of the Temple, Jews should no longer celebrate as they continue to do.[53] This rhetoric reveals that Ephrem uses his knowledge of contemporary Jewish practices to further his supersessionist argument that the time for Judaism has passed and that contemporary Jews themselves follow God's scriptural commands incorrectly.

Ephrem's writings also draw a clear distinction between Jews and Christians, implying that they are unmistakably separate communities with entirely dissimilar people. His rhetoric paints a picture of two wholly distinct communities precisely in the hope of creating that distinction, which would be consistent with Nicene Christianity, out of what appears rather to have been in his own context two much more fluid communities. Despite language that presents Jews and Christians as two clearly bounded, and widely separated, groups, Ephrem's references to some members of his "Christian" audience circumcising and joining in the Jewish Passover celebration imply that the relationship between Jews and Christians in Nisibis and Edessa was not as clear as Ephrem would have liked it to be. In his concern to promote Nicene Christianity as Roman orthodoxy,[54] Ephrem emphasizes the ideal of Gentile Christianity without any Judaizing elements, something that appears not yet to have been a clear reality in fourth-century Syria.

---

52. It is impossible to know for certain if some of his descriptions come directly from the scriptural passages on which the practices are based, or else also come from direct knowledge of the contemporary practices themselves. (See, for example, the following: on circumcision, see *SdF* 3.169, 179, 237–71; on atonement, see *Ieiun.* 2.1; on fasts, see Ephrem's series of *Hymns on Unleavened Bread*; on festivals, see *Ieiun.* 5.6–7, *Res.* 4.1, *Cruc.* 1.2ff.; on the Sabbath, see *SdF* 3.179, 217; on food laws, see *SdF* 3.99; on tithing, see *SdF* 3.217; and on prayer, see *Ieiun.* 2.1.) Nonetheless, Ephrem does include many references to these practices without explanation, suggesting that his audience may already have been familiar with them. For further discussion, see Shepardson, "In the Service," 63–71.

53. See Christine Shepardson, "Paschal Politics: The Temple's Destruction Deployed by Fourth-Century Christians," *VC* 62, no. 3 (2008): 233–60.

54. See Griffith, "Deacon," as well as the discussion in the following chapters.

In the late nineteenth century, Samuel Krauss observed, "In passionate hatred of the Jews, in contempt and active hostility towards the people of the covenant, Ephraem of Syria surpasses all the Church Fathers who came before and all those who went after him. His voluminous writings are filled with rage and animosity against the Jews."[55] Krauss calls Ephrem's texts "envenomed productions," and notes the bitterness of his polemic (particularly in contrast to that of Aphrahat).[56] He does not go into detail about the possible causes of this hatred, but does suspect that it is spurred by "the power of resistance shown by the old creed" of Judaism in Ephrem's immediate Syrian surroundings.[57] In the 1960s Stanley Kazan interpreted Ephrem's writings very much at face value, determining that Ephrem's anti-Jewish polemic was driven by an immediate and serious threat posed by Jews in Nisibis to the Christians in that community.[58] Kazan's interpretation, paralleled by Beck's early interpretation, was adopted by other more recent scholars such as Benin and Hayman.[59] The literalness with which Kazan interpreted Ephrem's anti-Jewish rhetoric produced some inaccurate descriptions of Ephrem and fourth-century Syria.[60]

Ephrem emphasizes, in the interest of maintaining the boundaries of Nicene orthodoxy, that Jews and Christians must be two clearly distinct communities. Since he appears to be in the process of drawing boundaries between "Jew" and "Christian" that were not yet distinct in the ways he wished, it is important to determine how he distinguishes the two from each other. One of the most frequent ways in which he does this is through the pairs of mutually exclusive categories that he links with the two groups. For example, throughout his writings, Ephrem refers to Jews as "the circumcised" and "the People," the group that God has rejected because they rejected and denied God's Son, as opposed to the uncircumcised "peoples," as he refers to the (Gentile) Christians, those who recognize and worship God's Son.[61] In fact, Ephrem sometimes uses these contrasting categories of circumcised and uncircumcised side by side in order to emphasize that they are, by definition, mutually exclusive, thereby implying that the groups to which he applies

---

55. Krauss, "Jews," 88–89.

56. Krauss, "Jews," 90.

57. Krauss, "Jews," 89.

58. Kazan (1963), 89–90.

59. See Benin, "Commandments," 142–45; and Hayman, "Image," 433.

60. Other scholars refer more critically to Ephrem's anti-Judaism, but still have not traced its complexity. See, for example, McVey, "Anti-Judaic"; Griffith, "Deacon"; Darling, "Church."

61. See, for example, de Dom. nos. 7; Cruc. 5.5; Virg. 20, 27, 44; Eccl. 51.7, 49.15; CJ 1.16, 2.7; HdF 44, 56, 87; Nat. 25.7. See also Darling, "Nations," 111–21; and Robert Murray, Symbols of Church and Kingdom: A Study in Early Syriac Tradition (Cambridge: Cambridge University Press, 1975), 41–68. Compare also the language of the Didascalia.

them, namely, Jews and Christians respectively, must also be mutually exclusive.[62] Ephrem further emphasizes this separation by his use of pronouns, using first- and second-person pronouns, as well as familiar vocatives such as "my brothers," to address his audience, in contrast to the third-person pronouns with which he regularly refers to the Jews.[63] This use of pronouns emphasizes a familiar common "we" that includes the Christian Ephrem and all those who hear him, as opposed to a foreign "they" of the Jews. Ephrem thus distances the category "Jew" from that of "Christian," making the Jews an incompatible "other" to the Christian "self."[64]

One other way in which Ephrem rhetorically separates Jews and Christians is through his recitation of a negative Jewish history for Jews, and a positive Gentile history for Christians.[65] This comes through most clearly in Ephrem's recurring references to the negatively portrayed Jewish leaders in the New Testament Gospel narratives as the immediate ancestors of contemporary Jews, and to the positively portrayed Gentile magi in Matthew 2 as the immediate forerunners of Christians.[66] Thus Ephrem implies that the category of Christian is simply a subset of the category Gentile. Christians are Gentiles, Ephrem implies, and therefore can never be Jews.

This last claim is particularly interesting because it comes from eastern Syria. Scholars have traditionally, at least since F. C. Burkitt wrote *Early Eastern Christianity* in 1904, described Syriac Christianity as particularly "Jewish" in character, while some have gone further and argued that Syriac Christianity represents a "Jewish-Christianity"[67] that originally arrived directly from

---

62. See, for example, Ephrem, *Virg.* 44.

63. For Ephrem's use of the second-person pronoun, see, for example, *SdF* 3.15, 19, 25, 87, 229; for the vocative, see, for example, *Azym.* 19.11, 16; and for examples of his use of the third-person to refer to the Jews, see *SdF* 3.247–50, 267–70, 289.

64. For a discussion of the self/other dichotomy, as well as the danger of the proximate other, see Jonathan Z. Smith, "What a Difference a Difference Makes," in *"To See Ourselves as Others See Us": Christians, Jews, "Others" in Late Antiquity,* eds. Jacob Neusner and Ernest Frerichs (Chico, Calif.: Scholars Press, 1985), 3–48. Ephrem's rhetoric here again demonstrates precisely the constructive language that Boyarin discusses *(Border Lines).* Numerous recent works have contributed significantly to understanding the complexity of Christian/Jewish relations in late antiquity. In addition to Boyarin *(Border Lines),* see especially Charlotte Fonrobert, "The *Didascalia Apostolorum:* A Mishnah for the Disciples of Jesus," *JECS* 9, no. 4 (2001): 483–509; Judith Lieu, *Neither Jew Nor Greek? Constructing Early Christianity* (New York: T&T Clark, 2002); and Adam Becker and Annette Yoshiko Reed, *The Ways that Never Parted: Jews and Christians in Late Antiquity and the Early Middle Ages* (Tübingen: Mohr Siebeck, 2003); ter Haar Romeny, "Hypothesis."

65. See also the discussion in chapter 3.

66. See, for example, Ephrem, *SdF* 6.91–159; *Nat.* 21, 23, 24, 26; *HdF* 7.

67. One of the fundamental problems in any discussion of Jewish-Christianity is in defining

Jerusalem in the first century.[68] In fact, Ephrem's writings themselves often serve as one important witness to both of these claims.[69]

---

just what scholars mean by the term "Jewish-Christian." Scholars have used this word to refer to Jews who believe Jesus is the Messiah, Christians of Jewish background, Gentile Christians who follow food and purity laws and practice circumcision, any Christian who follows "Jewish" practices, or any combination thereof. Recently more scholars have recognized this problem and have presented their working definitions more clearly (see, for example, Alan Segal, "Jewish Christianity"). Other scholars have not, however, and as Joan Taylor has critiqued, some even use more than one definition within their work (Joan E. Taylor, "The Phenomenon of Early Jewish-Christianity: Reality or Scholarly Invention?" *VC* 44 [1990]: 313–34). Alan Segal and Simon Mimouni have also recently addressed the problem of scholarship on "Jewish-Christianity," and the vagueness of the term. Segal's work demonstrates a more careful and nuanced use of sources in an attempt to reconstruct the history of the early Jerusalem church (Segal, "Jewish Christianity"). Mimouni, on the other hand, challenges the construction of Syriac Christianity as necessarily and innately "Jewish-Christian" and a product of Jerusalem Christianity (Mimouni, "Judéo-christianisme"). See also J. Carleton Paget, "Jewish Christianity," in *The Cambridge History of Judaism*, vol. 3 (Cambridge: Cambridge University Press, 1999), 731–75; Robert Kraft, review of *Théologie du judéo-christianisme*, by Jean Daniélou, *JBL* 79 (1960): 91–94; Marcel Simon, "Problèmes du judéo-christianisme," in *Aspects du judéo-christianisme: Colloque de Strasbourg, 23–25 avril, 1964* (Paris: University of France Press, 1965), 1–17; Georg Strecker, "On the Problem of Jewish Chrsitianity," appendix 1 in Walter Bauer, *Orthodoxy and Heresy in Earliest Christianity* (*Rechtgläubigkeit und Ketzerei im ältesten Christentum* [Tübingen: Mohr, 1964]; Philadelphia: Fortress Press, 1971), 241–85; Robert Kraft, "In Search of 'Jewish Christianity' and its 'Theology': Problems of Definition and Methodology," *RSR* 60 (1972): 81–96; Marcel Simon, "Réfléxions sur le judéo-christianisme," in *Christianity, Judaism and Other Graeco-Roman Cults* 2, ed. Jacob Neusner (Leiden: Brill, 1975), 53–76; Bruce Malina, "Jewish Christianity or Christian Judaism: Toward a Hypothetical Definition," *JSJ* 7 (1976): 46–57; S. K. Riegel, "Jewish Christianity: Definition and Terminology," *NTS* 24 (1977–78): 410–15. See particularly the essays in the recent work edited by Becker and Reed, *The Ways that Never Parted;* as well as Boyarin, *Border Lines.* This is not to say that there is no relation to Judaism in Syriac Christianity, only to warn of the baggage that comes in tracing that relationship through a history of "Jewish-Christianity."

68. F. C. Burkitt, *Early Eastern Christianity* (London: John Murray, 1904). These beliefs pervade earlier scholarship on the origins of Syriac Christianity. For a few of the numerous possible examples, see Jean Daniélou, *Les manuscrits de la Mer Morte et les origines du christianisme* (Paris: Desclée, 1957), 110–14; Jean Daniélou, *Théologie du judéo-christianisme* (Paris: Desclée, 1958); J. C. L. Gibson, "From Qumran to Edessa or the Aramaic Speaking Church before and after 70 A.D.," *The Annual of Leeds Oriental Society* 5 (1966): 24–39; L. W. Barnard, "The Origins and emergence of the Church in Edessa during the First Two Centuries A.D.," *VC* 22 (1968): 161–75; Gilles Quispel, "The Discussion of Judaic Christianity," *VC* 22 (1968): 81–93; N. Séd, "Les hymnes sur le Paradis de saint Ephrem et les traditions juives," *Le Muséon* 81 (1968): 455–501; Hans-Joachim Schoeps, *Jewish Christianity: Factional disputes in the early Church,* trans. Douglas R. A. Hare (Philadelphia: Fortress Press, 1969); A. F. J. Klijn, "The Study of Jewish Christianity," *NTS* 20 (1973/1974): 419–31; Murray, *Symbols,* 4; Robert Murray, "The Characteristics of the Earliest Syriac Christianity," in *East of Byzantium: Syria and Armenia in the Formative Period,* eds. Nina Garsoïan, Thomas Matthews, and Robert Thomson (Washington, D.C.: Dumbarton Oaks, 1982), 5; Alan F. Segal, "Jewish Christianity," in *Eusebius, Christianity, and Judaism,* eds. Harold Attridge and Gohei Hata (Detroit: Wayne State University Press, 1992), 326–51. See also the discussion below, including the challenges raised by Han J. W. Drijvers, "Edessa und das jüdische Christentum," *VC* 24 (1970): 3–33; and Mimouni, "Le judéo-christianisme syriaque." See also Haar Romeny, "Hypothesis"; Boyarin, *Border Lines.*

69. For a discussion of this problem, see Shepardson, "Syria, Syriac, Syrian: Negotiating

There is persuasive evidence that early Syriac Christianity did have connections to local Judaism, and that there were Judaizers among fourth-century churchgoers, as well as a respect among many early Syrian Christians for Jewish Scripture, scriptural interpretation, and traditions.[70] More recent work in these areas has shifted the focus from using the undifferentiated term "Jewish-Christianity" to describing instead a more complex relationship between Judaism and early Christianity in Syria.[71] Syriac-speaking Jews and Christians shared a language, traditions, and Scripture that gave some common elements to their respective worship services. Michael Weitzman's work on the Jewish origins of the Syriac version of the Old Testament (the Peshitta) has added considerably to the continuing debate about how best to characterize the relationship between early Syriac Christianity and Judaism. Weitzman argues that the Peshitta was originally the text of a group within Syrian Judaism that gradually grew together with Syriac Christianity, so that over time these Jews' Bible became part of Syriac Christianity's Scripture.[72]

East and West in Late Antiquity," in *Blackwell Companion to Late Antiquity*, ed. Philip Rousseau (Blackwell, 2008, forthcoming).

70. This will become clearer in the textual analysis of Ephrem's writings below. In addition, however, scholars use texts such as the *Didascalia*, whose origins scholars have traced to Syria and whose language suggests a favorable and deeply rooted connection with Judaism, to reconstruct early Syriac Christianity as closely tied to local Judaism. For a more recent and nuanced discussion of the *Didascalia*, see Charlotte Fonrobert, "The *Didascalia Apostolorum*: A Mishnah for the Disciples of Jesus," *JECS* 9, no. 4 (2001): 483–509. Scholars such as Michael Weitzman offer further support for this hypothesis through their study of Syriac Scripture in late antiquity (Michael P. Weitzman, *The Syriac Version of the Old Testament: An Introduction* [New York: Cambridge University Press, 1999]). Furthermore, scholars have discussed in detail Ephrem's own relationship to Jewish exegesis. R.-M. Tonneau argues that Ephrem was not only strongly influenced by Jewish exegetical methods, but that Ephrem in fact used Jewish haggadic traditions in his writings ("'Moïse dans la tradition syrienne," in *Moïse, l'homme de l'Alliance* [New York: Desclée, 1955], 253). Séd also argued for the influence of Jewish exegesis on Ephrem ("Les hymnes sur le paradis de saint Ephrem et les traditions juives," *Le Muséon* 81 [1968]: 455–501). Compare also the references above regarding the relation of Ephrem's commentaries to Jewish exegetical texts.

It is interesting to note that Ralph Hennings observes about Eusebius of Emesa, who was born in Edessa, that in his (Greek) biblical commentaries he also appears to have shared exegetical traditions with contemporary Jews, while including anti-Jewish rhetoric in his homilies (Ralph Hennings, "Eusebius von Emesa und die Juden," *Journal of Ancient Christianity* 5, no. 2 [2001]: 240–60). John Chrysostom's Greek Syrian texts also mention his Christian congregants' respect for the synagogue and Jewish Scripture. See Shepardson, "Controlling Contested Places: John Chrysostom's *Adversus Iudaeos* Homilies and the Spatial Politics of Religious Controversy." *JECS* 15, no. 4 (2007): 483–516.

71. In particular, see the essays in Becker and Reed, eds., *The Ways that Never Parted;* as well as Boyarin, *Border Lines*; Fonrobert, *"Didascalia"*; and Lieu, *Neither Jew*.

72. See Michael Weitzman, "From Judaism to Christianity: The Syriac version of the

Rouwhorst also supports the view that some Syriac Jewish traditions found their way into Syriac Christianity. He argues that early Syriac Christianity retained traces of "Jewish" architecture and liturgical traditions, including the presence of a *bema,* regular readings from both the Torah and the Prophets during the Eucharist, the language of the Eucharist prayer, and Quartodeciman traditions (of celebrating Easter on the date of the Jewish Passover) until the fourth-century Council of Nicaea.[73] For these authors, their arguments explain the origins of the same shared scriptural traditions that also resulted in "Jewish" exegetical traditions in later writings, such as those by Ephrem.[74]

It is misleading, however, to use Ephrem's writings only to look back in time in order to reconstruct earlier Syriac Christianity, since he is so actively engaged in his own fourth-century context. By rhetorically forcing Jews and Christians into two distinct groups with discrete histories, Ephrem implies that a person in his community has no room to slide easily between the two categories, but rather belongs necessarily only to one or the other. In his hymns, he leaves no doubt which of the two is the better option.[75]

Hebrew Bible," in *The Jews among Pagans and Christians in the Roman Empire,* eds. Judith Lieu, John North, and Tessa Rajak (New York: Routledge, 1992), 147–73; *Syriac Version.* Compare also the following works by Sebastian Brock: "Jewish Traditions in Syriac Sources," *JJS* 30 (1979): 212–32; "A Palestinian Targum Feature in Syriac," *JJS* 46 (1995): 271–82; "The Peshitta Old Testament: Between Judaism and Christianity," *Cristianesimo nella Storia* 19 (1998): 483–502; Haar Romeny, "Hypothesis."

73. See G. Rouwhorst, "Jewish Liturgical Traditions in Early Syriac Chrsitianity," *VC* 51 (1997): 74–82. See also C. W. Dugmore, "A Note on the Quartodecimans," *Studia Patristica* 79, no. 4.2 (1961): 411–21; G. Rouwhorst, *Les hymnes pascales d'Ephrem de Nisibe: Analyse théologique et recherche sur l'évolution de la fête pascale chrétienne à Nisibe et à Edesse et dans quelques églises voisines au quatrième siècle,* Supplements to *VC* 7, no. 1/2 (New York: Brill, 1989). Of course, this discussion calls into question Rouwhorst's assumption that such behavior ended with the injunctions of the Council of Nicaea in 325.

74. Compare also those of Eusebius of Emesa (see Hennings, "Eusebius"). Paul Feghali, on the other hand, denies that these exegetical similarities are the result of Jewish influence, and Han Drijvers argues that any "Jewish" elements of early Syriac Christianity were not due to Syriac Christianity beginning in the synagogue, but rather reflect Gentile Syriac Christians' later attraction to Jewish texts and traditions (see Feghali, "Targums"; Han Drijvers, "Syrian Christianity and Judaism," in *The Jews among Pagans and Christians in the Roman Empire,* eds. Judith Lieu, John North, and Tessa Rajak [New York: Routledge, 1992], 124–46). Regardless, the similarities in Ephrem's time remain.

75. Michel Foucault notably identified significant aspects of the power relations involved in narratives. See especially, Michel Foucault, *The History of Sexuality,* vol. 1, trans. Robert Hurley (New York: Random House, 1978). Scholars of ideology criticism likewise note the force that constructions of reality such as Ephrem's have on their context, often reifying the worldview that they promote in the very act of describing it. See, for example, Louis Althusser, "Ideology and Ideological State Apparatuses (Notes towards an Investigation)," in *Lenin and Philosophy and Other Essays,* trans. Ben Brewster (New York: Monthly Review Press, 1971), 127–86; Jorge Larrain,

Looking more closely at Ephrem's writings supports scholars' conclusions that relations between Jews and Christians were far more complex than Ephrem's idealized rhetoric of two separate communities portrays.[76] The third of Ephrem's *Sermons on Faith* and the nineteenth of his *Hymns on Unleavened Bread* are the sources in which this complexity becomes most clear, since in both these texts Ephrem implies that not only does he himself know something of contemporary Jewish practices, but also that members of his church audience visit the local synagogue. In fact, Ephrem goes so far as to accuse some in his audience of Judaizing by upholding Jewish law, including circumcision, and celebrating the Passover festival with local Jews. Certainly, these descriptions are a far cry from his binary rhetorical distinctions between Christians and Jews as "us" and "them," uncircumcised and circumcised, Gentiles and Jews.

In his third *Sermon on Faith* Ephrem discusses the origin of the commandments that were given to Jews and that he believes have since ended with the beginning of Christianity. He first claims that there have been different ages, each with their own set of regulations, so that in the time of the Jews (before the life of Jesus) there was an appropriate time for the laws of the Jews. Nonetheless, he writes, "At this time the commandments of the Sabbath, circumcision, and purification have ceased," arguing that these commandments are now outdated and have become harmful to people who no longer need them.[77] Using the metaphor of a physician treating a patient, Ephrem argues that the earlier commandments were medicines for illnesses that no longer exist; the medicine healed the people who were sick, but the medicine is harmful to those who are already healthy.[78] Ephrem thus acknowledges that Scripture describes these commandments, and that they were necessary and helpful in their time, at the same time that he argues that their time has since passed.

The Concept of Ideology (London: Hutchinson, 1979); Anthony Giddens, "Four Theses on Ideology," *Canadian Journal of Political and Social Theory* 7, no. 1–2 (1983): 18–21; John B. Thompson, *Studies in the Theory of Ideology* (Cambridge, Mass.: Polity Press, 1984); John B. Thompson, *Ideology and Modern Culture: Critical Social Theory and the Era of Mass Communication* (Stanford: Stanford University Press, 1990); Terry Eagleton, *Ideology: An Introduction* (New York: Verso Press, 1991); Jorge Larrain, *Ideology and Cultural Identity: Modernity and the Third World Presence* (Cambridge, Mass.: Polity Press, 1994).

76. Compare Ephrem, *Virg.* 18.6.

77. Ephrem, *SdF* 3.179–80. All translations from these sermons are from the Syriac text in Edmund Beck, ed., *Des Heiligen Ephraem des Syrers Sermones de Fide,* CSCO 212, SS 88 (Louvain, 1961). Compare also the language of the temporary "second legislation" throughout the *Didascalia.*

78. Again, we see Ephrem using the metaphor of a physician.

The reason for Ephrem's concern soon becomes more explicit. Ephrem insists, "Whoever at this time uses the commandments as an instrument is like a killer who cuts off healthy limbs," implying that he is concerned lest someone in his own time consider following the outdated commandments.[79] Ephrem in fact becomes more adamant still with his subsequent discussion in which he not only worries that someone might follow these outdated commandments, but chastises those who apparently do so. Ephrem forbids those in his audience either to follow the commandments themselves, or to coerce someone else in his audience to follow them:

[These commandments] were fitting for those that were stricken. Do not hurt the strong with them! They were established because of sicknesses. Do not strike the healthy with them! They are evil who hurt the hidden soul by manifest circumcisions. . . . For the sicknesses and the drugs of sacrifices, Sabbaths, and tithings ceased. . . . Do not run after the commandment that ceased, and its sickness has ceased! . . . Do not place upon your wounds drugs that are not suitable for yourself![80]

Ephrem thus implies that there are those in his audience who follow the outdated commandments and who wish to convince others in Ephrem's church to do so as well.

Ephrem elaborates on this charge, claiming against these misguided members of his audience, "The one who set the law is angry because he himself loosened, and yet you bind. The commandment that he gave has ceased for you, and yet you are keeping that which he loosed."[81] Becoming more specific about precisely which of these outdated commandments appears to be causing the most trouble in his contemporary congregation, namely, circumcision, Ephrem pleads,

Interrogate yourself a little, foolish one, concerning the observance of the law! What can circumcision do for the sin that dwells within? Sin dwells within your heart, and you, you circumcise your foreskin. You would do well to say thus: circumcision was proper in its time. . . . Do not therefore afflict yourself with circumcision, whose time has passed by. . . . See that the one who circumcised their bodies cried out to them, "Circumcise your hearts!" [cf. Jeremiah 4:4; Deuteronomy 30:6]. Why did he

79. Ephrem, *SdF* 3.189–192. In this passage, Ephrem uses the root for "to circumcise" [*gzr*] in order to describe the killer *cutting off* the healthy limbs, again drawing his audience's attention to the Jews.

80. Ephrem, *SdF* 3.195–200, 217–18, 221–22, 225–26. Compare the similar language in *Didascalia* 26.

81. Ephrem, *SdF* 3.229–32. Compare also the language of "bonds" and "binding" that permeates the *Didascalia* in reference to Jewish laws that Christians should not follow.

seek another circumcision? Because look! Their bodies had been circumcised. And if he seeks another circumcision, do not use the visible one![82]

Ephrem continues, naming not only circumcision, but also Sabbath observance as a pressing concern: "Let Sabbath and circumcision go, because these things have left you and passed by. You are guilty inside yourself, and you observe outward things. The soul, which is within, is destroyed, and Sabbath, which is outside, is observed."[83] Instead of Ephrem's binary oppositions, this text portrays a concern about those in his "Christian" audience who followed these "Jewish" traditions. While it is easy to categorize those whom Ephrem describes as Judaizing Christians, Ephrem's stark rhetoric ostensibly does not allow for this mixed category. Ephrem uses his sermons and hymns to construct two clearly distinct categories of Christians and Jews, neither of which has room for the overlapping of boundaries that he describes in chastising those in a Christian congregation who practice circumcision and respect the Jewish Sabbath.

In addition to this intimation of boundary permeability in his *Sermons on Faith*, Ephrem's *Hymns on Unleavened Bread* also include references to a similar situation. Particularly in Hymn 19, as seen briefly above, Ephrem not only discusses the Jews' unleavened bread and the accompanying festival, but as in Sermon 3 he also warns his audience against participating in the Jewish traditions. In Hymn 19 Ephrem describes the Jews' unleavened bread as "desirable," and at the same time warns of the danger of giving in to its temptation.[84] Ephrem again pleads with his audience, "Loathe the unleavened bread, you, my brothers, in which the symbol of Iscariot dwells! Moreover, flee, my brothers, from the unleavened bread because stench dwells within its purity," suggesting that Ephrem's (Christian) "brothers" are already dangerously close to the unleavened bread.[85] Ephrem continues, appealing to a familiarity between himself and his audience in order to authorize his concern for the well-being of those in his audience who would be "joined together in their festivals":[86] "Do not take, my brothers, that unleavened bread from the People whose hands are covered with blood. . . . Let us not eat, my brothers, along with the drug of life the unleavened bread of the People as a deadly drug. . . . The one who received [the Messiah's blood] in our [Eucha-

---

82. Ephrem, *SdF* 3.233–40, 259–60, 267–72.   83. Ephrem, *SdF* 3.281–86.

84. Ephrem, *Azym.* 19.6.   85. Ephrem, *Azym.* 19.11–12.

86. Ephrem, *Azym.* 19.26.

rist] offering has received the drug of life. The one who ate it with the People received a deadly drug."[87] In this hymn, Ephrem thus portrays a situation, much like the one he describes in Sermon 3, in which, addressing himself to a church audience, he worries that the traditions of the Jews will appeal to them, and he pleads with his audience not to participate in the festival. Those who do participate, he warns (thereby suggesting that there are, in fact, those who do), place themselves in great danger. Far from the two distinct categories implied by some of Ephrem's rhetoric, these appeals to his audience about their behavior suggest that identifying a "Jew" or a "Christian" in fourth-century Nisibis may not have been as easy as identifying the circumcised from the uncircumcised and the other clear-cut categories for which Ephrem's rhetoric wistfully yearns.

In light of Ephrem's own knowledge about contemporary Jews and Judaism and his intimations that some people in Nisibis attend both Ephrem's church services and Jewish Passover celebrations, Ephrem's rhetoric about Jews and Christians as two indisputably distinct contemporary communities is difficult to accept at face value. The picture that emerges instead is of distinct places of worship, with many people in Nisibis attending only one or the other, but with a visible minority periodically attending both. Along with this, we see that Ephrem's church congregation may have included people who were circumcised along with those who were not. Within this context, then, Ephrem's rhetoric of two distinct communities, defined by issues of practice and heritage, appears not to describe the context as it was, but rather to delineate clear Nicene boundaries that Christians will thereafter be able to patrol. As he will later do for "Nicene" and "Arian" Christianity, Ephrem here constructs "Christianity" and "Judaism" as mutually exclusive categories, praises the one while attacking the other, and defines where the borders of each community should be. Ephrem thereby forces his audience to distinguish clearly between the two, while at the same time threatening those in his "Christian" audience that if they are not careful, they will find themselves on the wrong side of the new Nicene chasm that insistently separates Easter from Passover, Christians from Jews, and God's people from those whom God has rejected.

---

87. Ephrem, *Azym.* 19.16–24.

Ephrem against Jews and Judaizing Christians

Ephrem has several different methods for persuading his audience to choose Christianity over Judaism when they confront the binary decision with which he presents them. Ephrem insults and criticizes the Jews in order to make them less appealing to his audience, contrasts them with Christians in order to highlight the differences that he sees, and warns his audience of the physical danger that Jews pose to them in order to frighten them away from Judaism if his other tactics are not sufficiently effective. These different aspects of Ephrem's anti-Jewish language reinforce the binary oppositions of Christianity versus Judaism, of light and truth versus darkness and evil, that Ephrem wants to instill in his audience, which as of yet experiences the more permeable communities in which church attendees sometimes celebrate Passover.

Critical Insults

Detailed poetic metaphors and descriptions are characteristic of Ephrem's writing style, and his anti-Jewish rhetoric is no exception. For example, Ephrem is particularly fond of using bodily descriptions of blindness and deafness to describe his belief that the Jews missed the coming of the Messiah and are deaf to God's wishes.[88] Likewise, Ephrem frequently describes the Jews as foolish. To Ephrem, the mind, the eyes, and the ears of the Jews are all shut up uselessly, with the result that the Jews, once God's chosen people, are now despised and hateful to God.

Ephrem describes different generations of Jews as foolish, deaf, dumb, and blind, sometimes literally blind in their sight and sometimes figuratively blind in their understanding.[89] As with his other anti-Jewish accusations, Ephrem attributes these negative characteristics not only to one particular generation of Jews, but to all Jews ever. Initially, Israel was blind in the desert when she did not see God in her midst, and so made the golden calf in order to have a visible god.[90] Ephrem elsewhere writes regarding Mt. Sinai, "While Moses

88. See, for example, Ephrem, *Nat.* 10.8; Brock, *Luminous*, 71–79. See also Aho Shemunkasho, "The Healing of Interior and Exterior Blindness in Ephrem," in *Studia Patristica XXXV* (Louvain: Peeters, 2001), 494–501.

89. This is a familiar biblical accusation against Israel, which is also frequently picked up by early Christian writers. See, for example, Isa 42, 43:8; *Didascalia* 21, 26.

90. Ephrem, *de Dom. nos.* 43. All quotations from *de Dom. nos.* are from the English translation by Joseph Amar in FC 91, with my own occasional changes based on the Syriac text in

was praying on the mountain, that blind People was indulging itself."[91] In his *Homily on our Lord,* for example, Ephrem compares this earlier blind generation to the generation of Jews in Jesus' time, particularly Simon the Pharisee from Luke 7.[92] This in turn leads Ephrem to an easy comparison to the "blind teachers who became the leaders of others," reminiscent of Jesus' condemnation of the Jewish scribes and Pharisees in Matthew 23.[93] Ephrem suggests, however, that not only the Pharisees, but all "Jews" during Jesus' time were blind.[94] For Ephrem the Jews' blindness has remained a timeless trait that also carries over into his own time. Ephrem describes in his own context "the blind People" that "hurried to the day of its fast."[95] Ephrem thus uses blindness as one of the defining traits of Jews throughout their history, from the time of Moses up through the fourth century.[96]

Along with these descriptions of the Jews' blindness, Ephrem also refers in other ways to their ignorance and lack of understanding, frequently referring to them as "fools." Ephrem writes, "Come, let us remember in the fast that which the fools had done in their fasts,"[97] and refers to "the foolish People," "the foolish scribes," and "the foolish synagogue."[98] Ephrem elaborates with criticisms that the Jews did not recognize the Messiah when he came,[99] and refers to the Jews as "that People whose understanding never matured."[100]

Edmund Beck, ed., *Des Heiligen Ephraem des Syrers Sermo de Domino Nostro,* CSCO 270, SS 116 (Louvain, 1966). See Ex 32, Isa 43:8.

91. Ephrem, *Ieiun.* 10.4.   92. Ephrem, *de Dom. nos.* 42–44.

93. Ephrem, *de Dom. nos.* 46.

94. Ephrem here seems surprisingly able to distinguish at his convenience "Jews" from Jesus and his followers, despite the fact that elsewhere Ephrem emphasizes Jesus' own Jewishness (see, for example, *de Dom. nos.* 50–59 and *Nat.* 26.11). Compare Ephrem, *Ieiun.* 5.7–10.

95. Ephrem, *Ieiun.* 1.12.

96. Ephrem also occasionally uses blindness to refer to other groups who oppose him. See, for example, *HdF* 8, 9, 27. In addition, Ephrem not only uses visual descriptions of blindness, but he also describes a deafness and ignorance that reflect the Jews' blind unknowing (see Ephrem, *Ieiun.* 26.4; 2.1). Ephrem elsewhere adds the Jews' muteness to these accusations (Ephrem, *Nat.* 24.14–15). Accusing the Jews of being deaf, dumb, and blind, Ephrem criticizes their rejection of the Messiah and describes it as their inability to see, hear, and praise God.

97. Ephrem, *Ieiun.* 5.6.

98. See, for example, Ephrem, *Eccl.* 49.13 and 57.13; *Eccl.* 32.2 and *Nat.* 24.11; *CNis.* 28.14; and *Azym.* 1.15.

99. See, for example, Ephrem, *Azym.* 4.20 and *Eccl.* 41.2. Compare also *Azym.* 18.6 and *Nat.* 3.10.

100. Ephrem, *CNis.* 62.21. All translations from this series of hymns are from the Syriac text in Edmund Beck, ed., *Des Heiligen Ephraem des Syrers Carmina Nisibena (I),* CSCO 218, SS 92 (Louvain, 1961); and Edmund Beck, ed., *Des Heiligen Ephraem des Syrers Carmina Nisibena (II),* CSCO 240, SS 102 (Louvain, 1963).

Combining these ideas, Ephrem criticizes the Jews through an allusion to the New Testament Gospel birth narratives:

The foolish scribes were not aware of even one advent . . . the one advent scattered the People whose understanding was blind . . . the redeemer shone forth to the blind, but they looked to others . . . they silenced the kithara of the spirit. . . . Since in Judea the announcers were silent, the magi sounded . . . behold, the fool reads in his Scriptures.[101]

According to Ephrem, the Jews stumble along in the dark, deaf, mute, blind, and uncomprehending the will of God. This anti-Jewish language furthers Ephrem's efforts to distinguish clearly between Christians and Jews, Christianity and Judaism, and to portray Jews and Judaism negatively in the process.

Continuing his emphasis on the physical senses, Ephrem also describes the Jews as a people that stinks, in sharp contrast to the pleasing aromas of paradise and Christ.[102] In his poetic writings, Ephrem consistently attributes sweet and pleasing smells to that which he values positively, such as paradise and Christ,[103] and foul odors to things and people whom he portrays negatively, such as Herod Antipas, the emperor Julian, and the Jews and their unleavened bread.[104] In his *Hymns on Unleavened Bread* Ephrem warns his audience, "Flee, my brothers, from the unleavened bread because stench dwells

---

101. Ephrem, *Nat.* 24.11–22.

102. This topic is itself worthy of much discussion, as demonstrated by Susan Ashbrook Harvey, *Scenting Salvation: Ancient Christianity and the Olfactory Imagination* (Berkeley: University of California Press, 2006). See also Constance Classen, David Howes, and Anthony Synnott, *Aroma: The Cultural History of Smell* (New York: Routledge, 1994); P. J. Botha, "The Significance of the senses in St. Ephrem's description of Paradise," *Acta Patristica et Byzantina* 5 (1994): 28–37; Susan Ashbrook Harvey, "St. Ephrem on the Scent of Salvation," *JTS* n.s. 49 (1998): 109–28; Susan Ashbrook Harvey, "Olfactory Knowing: Signs of Smell in the vitae of Simeon Stylites," in *After Bardaisan: Studies on Continuity and Change in Syriac Christianity in Honour of Professor Han J. W. Drijvers*, eds. G. J. Reinink and A. C. Klugkist (Louvain: Peeters, 1999), 23–34. I thank David Woods for bringing to my attention an interesting parallel passage in Ammianus Marcellinus (22.5.5). Rohrbacher suggests that this odor could be associated with leprosy (D. Rohrbacher, "Iudaei Fetentes at Amm. Marc. 22.5.5," *Mnemosyne* 58 [2005]: 441–42), but Woods emphasizes that Ammianus was most likely strongly influenced by Christianity (David Woods, "Strategius and the Manichaeans," *Classical Quarterly* 51 [2001]: 255–64), and has argued that Ammianus grew up in Syria, perhaps near Emesa (David Woods, "Ammianus Marcellinus and Bishop Eusebius of Emesa," *JTS* 54 [2003]: 585–91). As Woods has suggested informally, Ephrem's similar language may suggest that there may be an important cultural connection between these two authors' association of the Jews with bad odors.

103. See, for example, *HdP* 1.9, 6.6, 7.14, 11.10, and *SdF* 6.5.

104. See, for example, Ephrem, *Nat.* 4.70; *CJ* 2.9; and *Azym.* 19.

in its purity. For that putrid reputation that Moses described indeed dwells in the purity of that unleavened bread. Garlic and onions the People had desired [Numbers 11:5]. Their unleavened bread stank together with the eating of it,"[105] and in his *Hymns against Heresies* he praises the church that "rose above . . . the stench of the stinking Jews."[106] Ephrem elaborates further on this anti-Jewish rhetoric in his *Hymns on Nisibis* when he writes, "But if there is indeed a way, I will toss these bones of theirs out of Sheol, for they are making it stink. I myself am amazed at the Holy Spirit, how much it stayed within the People whose smell stank like its customs. Onions and garlic are proclaimers of their works [cf. Numbers 11:5]. Like its food, the mind of the People is filthy."[107] Describing the Jews in such forceful and descriptive language further promotes the negative picture with which Ephrem's rhetoric portrays them.

In addition to the emphasis on the senses, Ephrem also denigrates the Jews by attributing other unfavorable characteristics to them. For example, Ephrem describes the Jews as a jealous people: "the scribes were silent with envy, and the Pharisees with jealousy,"[108] and "jealous of you is the People that is aware that you will teach the peoples."[109] Ephrem thus implies that the Jewish leaders of Jesus' time knew that he was God's Son and the Messiah, and as a result of their jealousy, Ephrem claims, they were silent and did not acknowledge him. This jealousy that Ephrem attributes to the Jews of Jesus' time brought out and aggravated, he claims, the contentious stubbornness and pride that he attributes to the Jews throughout history. Ephrem's writings are filled with various references to the Jews as difficult, hard-hearted, and stiff-necked, having an ear of contention.[110] He accuses them of being "more stubborn than all people," adding that they are a contentious and unbelieving people who inappropriately rage and complain against God,[111] and he attributes this stubbornness to "the pride of the foolish Jews who boast that their heritage is

---

105. Ephrem, *Azym.* 19.12–14.

106. Ephrem, *CH* 56.8. Ephrem's language in these passages highlights his concern for purity for his community. See particularly, Mary Douglas, *Purity and Danger: An Analysis of the Concepts of Pollution and Taboo* (London: Routledge & Kegan, 1966).

107. Ephrem, *CNis.* 67.15–17.

108. Ephrem, *Nat.* 24.19.

109. Ephrem, *Virg.* 8.22.

110. Ephrem, *Virg.* 30; *Comm. Ex.* 4; *de Dom. nos.* 40; *HdF* 56.7. Compare Ezek 2:4, 3:7; Ex 32:9, 33:3, 33:5, 34:9; Deut 9:6, 9:13, 10:16.

111. See, for example, Ephrem, *de Dom. nos.* 41; *de Dom. nos.* 32; *SdF* 3.288; *CJ* 1.16; *Ieiun.* 10.8. Compare Deut 9:27, Judg 2:19, Ps 78:8.

in Jerusalem."[112] Likewise, in their rebelliousness and pride Ephrem accuses that the Jews slander, lie, and speak badly of God's Son.[113] Although Ephrem adopts this language from the Old Testament, in his hands it changes from an insider's criticism to the means by which those outside the (Jewish) community can insult and dismiss all Jews, through the words of their own prophets.

As a result of their disrespectful behavior, Ephrem argues, the Jews both have been shamed by God, and yet frequently display their contentiousness further by not being ashamed of their shameful actions. Ephrem assures his audience that the Jews have committed numerous shameful acts throughout history, including particularly their worship of the golden calf at Mt. Sinai and their crucifixion of God's Son.[114] Nonetheless, despite the shame that Ephrem claims the Jews incurred, he insists that the "stubborn" and "proud" people was not ashamed of its behavior. He notes that "it [the People] made a calf and was not ashamed,"[115] referring to the incident at Mt. Sinai, and with reference to the crucifixion he writes that the Jewish people "will both kill and commit adultery."[116] Ephrem charges that when the Jews murdered openly, behaving shamefully and yet were not ashamed, their shamelessness "surpassed that of animals."[117] Repeating this motif, Ephrem continues to slander his Jewish neighbors in the hope of persuading his audience of the important fact of, and nature of, a distinction between Christians and Jews.

Adding to the idea of the Jews' shame, Ephrem frequently describes the Jews' worship of the golden calf as an act of adultery against God, worshipping an idol after having betrothed themselves to God.[118] Ephrem thus relates the idea of the Jews' shame to this act of adulterous idolatry, and uses the resulting image in order to call the Jewish people an adulteress.[119] This adultery, added to the blood that Ephrem claims persists on the hands of the Jews ever after the

112. Ephrem, *Eccl.* 49.13. Compare also, *Ieiun.* 1.12, *Nat.* 24.20, *CH* 51.2, *Cruc.* 5.5, and *Eccl.* 43.20. All translations from these last hymns are from the Syriac text in Edmund Beck, ed., *Des Heiligen Ephraem des Syrers Hymnen de Ecclesia,* CSCO 198, SS 84 (Louvain, 1960).

113. Ephrem, *Ieiun.* 5.8, *Nat.* 10.5 and 14.13; *Ieiun.* 5.8; *de Dom. nos.* 21. Compare Deut 9:7, 9:24, 31:27; Ps 78:8; Isa 30:9, 65.2; Jer 13; Ezek 2.

114. See *Cruc.* 1, as well as the more in-depth discussion of these events in the following chapters.

115. Ephrem, *SdF* 3.356.

116. Ephrem, *Cruc.* 1.6. All translations from these hymns are from the Syriac text in Edmund Beck, ed., *Des Heiligen Ephraem des Syrers Paschahymnen,* CSCO 248, SS 108 (Louvain, 1964).

117. Ephrem, *Cruc.* 1.14.

118. This is a connection that is discussed in more detail below in chapter 3.

119. See, for example, Ephrem, *Cruc.* 1, *Res.* 3, *CJ* 2.

crucifixion, leads him also to refer to the Jews as bloody, defiled, filthy, and pol-luted.[120] These adjectives further contribute to Ephrem's vitriolic anti-Judaism. Rather than relying only on disagreements about theology or scriptural inter-pretation, Ephrem resorts to attacking through insults, repeatedly describing the Jews as a filthy and defiled people that stinks like garlic and onions.

These criticisms of the Jews throughout history lead Ephrem to explain, like the *Epistle of Barnabas,* that ever since the crucifixion God has perma-nently rejected the Jews, who thus lost their covenant and special relationship with God. Although Ephrem attributes the Jews' rejection by God to their stubbornness and rejection of God's Son, he also describes them in many of his texts as confused, astray, and in error.[121] More violently, Ephrem de-scribes the Jews after the crucifixion as dead and uprooted.[122] He says that because they rejected God, they have as a result also been rejected by God.[123] They have been disowned, destroyed, and spilled away as water in favor of the Gentiles (Christians) because they were unworthy.[124]

Combining all of these criticisms and insults of the Jews, Ephrem peri-odically in his writing resorts to outright condemnation of the Jews as "a contemptible flock."[125] He describes God as having made a marriage cov-enant with the Jews at Mt. Sinai, and the Jews instead worshipped the gold-en calf: "your father took the hateful synagogue (for a wife), she who com-mitted adultery with that calf, and because of her he hated her offspring."[126] Thus, Ephrem uses that one incident recorded in Scripture in order to claim that God hates the Jews up through his present day. Likewise, Ephrem refers to the Jews as "the children of the evil one [cf. John 8.44]," and as evil them-selves: "But the evil People that wants our death, enticing, gives us death in food."[127] Through these numerous vitriolic accusations, each of which rein-forces the others and is itself reinforced through frequent repetition through-out Ephrem's hymns—hymns which were themselves repeatedly sung in his church—Ephrem struggles to construct a divide between an allegedly Gen-

---

120. Ephrem, *Azym.* 19; *de Dom. nos.* 5 and *Virg.* 26.15; *CNis.* 67.17; *Virg.* 6.2.

121. See, for example, Ephrem, *Ieiun.* 1.12, 5.8; *HdF* 44, 56; and *Azym.* 1.19.

122. See Ephrem, *Virg.* 26.11 and *SdF* 6.68.

123. See Ephrem, *HdF* 44, 56, 87, 56, and *Nat.* 25.

124. See, for example, Ephrem, *Eccl.* 44.22; *Azym.* 2.13; *Cruc.* 5.5; and *Cruc.* 7.2 (compare *Ep. Barn.* 14.1, 4).

125. Ephrem, *SdF* 3.255. Ephrem here uses a word for flock that has the same root letters [*gzr*] as the word for circumcision, thereby undoubtedly adding another allusion to the Jews.

126. Ephrem, *CNis.* 27.9.

127. Ephrem, *Nat.* 3.8; *Azym.* 19.5.

tile community of uncircumcised Christians who are loved by God and a circumcised community of evil, contemptuous, blind, stubborn, stinking, and divinely rejected Jews.

Contrasting Communities

In addition to the anti-Jewish language discussed above, which primarily insults the Jews without always drawing a direct comparison to Christians, Ephrem also sometimes makes more explicit contrasts between Christians and Jews. Ephrem might hope that criticizing and insulting the Jews would make Judaism a less attractive option for his audience. In order for his rhetoric to effect changes in his community, however, he also depicts two clearly distinct communities, Judaism and Christianity, out of his current context in which those lines appear to have been blurred. It would only be by positing two radically separate options that his audience could be compelled to reject one and choose the other. The poetic contrasts throughout Ephrem's writings aid in presenting Judaism and Christianity as binary opposites, without allowing for anything in between.

Ephrem uses sharp contrasts between bitter and sweet, dark and light, and hidden and revealed to characterize actions and groups of people in sharp contrast to each other. Ephrem writes, "from the bitter ones [Jews], [came] the sweet fruit [the Lord]; and from killers, [came] the Physician who healed all," describing the Jews as bitter and murderers in contrast to "the Lord," the sweet physician.[128] Ephrem echoes this contrast between sweet and bitter in others of his writings, such as regarding Paul in the *Homily on Our Lord:* "He who was full of the bitter will of the Jews, the sweet preaching of the cross was filling him. But when the bitterness of the crucifiers had filled [him], he troubled the churches in his bitterness. But when he was filled with the sweetness of the Crucified, he made bitter the synagogues of the crucifiers."[129] Ephrem elsewhere uses sweet not in contrast to bitter tastes, but rather in contrast to the stench that he associates with the Jews.[130] Likewise, Ephrem characterizes the Jews as dark, in contrast to Christian light, and sometimes combines this with descriptions of things hidden and things

128. Ephrem, *HdF* 12.9. (Compare again the pericope of the dead lion in Judg 14.) All translations from these hymns are from the Syriac text in Edmund Beck, ed., *Des Heiligen Ephraem des Syrers Hymnen de Fide,* CSCO 154, SS 73 (Louvain, 1955).

129. Ephrem, *de Dom. nos.* 25. Compare *CNis.* 11.22; *Eccl.* 38.2; *Azym.* 19; *Virg.* 11.3, 44.13–15, 49.9.

130. See, for example, Ephrem, *Virg.* 11.14; *Nat.* 19.1, 22.28, 28.8; *HdP* 11.12–13.

revealed. Ephrem describes, "the People grew darker like the sun,"[131] in direct contrast to the light of Christian truth.[132] These contrasts rely heavily on sensory images and conjure up a distasteful and dark image of the Jews in sharp contrast to the sweetness and light of Christian truth.

Playing on the idea of darkness versus light, Ephrem also periodically uses language of what is seen and unseen, hidden and revealed, to accuse the Jews of hypocrisy. Ephrem traces this theme back at least as far as the Jews' exodus from Egypt, explaining that the golden calf was merely an excuse to practice openly the idolatry that the Jews secretly had brought with them out of Egypt: "For that idolatry that they stole in their hearts and brought out from Egypt, when it came out in the open, it openly killed those in whom it was dwelling secretly."[133] Ephrem elaborates later in this homily that the Jews made the idol "that they might also worship openly what they had been secretly worshipping in their hearts."[134] In his *Hymns on Crucifixion* Ephrem compares this incident in the wilderness to the Jews' refusal to recognize the Messiah.[135] Knowing that Israel had chosen the visible calf over their invisible God, Ephrem explains, God sent God's Son "clothed with a body" so that he would be visible to God's people, but the Jews, not recognizing him, rejected and killed him.[136]

Continuing to use the distinction between what is hidden and what is revealed, Ephrem charges that contemporary Jews' actions are not what they appear to be. He accuses them of being hypocritical in their actions: "For the blind People hurried to the day of its fast in pride and astray. A fast in its mouth, an idol in its heart; prayer on its lips, augury in its mind; its belly empty of bread, and full of lying. Washing its hands every day, and the concealed blood that is on them calling out against them";[137] and likewise describes them as "outside, beautiful and healthy, and inside, putrid and decaying."[138] The same hypocrisy is true not only for their fasts, Ephrem claims, but also for their Passover celebrations, whose purity they turn to impurity, as well as their circumcision, which is uncircumcision since it does not include the circumcision of the Spirit.[139]

Ephrem often contrasts this alleged Jewish hypocrisy to the virtuous be-

---

131. Ephrem, *Cruc.* 6.16. Compare also *Azym.* 15.20, *Nat.* 1.71–72, 24.12. See also J. Martikainen, *Das Böse und der Teufel in der Theologie Ephraems des Syrers: Ein systematisch-theologishe Untersuchung* (Abo: Abo Academy Research Institute, 1978).

132. See Ephrem, *Nat.* 24.12, *HdF* 8.5–6, and *CH* 43.10. See Brock, *Luminous*, 27–29.

133. Ephrem, *de Dom. nos.* 6.   134. Ephrem, *de Dom. nos.* 17.

135. Ephrem, *Cruc.* 1.16–17.   136. Ephrem, *Cruc.* 1.16.

137. Ephrem, *Ieiun.* 1.12.   138. Ephrem, *CH* 51.9.

139. See Ephrem, *Azym.* 21; *Virg.* 44.17–19.

havior of Christians, or to those scriptural figures such as Moses, whom Ephrem claims for Christian history. For example, Ephrem chastises, while "Moses taught; the People apostasized," and with respect to God's Son, "today the People mock him, and the peoples know him."[140] Again, Ephrem identifies this behavior as early as the time of Moses: "While Moses was praying on the mountain, that blind People was indulging itself. With Moses, a fast of atonement; with the People, the sweet scent of idolatry; Moses together with the One on High; the People together with the calf; the Spirit within Moses, and Legion within the People."[141] More elaborately, however, Ephrem details in several different hymns the rejection and silence of "the People" in comparison to those who did recognize and praise God's Son, and notes God's rejection of the Jews and adoption of the Gentiles that resulted from their behavior.[142] While those who were not expecting him praised and welcomed him, Ephrem claims, the Jews whose prophets predicted him did not recognize him and killed him. Even the stones cried out in recognition, but the Jews remained silent.[143]

Explaining the results of the Jews' silence and of the Gentiles' praise, Ephrem writes,

The People have the voice and the reading; the peoples have the shining forth and the explanation. They have the books and we have the deeds; they have the branches and we their fruits. The scribes read in books; the magi saw in actions the flash of that reading. . . . The simple believers recognized two advents of Christ, but the foolish scribes were not aware of even one advent. Yet the peoples received life from one and there at the other they will be revived. The one advent scattered the People whose understanding was blind; the second will blot out its memory.[144]

Again, as in his other rhetoric, Ephrem explains that as a result of their own actions the Jews have been rejected and replaced by Gentiles, that is, Christians. Contrasting these behaviors both helps Ephrem to depict Christianity and Judaism as two distinct categories, and at the same time associates only uncircumcised Gentiles with Christianity.

In addition to these sharp contrasts, Ephrem also refers to Jews as dead and barren, as opposed to Christian youth and fruitfulness,[145] and describes,

---

140. Ephrem, *Virg.* 49.13; *Cruc.* 8.9.   141. Ephrem, *Ieiun.* 10.4.
142. Ephrem, *Nat.* 24.14–20. Compare also Ephrem, *Virg.* 19.2–4, 20.9, 26.11–14; and *Nat.* 23–9–10.
143. Ephrem, *Eccl.* 41. Compare also *Nat.* 24.
144. Ephrem, *Nat.* 24.4, 11. Compare also *Virg.* 44, *Cruc.* 4.10–13; and *Ieiun.* 5.7–10.
145. Ephrem, *Virg.* 26.11 and 35.13.

"The Gentiles were gleaming and purified and cleansed, but the People were blackened and defiled by that blood."[146] These themes of youth and age come out also in Ephrem's *Hymns on Unleavened Bread* in which he presents a lengthy series of descriptions that contrast both the Christian Eucharist, "the drug of life," and unleavened bread, "a deadly drug," as well as the Christians and Jews to whom each belongs:[147]

Woe to the People that became old, with the unleavened bread. . . . Woe to the unleavened bread, which little by little led those who ate it toward unbelievers. . . . That symbol of the Son, Moses hid within that unleavened bread as a drug of life. He washed away the drug of life from the unleavened bread and gave it to Judas as a deadly drug. Therefore the deadly drug also of Iscariot each received from that unleavened bread.[148]

In this series of hymns, Ephrem locates the negative qualities that he attributes to the Jews in their unleavened bread. As with the anti-Jewish insults about the blind stubbornness of the Jews, these colorful contrasts that permeate Ephrem's writings work to address what he understood to be a problematic comfort among some in his audience in blending what he taught are elements of two separate religions, Judaism and Christianity. By tainting the Jews with insults and defining an impassible chasm between Jews and Christians, Ephrem's rhetoric compels his audience to distinguish between the two, and to recognize Christianity as unquestionably superior.

Dangerous Liaisons

One final tactic that Ephrem employs in his anti-Jewish rhetoric is not only to insult the Jews and to emphasize a clear distinction between Jews and Christians, but also to define the Jews as dangerous killers who have in the past threatened their own leaders, even their own Messiah, and who now, in Ephrem's time, likewise pose a physical threat to God's people, Christians. Given Ephrem's frequent appeals to Scripture, it is no surprise that his texts contain many Scripture-based accusations against the Jews.[149] Drawing on the scriptural history of Israel's struggles against prophets, and of Jewish leaders' role in the crucifixion in the New Testament Gospels, Ephrem uses the epithets "crucifiers" and "murderers" as synonyms for "the [Jewish] Peo-

---

146. Ephrem, *Virg.* 26.15.   147. Ephrem, *Azym.* 17–19.

148. Ephrem, *Azym.* 18.12–17.

149. The scriptural basis for much of Ephrem's language provides the framework for a fuller discussion in chapter 3.

ple," frequently referring to them in this way without further elaboration. In his writings Ephrem repeatedly refers to the Jews simply as "the crucifiers," identifying the entire people for all time as the murderers of Christ.[150] Elsewhere Ephrem refers to the Jews more generally as "killers," referring to the crucifixion but also to earlier attacks on prophets, and implying that Jews also are dangerous to the world at large, including Christians.[151] In his *Sermons on Faith,* Ephrem writes about the Jewish people:

Having tasted much blood, it was not able to stop killing. Then it killed openly; now it kills secretly. . . . It has no prophets to kill openly. . . . It clothed itself with those prophets whom it then had killed. It clothed itself with them . . . so that it might kill with them while disputing. It killed the body of the prophets and was clothed with the voices of the prophets, so that instead of the prophets it might kill those who read in the Prophets.[152]

Just as the Jews have in the past killed their own prophets, Ephrem warns, they now threaten Christians who read these same Prophets.[153] Within Ephrem's context, this language about the danger that Jews posed would have offered incentive to the people in Ephrem's audience to remain within what Ephrem's describes as the safe haven of his church rather than risk their very lives at the hands of the murderous Jews.

In addition to these two specific claims of "killing" and "crucifying," Ephrem frequently uses other vocabulary to convey the same message. He calls the Jewish people a butcher who "slaughtered the prophets,"[154] and claims that they stabbed "the true ones, Moses and the prophets."[155] Primarily, however, he repeatedly recounts the New Testament Passion Narrative throughout his writings, emphasizing again and again the abuse and brutality that the Jews allegedly carried out. Ephrem notes that "the crucifiers . . . mocked our Lord,"[156] and elsewhere gives the specifics: they mocked him, hit him with a reed, and pounded in the nails. Ephrem writes, "They hung the

150. For Ephrem's repeated references to the Jews as crucifiers, see, for example, Ephrem *de Dom. nos.* 13, 25, 26, 33; *Cruc.* 5.1, 8.7; *Azym.* 1.11, 18; *Virg.* 11.17, 12.30, 21.3, 26.14, 28.11, 30.11, 34.7, 35.13, 36.3–4, 37.9; *Nat.* 3.8; *CJ* 4.18, 24; *CH* 38.5 and 51.2; *CNis.* 29.1, 42.9; *HdF* 39.1, *HdF* 87.10.

151. For references to Jews as killers, see, for example, Ephrem, *SdF* 3.392; *de Dom. nos.* 13, 26; *Azym.* 1.7; *Virg.* 8.20, 8.22, 20.3, 28.7, 30.10; *Nat.* 6.23, 24.17; *CJ* 4.24; *HdF* 12.9.

152. Ephrem, *SdF* 3.329–348. Compare Ephrem, *Azym.* 19; *Comm. Diat.* 2.7.

153. This is another common Christian accusation. See the more in-depth discussion of Ephrem's use of the Prophets in chapter 3.

154. Ephrem, *SdF* 3.379–382. Compare also his use of the word "slaughter" to refer to the killing of Christ in *Azym.* 2.3, 3.1.

155. Ephrem, *CNis.* 27.10.

156. Ephrem, *HdF* 39.1. Compare also Ephrem, *Cruc.* 1.5–14, 5.5, 8.9.

circumcised one," and "with a reed they beat him."[157] Ephrem also emphasizes that the Jews pounded nails into him at the crucifixion, referring to the nails
"that they thrust into him."[158] Putting the many actions together, Ephrem describes "the spitting . . . the vinegar and thorns, nails and wood, garments and
reed, and the spear that struck him."[159] Ephrem identifies this crucifixion as
"the evil that their hands had done," namely, the murder, as Ephrem describes
it, not only of their Messiah, but in fact of God: the Jewish people "hung God
upon the cross."[160] Highlighting the crucifixion as not only a key moment in
the history of the world, but also as a turning point in the history of the Jews,
Ephrem emphasizes the threat that the Jews pose by reminding his audience
week after week through his hymns and sermons about the murderous nature
that he attributes not only to the Jews of Jesus' generation, but to all Jews of
all generations, including those in fourth-century Syria.

Although these descriptions of the crucifixion are themselves enough to
construct an image of Jews as a deadly threat, Ephrem reinforces this picture
further by his emphasis on blood. Matthew 27:24–25 claims that when Jesus
was on trial before Pilate, "when Pilate saw that he could do nothing, but
rather that a riot was beginning, he took some water and washed his hands
before the crowd, saying, 'I am innocent of this man's blood; see to it yourselves.' Then the people as a whole answered, 'His blood be on us and on our
children!'"[161] Ephrem capitalizes on this scriptural image in order to conjure
up a depiction of a crowd of Jews with bloodied hands after the crucifixion.
For example, Ephrem refers to "Israel who killed you, and who is marked
with your blood."[162] These bloody descriptions emphasize the violence as
well as the defilement of the Jews whom they purport to describe.

---

157. Ephrem, *Cruc.* 5.5, 13. For other references in Ephrem to the Jews hitting Jesus with a
reed, see *Cruc.* 4.10, *HdF* 87.13.

158. Ephrem, *CH* 39.11. Compare Ephrem, *Azym.* 20. refrain; *Virg.* 8.23, 30.10.

159. Ephrem, *HdF* 87.16. See also *Azym.* 18.4; *Ieiun.* 5.7.

160. Ephrem, *SdF* 3.359 and *Ieiun.* 5.6. Compare also *de Dom. nos.* 5–6. Ephrem was not the
only early Christian writer to accuse the Jews of deicide. The earliest extant text that raises the
charge of killing Christ to the accusation of killing God is Melito of Sardis's second-century
homily *Peri Pascha* 96.

161. All scriptural quotations are from the NRSV. Ephrem could have known this passage
from the Old Syriac version of the New Testament (see George Kiraz, *Comparative Edition of
the Syriac Gospels: Aligning the Sinaiticus, Curetonianus, Peshîttâ and Harklean Versions*, vol. 1: *Matthew* (New York: Brill, 1996), 433–34. Although Ephrem's *Commentary on the Diatesseron* does not
include this Matthean passage explicitly, Ephrem's comments on the *Diatesseron* text do refer to
the content of the passage (*Comm. Diat.* 21.10; compare also *Azym.* 19.25).

162. Ephrem, *de Dom. nos.* 5.

It was not only the Jews of his own time that Ephrem accused of this bloody crime, but rather all Jews ever after the crucifixion. Ephrem writes, "Pilate washed and cleansed his hands, so that the People were guilty of bespattering its hands. . . . in order to shame the daughter of Zion, whose head remained uncovered and whose hands were defiled with the precious blood."[163] This language of the Jews' hands being defiled with blood creates a vivid picture for Ephrem's audience. In fact, the refrain in one of Ephrem's *Hymns on Unleavened Bread,* which would have been repeated again and again as the hymn was sung, echoes this bloody image: "Blessed is the one who rejected the People and its unleavened bread because its hands were defiled with the precious blood."[164] Likewise, Hymn 19 of this same series, given in its entirety above, also emphasizes the bloodiness of the Jews' hands. Through this emphasis on *all* Jews' participation in the crucifixion, as well as on the bloody defilement that followed, Ephrem heightens the gore of the image and also the danger of the threat that he claims contemporary Jews pose to his audience.

In addition to the crucifixion, Ephrem also uses other scriptural events to demonstrate the violent aggression of the Jews in all times. Ephrem describes the Jews as a people who persecutes and abuses innocent people: "Moses in his time [the People] persecuted; their Lord in his time they crucified."[165] Elsewhere Ephrem elaborates, listing several different specific examples, often from Scripture, at one time. For example, in his *Hymns on Fasting* Ephrem accuses the Jews of persecuting others: "you devour the orphan; . . . you strip the widow; . . . you subject the free to a yoke."[166] The charge of eating children recurs in another hymn when Ephrem applies some of the least flattering moments in the scriptural history of Israel to contemporary Jews:

But it was not death that crucified Jesus, but rather it was the People. How hateful therefore are the People. . . . In a pit of filth they threw Jeremiah [Jeremiah 38:6]. . . . They battered Naboth with stones like a dog [1 Kings 21:13]. . . . The Hebrews ate their own children in hunger [2 Kings 6:28–29]. . . . The greedy Hebrews ate their children. . . . They slew the sons of the prophets and the prophets and threw [them] away. . . . How many deaths instead of the one death there was among the People.[167]

163. Ephrem, *Azym.* 13.11, 23. Compare also *Virg.* 30.10 in which Ephrem describes that the Jews pierced Jesus' side on the cross, and then "wash their hands with your blood."

164. Ephrem, *Azym.* 17, refrain. Compare also *Azym* 19.

165. Ephrem, *SdF* 3.317–18. Compare also *Virg.* 19.4, 20.2, 21.3, *Eccl.* 32.6, *Ieiun.* 5.6, and *Nat.* 7.6.

166. Ephrem, *Ieiun.* 2.1.

167. Ephrem, *CNis.* 67.2–10. There are also numerous New Testament passages that describe the Jews as a dangerous group: for example, John 8:44; Matt 21:33–44, 22:6, 23:29–36; Heb 11:32–38.

Through these accusations, Ephrem emphasizes the danger that Jews pose, granting authority to his claims by basing them on the very texts that Jews and Christians share.

Having described the Jews in so many negative ways throughout his writings, making them appear foolish, blind, and rejected as well as dangerous and bloodied murderers, Ephrem occasionally warns his audience explicitly about their own immediate danger and how they might save themselves from the threat that the Jews pose. Ephrem describes a dangerous fury of the Jews that threatens contemporary Christians, and also the "deadly drug" of the unleavened bread with which the Jews allegedly entice Christians to join in their festivals. Ephrem explains that God originally gave circumcision to the Jews "so that the revealed sign that he set upon them might restrain the vehemence of [the flock's] fury,"[168] suggesting the uncontrolled danger that lurks in them. Likewise, his references to contemporary Jews' unleavened bread as "a deadly drug" further builds the image of the danger of interacting with the Jewish community, particularly during their festivals.[169]

Whereas his other anti-Jewish rhetoric forces a separation between two communities, and values one negatively and the other positively, in this language of warning Ephrem explicitly instructs his audience as to what they must do to save themselves, namely, distance themselves from the threat by harboring themselves in the safety of Ephrem's church. One place in which Ephrem is particularly explicit about the danger that he claims contemporary Jews pose to those in his congregation is in the third of his *Sermons on Faith*. Although he frequently describes Christians and Jews as two unmistakably distinct communities, this sermon is one of the places that suggests this dichotomous anti-Jewish rhetoric does not merely describe the situation as it already is, but prescribes what he hopes it will become. Ephrem exhorts,

The commandments that these unbelieving [People] did not keep in their time, they now compel us to keep. . . . They seek to tear to pieces the limbs of the healthy. . . . Having tasted much blood, it was not able to stop killing. . . . for they circle sea and land that they might lead a companion to Gehenna [Matthew 23:15]. . . . Flee from it, weak one! Your death and your blood are nothing to it. It received the blood of God. Will it really be afraid of yours? . . . [The People] slaughtered these prophets like innocent lambs. The physicians came to them; [the People] became a butcher to them. Flee and escape from the madness! Run and take refuge in Christ![170]

168. Ephrem, *SdF* 3.249–50.
169. See, for example, Ephrem, *Azym.* 18.9, 11; 19.7, 9, 22, 24.
170. Ephrem, *SdF* 3.287–96, 329–34, 349–52, 379–84. Compare also *Azym.* 19.

Ephrem uses anti-Jewish language in this sermon not only to underscore the danger that Jews pose, but, as he did in number 19 of his *Hymns on Unleavened Bread,* also to warn his audience about the immediacy of the threat to them personally, and to tell them what to do to rescue themselves. Taken together with the rest of Ephrem's anti-Jewish language, these warnings appeal to Ephrem's audience to flee from the abhorrent, dangerous, and divinely rejected Jews, from their synagogues, their festivals, and their community, and to harbor themselves within the safety of Christ and Ephrem's Christian church and teachings. Through this rhetoric Ephrem describes a physical threat to his audience to match the theological danger that Ephrem feels they face in what he sees as too close a connection with Judaism.

Miriam Taylor has noted that some contemporary scholars appear to validate early Christian anti-Jewish rhetoric by explaining it as a reaction to an aggressive Jewish threat, a picture that relies on a misrepresentation of Judaism.[171] In the case of Ephrem's writings, this interpretation also overlooks the full rhetorical force of his descriptions within fourth-century Syriac Christianity. Ephrem's writings are not an "objective" or disinterested description of history or of his local social and political situation; rather, Ephrem's Christian rhetoric is itself attempting to effect certain behavior within his audience by presenting his descriptions of his context through his own particular lens.[172] Ephrem uses Gospel narratives to construct a history that leads up to the description of the threatening proselytism of contemporary Jews, permanently stained by their murder of Christ. Himself proselytizing for Nicene Christianity, Ephrem presents a forceful "proof" of the Jews' depravity and of the invalidity of Judaism that serves to highlight that Nicene Christianity, with Ephrem as its interpreter, is the only good, right, and safe religious community in which to participate in a time of intra-Christian conflict.

Ephrem's sermons and hymns address a congregation that appears to have included some who participated in local Jewish festivals. While there is evidence for Jews living in fourth-century Nisibis and Edessa, and Ephrem's writings themselves imply further evidence of this, Ephrem's anti-Jewish rhetoric reveals more about Ephrem's Christianity than it does about fourth-century Judaism. Ephrem's Scripture-based anti-Jewish rhetoric attempts to

171. M. Taylor, *Anti-Judaism.*

172. I have found the vocabulary of ideology criticism particularly useful in analyzing the constructive power of Ephrem's rhetoric in this regard. See Althusser, "Ideology"; Larrain, *Concept of Ideology*; Giddens, "Four Theses"; Thompson, *Studies*; Thompson, *Ideology*; Eagleton, *Ideology*; Larrain, *Ideology.*

coerce those in his congregation to unify themselves into a tight-knit group with clear community boundaries, conveniently united under the Nicene control of Ephrem's own church community, and clearly distinguished from "Jews" whom Ephrem portrays so negatively and threateningly. Describing the immorality of all Jews and the invalidity of contemporary Judaism, Ephrem's texts shape and naturalize a dire social situation that he uses to advocate a fear-driven group cohesion, and clear imperial Nicene boundaries for his Syriac Christian community. While some scholars have used Ephrem's numerous hymns to reconstruct active local Jewish proselytism in Ephrem's community,[173] this examination reveals that Ephrem's writings reflect more about the "proselytizing" efforts of the Christian Ephrem as, wielding scriptural authority and anti-Jewish rhetoric, he struggled to fit his local Christian community into an imperial mold of Nicene Christianity.

Syriac and Greek Anti-Judaizing

Just as Ephrem draws on a deep history of Christian anti-Jewish language for his poetry, so too his fourth-century concerns about Judaizing Christians echo the concerns of several other fourth-century texts. Ephrem's anti-Judaizing language did not exist in a vacuum; anti-Judaizing discussions also appear, for example, in the *Didascalia,* in the Syriac *Demonstrations* of Aphrahat from the 340s,[174] and in a series of eight Greek homilies by another Syrian, John Chrysostom (ca. 349–407).[175] The striking similarities, particularly between Ephrem and John Chrysostom, suggest both the presence of fourth-century Christians celebrating Jewish holidays, to the consternation of pro-Nicene leaders, and the relationship of Ephrem's Syriac hymns to Greek Christian rhetoric.

Despite some uncertainty about the date and place of the *Didascalia's* origin, scholars are largely agreed that the third-century Greek text originated

---

173. See, for example, Beck, *Reden,* 118–19; and J. B. Morris, *Select Works of St. Ephrem the Syrian* (Oxford, 1847), 396n.

174. Aphrahat's *Demonstrations* range in date from ca. 336–345, but the ones that are most useful in this comparison are from 343–344 (Jacob Neusner, *Aphrahat and Judaism,* 3–5).

175. The Greek writings of the Syrian Eusebius of Emesa (ca. 300–359) also make an interesting comparison, although his arguments are not as similar to Ephrem's as are those of Aphrahat and John Chrysostom, and less is known about his context in Emesa. See R. B. ter Haar Romeny, *A Syrian in Greek Dress: The Use of Greek, Hebrew, and Syriac Biblical Texts in Eusebius of Emesa's* Commentary on Genesis (Louvain: Peeters, 1997).

in Syria and was translated into Syriac and Latin by the early fourth century.[176] The language of this text provides an important reference for Ephrem's fourth-century Syriac rhetoric, as both express deep concern that some in their Christian audience inappropriately participate in the rituals of "the People," the texts' designation for the Jews. The *Didascalia's* criticism of those who continue to keep some of the "bonds" that are associated with "the second legislation" foreshadows Ephrem's sharp criticisms of those who follow Jewish law and festival practices, and his references to the different times for different laws. Ephrem's accusations that the Jews are blind, killed the Messiah, disobeyed God, and went astray further echo the concerns and vocabulary of the *Didascalia,* whose fourth-century Syriac translation may well have been familiar to Ephrem.[177] While the *Didascalia* does not have as concrete a context as Ephrem's, John Chrysostom's, and Aphrahat's writings do, its language and anti-Judaizing concerns remain significant for contextualizing Ephrem's similar accusations.

Like the *Didascalia,* Aphrahat's texts also contain language that sheds light on the breadth of the concern regarding Judaizing that Ephrem addresses. Like Ephrem, Aphrahat wrote in a context that contained an active contemporary Jewish community. Aphrahat, a church leader in Persia, wrote his Syriac *Discourses* in the middle of the fourth century, during Shapur II's persecution of Christians. Aphrahat describes local Jews' harassment of Christians at this time, suggesting that Jews challenged the validity of Christianity based on its persecuted status and raised up Judaism as a better (and safer) alternative.[178] For example, in Demonstration 21, *On Persecution,* Aphrahat notes, "I heard a reproach that has greatly grieved me, for the unclean ones say, 'This people which is gathered together from all the peoples has no God.' Thus say the unjust ones: 'For if they had a God, why does he not demand the vengeance of his people?' A thick darkness thickens about me even more when even the Jews reproach us and magnify themselves over the children of our

176. Arthur Vööbus, *The Didascalia Apostolorum in Syriac,* CSCO 402, SS 176 (1979), 23; R. H. Connolly, *Didascalia Apostolorum* (Oxford: Clarendon Press, 1929); Charlotte Fonrobert, *"Didascalia."*

177. Chapter 3 discusses the parallels in these texts' concern for Exodus 32 as a pivotal moment in Jewish history.

178. See, for example, Aphrahat, *Dem.* 12.12, 15.1, 18.1, 21.1. For discussion of Aphrahat's relation to Judaism, see Gavin, "Aphraates and the Jews"; Williams, *Adversus Judaeos;* Neusner, *Aphrahat;* Snaith, "Aphrahat and the Jews"; Hayman, "The Image of the Jew"; Benin, "Commandments"; Koltun-Fromm, "Jewish-Christian Polemics"; Koltun-Fromm, "A Jewish-Christian Conversation"; Becker, "Anti-Judaism."

people."[179] Within this context, Aphrahat coaxes his Christian audience to maintain their Christian faith and not be swayed by the Jews, and he laments that "greatly troubled are the minds of the simple and unlearned [Christian] people" about *kashrut,* and notes that there are members of the church who "are vexed concerning this time of the Passover."[180] While Aphrahat's anti-Jewish rhetoric is muted in comparison to Ephrem's vehement hostility, he nonetheless similarly uses it in order to try to persuade Christians who might be tempted to turn to Judaism to remain with the Christian church.[181]

Likewise, in his *Discourses against Judaizing Christians,* given in Antioch in 386 and 387, John Chrysostom is explicit about the contemporary problems that occasion his sermons.[182] He writes, "The festivals of the pitiful and miserable Jews are soon to march upon us one after the other and in quick succession: the feast of Trumpets, the feast of Tabernacles, the fasts. . . . if I should fail to cure those who are sick with the Judaizing disease, I am afraid that . . . some Christians may partake in the Jews' transgressions."[183] These discourses were allegedly prompted by the approach of Jewish festivals and

179. Aphrahat, *Dem.* 21.1. All quotations from Aphrahat are my translations from the Syriac in PS 1, with consultation of the English translation in Neusner, *Aphrahat.*

180. Aphrahat, *Dem.* 15.1, 12.12.

· 181. Eusebius of Emesa's homilies also try to convince his audience of the validity of Christianity over Judaism (see Hennings, "Eusebius").

182. See Lukyn Williams, *Adversus,* 132–38; G. Richter, "Über die älteste Auseinandersetzung der syrischen Christen mit den Juden," *ZNW* 35 (1936): 101–14; Fred Allen Grissom, "Chrysostom and the Jews: Studies in Jewish-Christian Relations in Fourth-century Antioch" (Ph.D. diss., Southern Baptist Theological Seminary, 1978); Wayne Meeks and Robert Wilken, *Jews and Christians in Antioch in the First Four Centuries of the Common Era* (Missoula: Scholars Press, 1978); Paul W. Harkins, "Introduction" (FC 68), xxi–lxii; Robert L. Wilken, *John Chrysostom and the Jews: Rhetoric and Reality in the Late 4th Century* (Berkeley: University of California, 1983); Klaas Smelik, "John Chrysostom's Homilies against the Jews: Some Comments," *Nederlands theologish tijdschrift* 39 (1985): 194–200; Kinzig, "Non-Separation," 35–43; Adolf Ritter, "John Chrysostom and the Jews: A Reconsideration," in *Ancient Christianity in the Caucasus,* ed. Tamila Mgaloblishvili (Surrey, England: Curzon, 1998), 141–54, 231–32; Pieter van der Horst, "Jews and Christians in Antioch at the End of the Fourth Century," in *Christian-Jewish Relations through the Centuries,* eds. Stanley Porter and Brook Pearson (Sheffield: Sheffield Academic Press, 2000), 228–38. See also the numerous works on John Chrysostom more generally, such as J. N. D. Kelly, *Golden Mouth: The Story of John Chrysostom—Ascetic, Preacher, Bishop* (London: Duckworth, 1995). Scholars agree that there is strong evidence of a significant and visible Jewish community in Antioch during Chrysostom's lifetime. See also Christine Shepardson, "Controlling Contested Places: John Chrysostom's *Adversus Iudaeos* Homilies and the Spatial Politics of Religious Controversy," *JECS* 15, no. 4 (2007): 483–516.

183. Chrysostom, *Discourses* 1.1.5. All quotations from John Chrysostom's *Discourses against Judaizing Christians* are from Paul Harkins's English translation (FC 68), with consultation of the Greek text in PG 48. It is worth noting that this English translation contains the page references to the corresponding Greek text in the PG.

fasts, and by Chrysostom's knowledge that there were those in his congregation who had in the past joined the Jews in these celebrations, and whom he anticipated would do so again.[184] Chrysostom insists, however, that these Judaizers wish to be identified as Christians: "You profess you are a Christian, but you rush off to their synagogues."[185] Chrysostom thus acknowledges that there are those he calls Christians who participate in Jewish festivals and, like Ephrem, he pleads with his church audience that the Judaizers cease their harmful behavior.

This apparently close proximity of Christians and Jews, without clearly distinct community boundaries between the two where the church leaders would like them to be, led each of these authors to argue against Jews, Judaism, and Judaizing. In the same way that Ephrem denounces the Jews as foolish and blind, and insultingly describes them as an adulteress, so too Aphrahat calls them "wanton," "uprooted," "boastful," "rebellious . . . [and] rejected,"[186] and Chrysostom describes them as "in darkness," "obstinate," and "in error," and refers to their synagogue as "not only a brothel and a theater; it also is a den of robbers and a lodging for wild beasts."[187] Like Ephrem, Chrysostom also warns about the danger that Jews and Judaizers pose to true Christians. Chrysostom writes, "Do you see that demons dwell in [Jews'] souls and that these demons are more dangerous than the ones of old? . . . Do you not shudder to come into the same place with men possessed, who have so many unclean spirits, who have been reared amid slaughter and bloodshed? . . . They became more savage than any wild beast."[188] In these ways, these authors attempt to coerce their audience into construing Judaism as a dangerous and unacceptable antithesis to Christianity, in order that their congregants might stop participating in Jewish celebrations.[189]

This comparison further demonstrates Ephrem's coherence within Greek Christianity, which scholars earlier disputed.[190] In the early twentieth century, F. C. Burkitt influenced decades of scholarship by describing Ephrem and

---

184. See Wilken, *Chrysostom*; Grissom, "Chrysostom"; and Paul Harkins' "Introduction" to his translation of Chrysostom's *Discourses* (FC 68), xxi–lxii.

185. John Chrysostom, *Discourses* 8.8.9.

186. Aphrahat, *Dem.* 18.1, 19.1, 16.8 and 15.8, 19.3 and 11.1.

187. John Chrysostom, *Discourses* 1.2.1; 8.5.4; 2.1.5; 1.3.1. See also Wilken's commentary on the invective of these Discourses (Wilken, *Chrysostom*, 95–127; cf. Grissom, "Chrysostom"). Compare also Eusebius of Emesa, *Hom.* 19.

188. John Chrysostom, *Discourses* 1.6.7 (see also 1.1.6, 1.5.7–8, 2.2.1, 3.2.6, 8.3.10, 8.8.9).

189. See Shepardson, "Paschal Politics."

190. See Shepardson, "Syria, Syriac, Syrian."

Syriac Christianity as utterly separated from the Greek world to the west, facilitating eastern Syria's isolation from studies on the Roman Empire.[191] More recent scholars have tempered this picture,[192] and critical works such as those by Sidney Griffith, Thomas Koonammakkal, and Ute Possekel argue persuasively that despite Ephrem's own denunciation of "the poison of the Greeks," he was duly influenced by the Roman Empire as a whole, as well as by the language and concepts of Greek philosophy.[193] Griffith has issued a heart-felt plea to end this misrepresentation:

> The time is long overdue for scholars to stop repeating the supposed truism that Ephrem knew no Greek, and to consider the likelihood that far from being among the last exponents of a purely Semitic Christianity, Ephraem of Nisibis and Edessa was actually one of the first in a long line of astonishingly successful Syrian writers who knew how to state the faith of the "orthodox" church of Nicaea in a flawless Syriac idiom that left nothing wanting in the pledge of allegiance to the orthodoxy of the church in the Roman Empire.[194]

191. Burkitt, *Early Eastern Christianity*. Compare also Robert Murray's earlier works, such as "Ephrem Syrus," *Catholic Dictionary of Theology*, vol. 2 (New York: Nelson, 1967), 220–23. Murray later retracted his earlier claims, and referred instead to the "hybrid" context of Ephrem's world (Murray, "Characteristics," 3–16). Peter Bruns argues that Ephrem's anti-Arian arguments actually led him to a deep aversion of everything Greek (Peter Bruns, "Arius hellenizans?—Ephräm der Syrer und die neoarianischen Kontroversen seiner Zeit," *ZKG* 101 [1990]: 47, 56). Bruns claims that Ephrem did not know Greek, and was actively hostile to it from the position of his "Semitic" Syriac church. Traditionally, scholars have assumed almost no contact with the Greek-speaking Roman Empire, reveling in Syriac Christianity as a "pure" and unadulterated example of "Semitic" Christianity such as Jesus himself began and his immediate followers practiced. As recently as 1996, Valavanolickal advocated this claim (Valavanolickal, *The Use of the Gospel Parables*).

192. Sebastian Brock has described Ephrem as a meeting point between the Greek and Syriac churches (*Luminous*, 13–21; cf. "From Antagonism to Assimilation: Syriac Attitudes to Greek Learning," in *East of Byzantium: Syria and Armenia in the Formative Period*, eds. Nina Garsoïan, Thomas Mathews, and Robert Thomson [Washington, D.C.: Dumbarton Oaks, 1982], 17–33). See also Sebastian Brock, "Greek and Syriac in Late Antique Syria," in *Literacy and Power in the Ancient World*, eds. A. K. Bowman and G. Woolf (Cambridge: Cambridge University Press, 1994), 149–60. While Brock does not think that Ephrem knew much Greek, he does believe that Ephrem would have been at least somewhat familiar with both Greek language and thought (see also Brock, *From Ephrem*).

193. Ephrem, *HdF* 2.24. Thomas Koonammakkal has written a persuasive article challenging the traditional picture of Syriac Christianity as entirely removed from Greek influence (Thomas Koonammakkal, "St. Ephrem and Greek Wisdom," in *VI Symposium Syriacum, 1992*, ed. René Lavenant [Rome: Pontificio Istituto Orientale, 1994], 168–76). Koonammakkal notes that Ephrem's references to "the poison of the Greeks" is a rhetorical device to critique a particular aspect of Greek philosophy, and is not a larger commentary on Greek language and life. Sidney Griffith's work echoes this critique of earlier scholarship. See, for example, Sidney Griffith, "Deacon," 27–29; "The Marks of the 'True Church'"; "Setting Right." Ute Possekel has also significantly added to this discussion: Ute Possekel, *Evidence of Greek Philosophical Concepts in the Writings of Ephrem the Syrian* (Louvain: Peeters, 1999).

194. Griffith, "Setting Right," 114.

While Ephrem wrote in Syriac, given the multilingual nature of his context, we can no longer imagine that he was wholly unfamiliar with the Greek language or with hellenistic ideas, and his relation to Greek anti-Jewish and anti-Judaizing texts contributes to this picture.[195]

Conclusion

The evidence for visible Jewish communities in Nisibis and Edessa during Ephrem's lifetime means that we must take this reality into account in order to understand his anti-Jewish language. A close examination of Ephrem's anti-Jewish rhetoric suggests that he, like other fourth-century Christian leaders such as Aphrahat and John Chrysostom, faced a congregation that included people who both participated in Jewish festivals and attended church services.[196] Ephrem therefore seems to address some uncritical local "Christian" participation in what he wants to distinguish as a particularly "Jewish" holiday. Although Ephrem uses numerous rhetorical methods to create distance between Judaism and Christianity, and between Jews and Christians, this analysis of his language suggests that more fluidity still existed between the two groups than Ephrem would have liked. Much of Ephrem's anti-Jewish rhetoric thus appears to stem from what we might term boundary anxiety, a desire to define the boundaries of "Christianity" in his context by delineating what behaviors are and are not acceptable for members of a (Nicene) Christian community.[197]

While scholarship has traditionally separated the study and history of Syriac Christianity from that of early Greek and Latin Christianity, Ephrem's anti-Jewish rhetoric reflects the efforts of a fourth-century deacon working to bring his local Christianity in line with his vision of the orthodoxy of the empire, Nicene Christianity. This effort certainly was not unique to Syria, although Ephrem's particular focus on clearly distinguishing Judaism from Christianity and forbidding Judaizing behavior within his congregation is closely tied to his Syrian context. This anti-Jewish rhetoric is perhaps most plausibly understood as an attempt to define proper social behavior and boundaries for an as-yet permeable Syriac "Christianity" that he is determined to make comply with the Nicene Christianity that he imagines

---

195. See also Shepardson, "Syria, Syriac, Syrian."
196. See also Shepardson, "Paschal Politics."
197. See also Boyarin, Border Lines.

will one day be synonymous with the Roman Empire itself. Ephrem's use of anti-Jewish rhetoric to depict contemporary Jews as dangerous and Judaism as divinely rejected is therefore a strong proselytizing effort to establish clear Nicene boundaries around his community, while convincing Nisibis's and Edessa's church attendees that in order to be Christian, they must be within that community under Nicene control. Ephrem's anti-Jewish language argues against Jews and Judaizers, and also against Christian opponents whom Ephrem claims equally challenge Nicene orthodoxy by resembling the Jews not in their physical actions, but in their theological subordination of the Son.

CHAPTER THREE

৩৩

Ephrem's Use of Scriptural History

While Ephrem's anti-Judaizing language and concerns for the Judaizing behavior of his local church audience represent one significant means by which
he attempts to assert the framework of Nicene orthodoxy in his eastern Syrian context, it is by no means the only one by which he does so. Ephrem's arguments against those Christians whose teachings subordinate the Son too
much to the Father likewise struggle to promote Nicene Christianity as the
orthodoxy of the Roman Empire, and also use anti-Jewish language to do so.
In order that these "Arian" Christians can become "Jews" in Ephrem's rhetorical accusations, his definition of "Jews" must be one that does not rely solely
on his audience's interaction with members of the contemporary local synagogue.[1] Since Ephrem does not accuse these particular Christians of Judaizing in their physical behavior, he must draw on a broader definition of Jews
and Judaism in order to conflate these Christians with the Jews. Ephrem ac-
complishes this rhetorical twist through his complex interpretation of Christian Scripture. Ephrem's use of the two Testaments of Christian Scripture to
paint a very particular negative history for, and description of, "the People"
provides the framework for understanding how Ephrem then manipulates
this scriptural history in order to invalidate not only contemporary Judaism,
but also the teachings of "Arian" Christians.

---

1. Compare the discussion in Averil Cameron, "Jews and Heretics—A Category Error?" in
The Ways that Never Parted, eds. Adam Becker and Annette Yoshiko Reed (Tübingen: Mohr Siebeck, 2003), 345–60.

Scriptural Interpretation as Self-Definition

The relationship between Scripture and history is complex in any Christian account, which must, by its very nature, concurrently account for the world that Christians inhabit as well as for Christian salvation history. For Ephrem, Scripture is a detailed and accurate record of the history of the world. As such, Christian Scripture provides Ephrem not only with the history of God's interaction with humanity, but also more broadly with the events of human history in terms of different social groups and their behavior relative to one another as well as to the divine. Therefore, all of human history is sacred for Ephrem, and thus the right telling of that history is the provenance of the orthodox religious leaders of God's chosen people. Understanding himself to be one of these leaders, Ephrem narrates Scripture through his liturgical writings, and in the process presents a world history that has significant social ramifications within his own fourth-century community. Ephrem's use of Scripture to recount history produces a grand narrative that supports, and in fact culminates in, his own conclusions that the Jewish people forfeited God's divine favor through their creation of the golden calf at Mt. Sinai, and that Judaism after the crucifixion of Jesus is entirely defunct. Through such scripturally supported historical narratives, Ephrem constructs for his audience a world with distinct and divinely sanctioned social boundaries between Jews and Christians, and at the same time leaves no doubt that it is "Christians" rather than "Jews" who are God's chosen people. Outlining the rhetoric that supports and validates Ephrem's historical narrative reveals that he uses Scripture in order to "prove" to his audience that Jews are dangerous, blind, and divinely rejected, that Christians are now God's people, and that he is an authoritative interpreter of Scripture. Ephrem's anti-Jewish language participates in outlining an ideological framework that reifies that framework while purporting to describe the social, religious, and political situation in fourth-century Syria.[2]

Ephrem, like other fourth-century Christians, found himself in the ironic situation of needing to rescue Jewish Scripture (and God's covenant with

2. Ephrem similarly constructs scriptural arguments against groups other than Jews and Judaizers, particularly against the followers of Mani, Marcion, and Bardaisan (see especially Ephrem's *Prose Refutations*). This current discussion focuses explicitly on Ephrem's anti-Jewish language, but this rhetoric is undeniably part of Ephrem's larger polemical project, in which Christian Scripture plays a significant role.

Israel) from the Jews, while also denouncing contemporary Jews and Judaism. While this situation led to a tradition of Christian anti-Jewish polemic, it also made Christian interpretation of Scripture a complex and political enterprise.[3] Christian leaders negotiated the potential pitfalls of biblical exegesis in a variety of ways, but in a context of competing interpreters and interpretations, Christian leaders such as Ephrem had to present and defend, whether implicitly or explicitly, their particular reading strategy for Scripture. Christians had to justify and explain the related claims of their rightful possession of Jewish Scripture as well as their authority in explicating that Scripture. As one more example of this early scriptural skirmish, Ephrem's texts offer explicit commentary on his own Christian scriptural interpretation practices that allow him to trace a single line of salvation history from the creation of the world to the end of time, and to "prove" that it is Christians who are God's chosen people.

Along with explaining Scripture, Ephrem, as any biblical exegete, had to impress upon his audience that his interpretation was both valid and authoritative. Along with his comments about how to read Scripture, Ephrem also provided examples of invalid interpretations and interpreters. Ephrem's laments about the misinterpretations of the "blind" Jews;[4] of Mani, Marcion,

3. Of course, biblical exegesis is always political, and not just in conversation with Jews. See, for example, James L. Kugel and Rowan A. Greer, *Early Biblical Interpretation* (Philadelphia: Westminster Press, 1986); David Dawson, *Allegorical Readers and Cultural Revision in Ancient Alexandria* (Berkeley: University of California Press, 1992); Bart Ehrman, *The Orthodox Corruption of Scripture: The Effect of Early Christological Controversies on the Text of the New Testament* (New York: Oxford University Press, 1993); Marc Hirshman, *A Rivalry of Genius: Jewish and Christian Biblical Interpretation in Late Antiquity,* trans. Batya Stein (Albany: SUNY Press, 1996); Elizabeth A. Clark, *Reading Renunciation: Asceticism and Scripture in Early Christianity* (Princeton: Princeton University Press, 1999). See also Elizabeth A. Clark, *History, Theory, Text: Historians and the Linguistic Turn* (Cambridge, Mass.: Harvard University Press, 2004).

4. See, for example, Ephrem, *Ieiun.* 5.7; *Azym.* 21; and *Virg.* 28. All translations from Ephrem's *Hymns on Fasting* are from the Syriac texts in Edmund Beck, ed., *Des Heiligen Ephraem des Syrers Hymnen de Ieiunio,* CSCO 246, SS 106 (Louvain, 1964). All translations from Ephrem's *Hymns on Unleavened Bread, Hymns on the Crucifixion* and *Hymns on the Resurrection* are from the Syriac editions in Edmund Beck, ed., *Des Heiligen Ephraem des Syrers Paschahymnen,* CSCO 248, SS 108 (Louvain, 1964). Except for occasional changes of my own, all quotations of Ephrem's *Hymns against Julian, Hymns on the Nativity* and *Hymns on Virginity* are from the English translation by Kathleen McVey (*Ephrem the Syrian: Hymns,* ed. and trans. Kathleen McVey [New York: Paulist Press, 1989]). My own changes are made from the Syriac text in Edmund Beck, ed., *Des Heiligen Ephraem des Syrers Hymnen de Nativitate (Epiphania),* CSCO 186, SS 82 (Louvain, 1959); Edmund Beck, ed., *Des Heiligen Ephraem des Syrers Hymnen de Virginitate,* CSCO 223, SS 94 (Louvain, 1962); and Edmund Beck, ed., *Des Heiligen Ephraem des Syrers Hymnen de Paradiso und Contra Julianum,* CSCO 174, SS 78 (Louvain, 1957). Compare the earlier Christian texts discussed above that Ephrem's language echoes, such as in the writings of Justin Martyr, Origen, and the *Didascalia.*

and Bardaisan;[5] and of "searching" Christians who call the Son a creature[6] reveal that Ephrem was far from the only person in Nisibis and Edessa who was claiming to offer the correct interpretation of the texts of Christian Scripture. Of utmost interest to this discussion of the scriptural history that Ephrem presents, and the capital that his rhetoric possessed in his context, are his comments regarding scriptural interpretation and the Jews.[7]

For Ephrem Scripture, whether texts that were originally Jewish or that are specifically Christian, tells one coherent and harmonious story of the salvation of God's covenanted people. In his *Hymns on the Church* Ephrem refers to the two tablets that Moses received at Mt. Sinai (Exodus 24:12, 31:18) in order to describe the Old and New Testaments as mirror images of one other, with one common meaning: "Doubtless, one tablet was a copy of its companion. . . . And again he bound up there [in the tablets] a distant allegory of the two coming Testaments that would be given. . . . their sense is one. For just as [one] tablet is not divided from its partner, so too [one] Testament is not divided from its companion."[8]

This unity and coherence that Ephrem understands to be inherent in Christian Scripture allows him to call upon a unified voice of scriptural authority to support his arguments, so long as he is able to locate at least one prooftext from anywhere in Scripture. For example, Ephrem concludes one of his arguments against "heretical" Christian opponents by summarizing, "Therefore both Testaments persuade us that those who have faith never disputed or investigated, because they had faith in God."[9] Because Ephrem demonstrates at least one biblical prooftext against his opponents' disputing and investigating, he calls upon the Bible itself, "both Testaments," to denounce them. Scripture is Scripture, for Ephrem, and while he recognizes that there are right and wrong interpretations of that Scripture, he sees the collection of texts, the New Testament and the Old, as a coherent and consistent story

---

5. See, for example, Ephrem, *Cruc.* 5.10–11, and especially Ephrem's arguments against Mani and his followers in his *Prose Refutations.*

6. See, for example, Ephrem, *SdF* 3 and *Virg.* 14.

7. I rely here on Pierre Bourdieu's concept of "cultural capital." Also, this discussion of the Jews will form a foundation for a related discussion about Ephrem's Christian opponents in the following chapter.

8. Ephrem, *Eccl.* 44.2–5. All translations from these hymns are from the Syriac text in Edmund Beck, ed., *Des Heiligen Ephraem des Syrers Hymnen de Ecclesia,* CSCO 198, SS 84 (Louvain, 1960). Compare also Ephrem, *Comm. Diat.* 6.11.

9. Ephrem, *HdF* 56.8. All translations from these hymns are from the Syriac text in Edmund Beck, ed., *Des Heiligen Ephraem des Syrers Hymnen de Fide,* CSCO 154, SS 73 (Louvain, 1955).

upon which he as an authoritative interpreter can draw in order to support his narrative of the world.

Given the diverse nature of the biblical texts, not only the distinction between those written before and those written after Jesus' lifetime, but also the seemingly contradictory information given about topics such as whether, and in what way, to circumcise,[10] it is not surprising that Ephrem, like others before him, turned to metaphorical and allegorical language in order to explain how it is that Scripture speaks with a unified voice to the learned interpreter.[11] Scholars have already devoted considerable attention to Ephrem's poetic use of symbolic, typological, and metaphorical language, as well as to his rich use of biblical language in his writings.[12] His poems and metri-

10. Compare, for example, Gen 17:10–14; Acts 15; Rom 2:25–29.

11. See again the scholarship by Dawson and Kugel on early Christian writers such as Origen and Clement of Alexandria.

12. See, for example, Edmund Beck, "Das Bild vom Spiegel bei Ephrem," OCP 19 (1953): 5–24; Edmund Beck, "Symbolum-Mysterium bei Aphrahat und Ephraem," OC 42 (1958): 19–40; Georges Saber, La théologie baptismale de Saint Ephrem (Kaslik, 1974), 21–32; Robert Murray, Symbols of Church and Kingdom (Cambridge: Cambridge University Press, 1975); Robert Murray, "The Theory of Symbolism in St. Ephrem's Theology," PdO 6/7 (1975/1976): 1–20; Bertrand de Margerie, "La poésie biblique de Saint Ephrem exégète Syrien (306–373)," in Introduction à l'histoire de l'exégèse: I. Les pères grecs et orientaux (Paris: Éditions de Cerf, 1980), 165–87; David Bundy, "Ephrem's Critique of Mani: The Limits of Knowledge and the Nature of Language," in Gnosticisme et Monde Hellénistique, ed. Julien Ries (Louvain la Neuve: The Catholic University of Louvain, 1982), 289–98; Sebastian Brock, "Clothing Metaphors as a Means of Theological Expression in Syriac Tradition," in Typus, Symbol, Allegorie bei den östlichen Vätern und ihren Parallelen im Mittelalter, ed. M. Schmidt (Regensburg: Pustet, 1982), 11–40; and in the same volume, Edmund Beck, "Zur Terminologie von Ephraems Bildtheologie," 239–77; André de Halleux, "Saint Ephrem le Syrien," Revue théologique de Louvain 14 (1983): 345–46; Pierre Yousif, L'eucharistie chez Saint Ephrem de Nisibe (Rome: Pontifical Institute, 1984), 31–39, 65–118, 269–94; N. el-Khoury, "The Use of Language by Ephraim the Syrian," Studia Patristica 16 (1985): 93–99; Pierre Yousif, "Exégèse et typologie bibliques chez S. Ephrem de Nisibe et chez S. Thomas d'Aquin," PdO 13 (1986): 31–50; T. Bou Mansour, "Etude de la terminologie symbolique chez Saint Ephrem," PdO 14 (1987): 221–62; N. el-Khoury, "Hermeneutics in the Works of Ephraim the Syrian," OCA 229 (1987): 93–100; T. Bou Mansour, La pensée symbolique de saint Ephrem le Syrien (Beirut: Bibliothèque de l'Université Saint Esprit, 1988); Margot Schmidt, "Alttestamentliche Typologien in den Paradieseshymnen von Ephräm dem Syrer," in Paradeigmata: Literarische Typologie des Alten Testaments, ed. Franz Link (Berlin: Duncker & Humblot, 1989), 55–81; Pierre Yousif, "Exegetical Principles of St. Ephraem of Nisibis," Studia Patristica 18, no. 4 (1990): 296–302; Sebastian Brock, The Luminous Eye: The Spiritual World Vision of Saint Ephrem the Syrian, rev. ed. (Kalamazoo: Cistercian Publications, 1992); C. McCarthy, "Allusions and Illusions: St. Ephrem's Verbal Magic in the Diatessaron Commentary," in Targumic and Cognate Studies: Essays in Honour of Martin McNamara, eds. K. J. Cathcart and M. Maher (Sheffield: Sheffield Academic Press, 1996), 187–207; A. S. Rodrigues Pereira, Studies in Aramaic Poetry (c. 100 B.C.E.–c. 600 C.E.): Selected Jewish, Christian and Samaritan Poems (Assen, Netherlands: Van Gorcum, 1997); Sidney Griffith, "Faith Adoring the Mystery": Reading the Bible with Ephrem the Syrian (Milwaukee: Marquette University Press, 1997), 30–37; Kees den Biesen, Simple and Bold: Ephrem's Art of Symbolic Thought (Piscataway, N.J.: Gorgias Press, 2006).

cal prose are rich with colorful and imaginative descriptions that led Robert Murray to refer to him as "the greatest poet of the patristic age and, perhaps, the only theologian-poet to rank beside Dante."[13] It is with the metaphorical language of symbols, signs, mirrors, and types that Ephrem explains the continuity between "the two Testaments."[14]

Ephrem refers several times to the "two Testaments," the first of which he calls "the Testament of Moses,"[15] and he frequently describes the characters and events of this first Testament as "symbols," "signs," and "types" of Christian parallels. Ephrem explains, "The Testament of Moses is like a mirror; it gave heed to our Lord. And whoever has sense concerning it looked here and there and saw there the symbol in the voice."[16] Ephrem adopts and emphasizes a foretelling of Christian truths out of the "Testament of Moses" in numerous other places, such as the early Christian description of the sacrifice of the Passover lamb as a symbol of Jesus' crucifixion.[17] Like other early Christians, in his *Commentary on Genesis* Ephrem explains that the plural pronoun for God in Genesis 3:22 demonstrates that Scripture "symbolically reveals the Trinity";[18] and in his *Hymns on Fasting* Ephrem sees Chris-

---

13. Robert Murray, "Ephrem Syrus," in *Catholic Dictionary of Theology,* vol. 2, ed. J. H. Crehan (New York: Nelson, 1967), 220–23. (Compare also Murray, *Symbols,* 31.) This is in direct contrast to the scornful evaluations of Burkitt and Segal, as noted in chapter 1. More recently, Sebastian Brock and others have echoed Murray's positive evaluation, which itself corresponds to some of the earliest Greek and Latin references to Ephrem and his poetry (cf. Sebastian Brock, "Introduction," in *St. Ephrem the Syrian: Hymns on Paradise* [New York: St. Vladimir's Seminary Press, 1990], 7–8; Jerome, *De vir. ill.* 115.1–2; Theodoret, *HE* 4.26; Sozomen, *HE* 3.16; Palladius, *Lausiac History* 40).

14. See, for example, Ephrem, *Eccl.* 44.3 (cf. *HdF* 56.8).

15. For Ephrem's references to "two Testaments," see, for example, Ephrem, *Cruc.* 3.5; *Azym.* 4.25; *Eccl.* 44; *HdF* 56. Ephrem names the first testament "the Testament of Moses" in Ephrem, *Ieiun.* 5.10; *Cruc.* 3.5; *Virg.* 9.2.

16. Ephrem, *Ieiun.* 5.10.

17. This imagery is, of course, already present in the New Testament itself. See, for example, the Passion Narrative of the Gospel of John, as well as 1 Cor 5:7.

18. Ephrem, *Comm. Gen.* 2.34 (FC 91). Compare also the following similar interpretations of the use of the plural first-person pronoun in Gen 1.26 in the texts of Greek Christian writers before Ephrem: *EpBarn* 6; Justin Martyr, *Dial.* 62; Irenaeus, *c. Haer.* 4.20.1; Tertullian, *Against Praxeas* 12; Ignatius, *Epistle to the Antiochenes* 2; Origen, *c. Celsus* 5.37. I have used the English translation of Ephrem's *Commentary on Genesis* and *Commentary on Exodus,* with occasional changes from my own consultation of the Syriac text in R. M. Tonneau, *Sancti Ephraem Syri in Genesim et in Exodum Commentarii,* CSCO 152, SS 71 (Louvain, 1955); *St. Ephrem the Syrian: Selected Prose Works,* trans. Edward Mathews and Joseph Amar, ed. Kathleen McVey, FC 91 (Washington, D.C.: The Catholic University of America Press, 1994). As noted in chapter 1, the authenticity of these commentaries has been the topic of some debate. Sten Hidal argues strongly for their authenticity (Sten Hidal, *Die Kommentare des Heiligen Ephräm des Syrers zu Genesis und Exodus mit besonderer Berücksichtigung inhrer auslegungsgeschichtlichen Stellung* [Lund: Gleerup, 1974]);

tian fasting foreshadowed in Jewish Scripture: "the Scriptures will become for us like a mirror, and we will see our fast in them."[19] For Ephrem Scripture demonstrates its continuity not in a repetitive series of explicit comparisons, but in the perfect reflection of the Old in the New. Ephrem claims about the Jews, "Indeed, the People will be shamed, for their Testament made a mirror for our Testament."[20] Like Christian writers before him, Ephrem claims that Christians inherit, and that Christianity fulfills, the prophecies made to the Jews.[21] As such, Christians like Ephrem appropriate the texts of the Jews, along with the right to interpret them. It is with this Christian claim to succession over Judaism and consequent inheritance of Jewish Scripture that Ephrem can say that the Scriptures are harmonious and unanimously point to Christian "truth."[22]

As a careful and well-versed reader of Scripture, however, Ephrem occasionally admits that seeing the New Testament in the Old is not always straightforward, and that Scripture allows for multiple interpretations.[23] It takes a "lucid eye" to be able to glean truth from the biblical texts.[24] Although Ephrem persistently refers to this continuity between the two Testaments that make up Christian Scripture, there are also times when as a Christian he wants to claim that parts of the Old Testament are no longer binding in a literal way. Ephrem criticizes the Jews for their clumsy understanding of Scripture: "The Jews are put to shame for they failed to study and seek out the reason for the law; instead they took up and dissolved the meaning of the commandments, clothing themselves without any understanding in the sounds of the words, for they did not labor to acquire that furnace of thought by which they might assay the truth and real meaning of Scrip-

---

Paul Feghali has since raised another challenge to the authenticity of the *Commentary on Genesis* (Paul Feghali, "Influence des Targums sur la pensée exégétique d'Éphrem?" *OCA* 229 [1987]: 71–82), but his arguments are not convincing and I use *Comm. Gen.* as an authentic text.

19. Ephrem, *Ieiun.* 1.7. Compare Justin Martyr, *Dial.* 15; Tertullian, *On Fasting.*

20. *Azym.* 4.25. Ephrem uses here the plural noun for Scriptures, even though he refers only to the Jewish Scripture. Compare also *Ieiun.* 5.10, and *Comm. Diat.* 14.13.

21. Although it is anachronistic to think of "Christianity" as something distinct from "Judaism" as early as the time of Paul, the argument that those who follow Jesus as the Messiah claim the inheritance promised to Jewish Israel begins even in the New Testament texts (see for example, Phil 3:2–21; Rom 9–11; the Matthean genealogy [Matt 1:1–17] and fulfillment prophecies [e.g., Matt 1:22–23]; Heb).

22. This claim also allows Ephrem to interpret the Prophets as speaking positively about Christianity, which he does by adopting their language and authority and using them against the Jews.

23. See Brock, *Luminous,* 46–51, and Ephrem, *Comm. Diat.* 1.18–19, 7.22.

24. Ephrem, *HdF* 67.8 (Brock, *Luminous,* 47). Compare also Schmidt, "Typologien," 66–69.

ture."[25] In this vein, Ephrem divides history into different epochs, each with its own challenges and understanding, and therefore each with its own religious requirements. In keeping with his argument for consistency, however, Ephrem explains that while the details of the requirements for each of these times differ slightly because of the specific context, the covenant that they represent remains the same.[26]

In more than one place in his writings Ephrem speaks of three different generations of people throughout the history of the world.[27] In his *Hymns against Heresies* Ephrem describes these three times as the "beginning" time of uncircumcision, the "middle" time of circumcision, and the "last" time to which "our Lord" gives the bread of life.[28] This description is similar to the periodization in the third of Ephrem's *Sermons on Faith,* in which he explains that in his own time the commandments of Sabbath, circumcision, and ritual purity have ceased: "To those of the earliest [time] they were not necessary because they were whole in knowledge; and they were also not necessary to those of the later [time] because they are whole in faith. They served those

---

25. Ephrem, *CH* 50.4. In this case, I have adopted Brock's English translation, with my own consultation of the Syriac (Brock, *Luminous,* 48).

26. Ephrem, *SdF* 3.93–187. The *Didascalia* frequently notes distinct times, with the "second legislation" applying to Jews, allegedly in order to stem their idolatry, but not to Christians.

27. Breaking history into different eras was a common practice in antiquity. Certainly Greco-Roman myths about the Golden, Silver, and Bronze Ages abounded. In contrast to these pagan mythologies, however, which portrayed a slow degradation in human history from the Golden Age through the Silver and Bronze Ages to the present, Christian chronologies generally traced salvation narratives, in which the present of Christian late antiquity was an improvement over the immediately preceding "Jewish" era under Mosaic law. In addition to noting the break in history caused by the advent of the Messiah, early Christian authors like Ephrem also noted an earlier break in history with God's covenant either with Abraham or with Moses, when Israel became God's chosen people. In the fourth century, these narratives became particularly useful in explaining the Christianization of the Roman Empire as an inevitable and divinely sanctioned stage in the natural progression of history. Eusebius of Caesarea presents a clear narrative of history in his *Preparation for the Gospel,* in which he describes three eras to human history: the early era of Noah and Abraham in which the "Hebrews" lived naturally in accordance with God's wishes; the middle era that began when Moses, a virtuous Hebrew, delivered God's law to the Jews who had been unable to live rightly without it; and the final Christian era in which Christ's teachings renewed the old religion of Abraham and annulled the Jewish law (*PE* 7–8). See also Pierre Yousif, "Histoire et temps dans la pensée de Saint Ephrem de Nisibe," *PdO* 10 (1981/1982): 3–33; Robin Darling, "The 'Church from the Nations' in the Exegesis of Ephrem," in *IV Symposium Syriacum, 1984,* eds. H. J. W. Drijvers et al. (Rome: Pontifical Institute, 1987), 111–21); Aryeh Kofsky, *Eusebius of Caesarea against Paganism* (Boston: Brill, 2000), 103–14.

28. Ephrem, *CH* 26.4–5. All translations from these hymns are from the Syriac text in Edmund Beck, ed., *Des Heiligen Ephraem des Syrers Hymnen contra Haereses,* CSCO 169, SS 76 (Louvain, 1957).

of the middle [time] alone."[29] The significance of these generations in the context of Ephrem's biblical interpretation is that Ephrem explains that each one had its own religious rules to live by, which in turn allows him to explain why Christians do not follow literally all of the laws laid out in the Old Testament of their own Scripture.[30]

Although Ephrem identifies these three generations, in practice he is most concerned with the second and third, since he understands his own time, generally speaking, to be still in the process of adapting to the transition between these two. In other words, according to Ephrem the coming of the Messiah brought to an end the "Jewish" generation, so that circumcision and purity laws became defunct, although the history and tradition of God's chosen people continues unbroken into Christianity. Ephrem speaks of two covenants: "A small covenant was given through Moses from the glorious mountain; [next,] a great covenant came forth from the small fold and filled the earth."[31] With the coming of the latter, the former Jewish dispensation was fulfilled:

The synagogue, which preceded, which came for a little while, both went out and was rejected, and she did not return to her house because he who clothed himself with the church is not willing to disrobe. And because the synagogue was corrupted there through the calf, he destroyed and broke the tablets so that he might teach her that she might be rejected. [Only] necessity designated that she remain until the completion of the age.[32]

29. Ephrem, *SdF* 3.183–187. It is interesting to note that sometimes (*CH* 26) it is the covenant of circumcision with Abraham (Gen 17) that distinguishes Ephrem's first time period from the second, whereas in other texts, such as here in his *Sermons on Faith*, he emphasizes instead the later Mosaic covenant that includes the Sabbath and ritual purity. As mentioned in chapter 1, Ephrem does not lay out systematic arguments in his liturgical writings. He uses both of these periodizations to the same end, without differentiating clearly between them. His emphasis elsewhere on the incident with the golden calf (Ex 32) suggests that Moses and Mt. Sinai play a crucial role in Ephrem's thought. (Compare also yet another way that Ephrem divides history in his *Commentary on the Diatessaron*: between Adam and Noah, God's people distinguished themselves from Cain's people; from Noah to Abraham, they promised not to eat blood; from Abraham to Moses, they practiced male circumcision; from Moses to Christ, they practiced the Mosaic law; and after Christ, there was a new covenant that would never end [*Comm. Diat.* 5.13].)

30. Ephrem, *SdF* 3.93–309. This also offers, as we shall see, further support for his claim that after the lifetime of Jesus, Judaism was passé (see, for example, Ephrem, *Eccl.* 44. 22–23).

31. Ephrem, *Cruc.* 3.5.

32. Ephrem, *Eccl.* 44.22–23. Compare the *Epistle of Barnabas* and the *Didascalia*, which similarly use the story of the creation of the golden calf as a defining moment in Jewish history, and the reason for the parts of the Jewish law that these texts claim their Christian readers need not follow.

Thus Ephrem reads Scripture from the position of the third of the genera-tions that he describes, which is why the Old Testament no longer stands on its own literally, but rather serves as a mirror that reflects the eternal truths of the New Testament.

Since Christianity's beginnings, of course, there have been Christians who presented what came to be called Christianity as the continuation and fulfill-ment of the history of Israel, so while Ephrem uses anti-Jewish language in a new context, this particular premise behind his language of fulfillment was far from new to Christianity.[33] Like Christian writers before him, Ephrem uses this notion of fulfillment in order to support his anti-Jewish narrative that the former Jewish ways are no longer valid and that those who follow them are in error. Ephrem writes,

> With the advent of our Sun, lamps served and passed away, and types and symbols ceased. With hidden circumcision, visible circumcision was abolished. . . . The Testa-ment of Moses awaited [Christ's] gospel. All the old things took flight and came to perch on his New Testament. . . . For his law is weak; it is unable to enclose the great flow of his symbols in the small bosom of its kings and priests. . . . Since the bosoms of the just were too small, he poured out [the flow of symbols]. . . . The prophets poured into it their glorious symbols. . . . For it is Christ who perfects its symbols.[34]

Ephrem elsewhere refers to "the keys of [Christian] doctrine which unlock all of Scripture's books."[35] What is new in the fourth century with authors such as Ephrem, however, is the particular combination of anti-Jewish themes and accusations that he uses, the effect to which he puts this Christian rheto-ric, and the results that it would have had in his fourth-century context. For Ephrem all of history, and all of Scripture, must be seen through the lens of Christianity, since Christianity represents the fulfillment of all that came be-fore. This ideological claim provides the framework for Ephrem's polemic against Jews as well as against his Christian opponents.

Despite his insistence on the replacement of the old generation with the new, Ephrem also insists that the important and salvific core of God's mes-sage is and always has been the same throughout the generations, regardless

33. The New Testament traditions already noted continued in later supersessionist Christian narratives such as in the writings of Ignatius of Antioch (e.g., *Letter to the Philadelphians*), Justin Martyr (e.g., *Dial.*), Melito of Sardis (e.g., *Peri Pascha*), Origen (e.g., *Peri Pascha* 32), Eusebius of Emesa (e.g., *Hom.* 18), and Eusebius of Caesarea (e.g., *HE* and *DE* 3–10).

34. Ephrem, *Virg.* 9.1–3, 6, 9, 15. This is a common theme in these writings. Compare, for ex-ample, *Virg.* 8 and 10.

35. Ephrem, *HdP* 6.1 (Brock, "Introduction").

of the words in which it is clothed in order to fit the particularities of each generation. In his *Commentary on Genesis* Ephrem explains,

To God who, through his Son, created the creatures from nothing. But he did not write these things down in the beginning because they were obvious to the understanding of Adam, and every generation handed down to the next just what it had learned from the previous. Because all went astray from God and all had forgotten that God was Creator, he wrote these things down through Moses for the Hebrew people. . . . In the desert Moses wrote down those things that had been manifested in Adam's mind at that very time he was in Paradise, through the ancient peoples who knew these things without their being written down, through the intermediate peoples who through the Scripture heard and believed them, and through the last peoples who came to the books of the middle ones, and even through those who stubbornly remained in their resistance and were not convinced.[36]

Thus the three generations had the same message, first through Adam, then through Moses, and finally through Jesus. While the form of the words changed from oral to written, and from written in one Testament to written in two Testaments, the core of the message itself remained the same.

Ephrem's anti-Jewish polemic relies on the larger ideological framework through which he views the history of his world, and for Ephrem it is Scripture that reveals the narrative of that human history. Working to make sense of history as told in Christian Scripture, Ephrem identifies two generations that have preceded his own (final) generation, including the most recent and most threatening Jewish generation that came to an end through the advent of "the Lord." Ephrem's interpretive blueprint requires a continual thread of God's promise to God's people and yet also includes the passing away of one generation in favor of another.

Ephrem's "Jews" and the "Testament of Moses"

Ephrem's multifaceted use of the "Testament of Moses" to present his narrative of history constructs community boundaries and positively- and negatively-valued histories for "Christians" and "Jews," respectively. Specifically, Ephrem's writings frequently rely on his particular reading of the narrative in Exodus 32 about the making and worship of the golden calf, as well

36. Ephrem, *Comm. Gen.* 44.3 (FC 91). In this commentary, Moses, and not Abraham, represents the division between the first and second generations: Adam represents the first generation, Moses begins the second generation with his reception of the written Law, and Christians represent the third generation with their second written Testament.

as his interpretation of several biblical prophets' chastisements of their own people. Ephrem's use of scriptural history to depict clear community borders helped to reify the boundaries and definitions of, and connotations associated with, social groups in his own fourth-century context in ways that were advantageous for Ephrem in his struggle to assert the local authority of Nicene Christianity.

"Whoring with the Calf": Ephrem's Use of Exodus 32

As demonstrated in chapter two, in his writings Ephrem points to countless faults of the Jewish people. In addition to the New Testament crucifixion story, the story to which Ephrem most frequently returns in order to prove the faithlessness of the Jews and to explain God's election of the Gentiles is Exodus 32, the creation of the golden calf at Mt. Sinai. For Ephrem, this story represents a definitive moment in the history of "the People" when they flagrantly annulled their covenant with God through what Ephrem condemns as adulterous idolatry. Ephrem is not the only early Christian writer to use this story in "proving" that the Jews lost their divine covenant.[37] Ephrem, however, weaves a particularly elaborate interpretation of this story through-

---

37. The early *Epistle of Barnabas* contains a similar narrative in which the creation of the golden calf proves to be the definitive moment in which the Jews permanently lost their hope for a covenant with God, at the very moment when Moses was on the mountain receiving the two tablets of God's commandments (*Ep. Barn.* 4, 14). Likewise, the *Didascalia* places a significant emphasis on the idolatry of the golden calf, and its results for "the [Jewish] People." Compare also Justin, *Dial.* 20.3, 21.1, 22.1; *Apost. Const.* 6.4.20; Origen, *Comm. Rom.* 2.14, as noted in Leivy Smolar and Moshe Aberbach, "The Golden Calf Episode in Postbiblical Literature," *Hebrew Union College Annual* 39 (1968): 96. Given its early transmission in Syriac, the *Didascalia* also serves as an important witness to this early Christian tradition (cf. *Didascalia* 26). For further comment, see also Pier Cesare Bori, *The Golden Calf and the Origins of the anti-Jewish Controversy,* trans. David Ward (Atlanta: Scholars Press, 1990).

Jewish writers in antiquity likewise recognized the potential danger posed by this biblical passage. As Smolar and Aberbach note, Josephus omits the creation of the golden calf in his history of the Jews (Josephus, *Antiq.* 3.5). See also P. S. Alexander, "The Rabbinic Lists of Forbidden Targumim," *JJS* 27, no. 2 (1976): 177–91; and I. J. Mandelbaum, "Tannaitic Exegesis of the Golden Calf Episode," in *A Tribute to Geza Vermes: Essays on Jewish and Christian Literature and History,* eds. P. R. Davies and R. T. White (Sheffield: Sheffield Academic Press, 1990), 207–33.

It is worth noting that Ephrem focuses almost exclusively on the golden calf at Sinai (with an exception in Ephrem, *Comm. Diat.* 11.8, when he links this calf with the two calves of Jereboam), although there have been readers from antiquity to the present who have noted the connection of this story to the biblical stories about Jereboam. See G. N. Knoppers, "Aaron's Calf and Jereboam's Calves," in *Fortunate the Eyes that See: Essays in Honor of David Noel Freedman in Celebration of His Seventieth Birthday,* eds. A. B. Beck et al. (Grand Rapids: Eerdmans, 1995), 92–104; Smolar and Aberbach, "Golden Calf"; Moses Aberbach and Leivy Smolar, "Aaron, Jereboam, and the Golden Calves," *JBL* 86 (1967): 129–40.

out his writings, creating an intricate anti-Jewish narrative that reflects his understanding of ancient Israel as well as of contemporary Christianity, Jews, and Judaism. Specifically, Ephrem describes that at Sinai God made a covenant with Moses that "the People" (with the exception of Moses) broke through their creation and worship of the golden calf. God maintained relations with the Jewish people until the time of Jesus for the sake of a faithful strand, including those such as Moses and the prophets, that preserved God's covenant until the birth of Jesus. With the fulfillment of Jewish prophecies in Jesus, however, this good seed emerged from within the otherwise blind, foolish, and unfaithful Jewish people, and God rejected them forever and created a new covenant with the Christian church, which consisted of the spiritual descendents of those earlier faithful few.[38] Ephrem thus effectively divides in two the Jewish people from Moses until Jesus: one, a pristine line of divine covenant inherited by Christians and represented at Sinai by Moses, and the other, a corrupt tradition preserved among contemporary Jews and represented at Sinai by the idolatrous masses, who defiled their covenant by "whoring with the calf."[39] It is this image of a coherent and soundly negative Jewish "other" that Ephrem deployed against non-Jewish opponents.

For Ephrem the idolatry of the golden calf was a manifestation of a defilement that took place earlier in Egypt.[40] The idolatry that they brought out

38. By Ephrem's time, a long tradition of Christian anti-Jewish polemic already existed to argue that Christians were the true inheritors of God's ancient covenant with Israel. This argument helped to alleviate any cognitive dissonance created by early "orthodox" Christians' strident efforts to distinguish themselves from contemporary Judaism while simultaneously claiming to be the legitimate heirs of promises made to Jews about Jews and recorded in Jewish Scripture. While the very nature of Ephrem's supersessionist argument necessitates some level of anti-Jewish language, in that it argues that Christianity has replaced Judaism as the valid fulfillment of Scripture, the particular ways in which each early Christian writer expressed the details of this shift varied, with some being more explicitly vitriolic toward contemporary Jews and Judaism than others. As David Brakke has rightly noted on this topic with respect to Athanasius, "Still, no Christian bishop, even one writing to the masses of ordinary Christians, after centuries of Christian anti-Jewish rhetoric, in a city shared with a living Jewish community, was required to fill his Easter letters—or his other writings for that matter—with attacks on Jews. No matter how 'intrinsic to Christian teaching' such anti-Judaism was, Athanasius chose to use anti-Jewish rhetoric for particular ends. Historians should try to elucidate these ends and to give such rhetoric its social, political, and ideological context, if not its subjective motivations" ("Jewish Flesh and Christian Spirit in Athanasius of Alexandria," *JECS* 9, no. 4 [2001]: 456).

39. Ephrem, *Nat.* 14.19.

40. Although Ephrem highlights the idolatry in the wilderness and describes the worship of the golden calf as a permanent stain on the Jewish people, he does not describe idolatry itself as inherent to the Jews. Rather, for Ephrem the original purity of the Jews' ancestors was permanently defiled during their sojourn in Egypt. Ephrem describes it as "that idolatry that

of Egypt remained hidden for a time until its revelation with the calf. In his *Homily on our Lord,* Ephrem explains, "For that idolatry that they concealed in their hearts and brought out of Egypt, when it came out openly, killed openly those in whom it was dwelling secretly. . . . For Moses was removed from them for a little, so that the calf that was before them might be seen, that they might worship it openly; because they had been secretly worshipping it also in their hearts."[41] In this respect, Ephrem understands the creation and worship of the golden calf not as a spontaneous whim that might be attributed to unusual circumstances, but as merely the revelation of the paganism that secretly festered within the Jewish people from their sojourn in Egypt. The idolatry with the golden calf, then, was not a momentary lapse, but rather a glimpse into this people who had changed from a state of purity to one of impurity.[42]

Although Ephrem's hymns contain numerous references to the story in Exodus 32, it is in the third of his *Hymns on the Resurrection* and the first of his *Hymns on the Crucifixion* that he discusses it most explicitly. For Ephrem, God's covenant did not end with God's rejection of the apostasized Jews.[43] In these two hymns Ephrem acknowledges that the Jews formerly were God's chosen people, places the blame for their loss of God's covenant on their

---

they concealed in their hearts and brought out from Egypt" (Ephrem, *de Dom. nos.* 6). (All quotations from *de Dom. nos.* are from the English translation by Joseph Amar [FC 91], with my own occasional changes based on the Syriac text in Edmund Beck, ed., *Des Heiligen Ephraem des Syrers Sermo de Domino Nostro,* CSCO 270, SS 116 [Louvain, 1966].) For Ephrem, Egypt is a haven of idolatry, paganism, error, and avarice (respectively, Ephrem, *de Dom. nos.* 6, 17; *Azym.* 3.9, 10). Ephrem writes that before Moses led his people through the Red Sea "the leaven of Egypt was hidden among the People" (Ephrem, *Virg.* 49.7). Elsewhere, Ephrem explains that "the People bore when it went out the leaven of paganism together with the unleavened bread" (Ephrem, *Azym.* 17.2), despite Moses' warning that they not "hide the leaven of the Egyptians within their mind" (Ephrem, *Azym.* 17.4).

41. Ephrem, *de Dom. nos.* 6, 17.

42. In his *Commentary on Exodus,* Ephrem excuses Aaron, who remained at the foot of Mt. Sinai, by explaining that he allowed the creation of the calf "lest Aaron also die and they be liable for a blood feud for his murder at their hands, and lest they make many calves for themselves instead of just one, and lest they return to Egypt" (Ephrem, *Comm. Ex.* 32.2 [FC 91]). While this narrative portrays the golden calf as a better option than certain others, and rescues Aaron's reputation, it does not change for Ephrem the fact that these ancestors of the Jews were defiled by their time among the idolatrous Egyptians and that as a result the Jews' ancestors, in their state of impurity, turned to idolatry, and in doing so abandoned their covenant with the God of Israel. As noted briefly in chapter 1, there are some differences in emphasis between Ephrem's use of Exodus in his hymns and in his *Commentary on Exodus.*

43. Ephrem does not appear to be actively awaiting a future in which Jews will return to Israel, as Paul describes in Rom 9–11. By the fourth century, despite any apparent overlap in his Syrian church, Ephrem describes Jews and Christians as antithetical to one another. Jews are, by definition, not-Christian, and Christians are not-Jews.

conscious decision to break it, and describes God's consequent election of the Gentiles, which Ephrem equates with the (Nicene) Christian church. Noting that the Jews broke their marriage-like covenant with God, Ephrem rejoices in the subsequent Christian covenant: "Blessed is he who betrothed the church of the nations."[44] For Ephrem, the validity of Christianity and the unhappy state of contemporary Judaism are equally the direct result of the creation and worship of the golden calf at Mt. Sinai.

Although the retelling of the story of the creation of the golden calf is itself sufficient to call to mind for Jews and Christians who were familiar with the biblical passage a costly error in the history of the people of Israel, the specific language with which Ephrem portrays the biblical account enhances the folly of the crowd's actions more so than in other early Christian retellings. The charge that Ephrem levels against the Jews through the use of this story is simultaneously that of both idolatry and adultery.[45] These two are inextricably linked for Ephrem (as well as for the biblical prophets) in that the more literal idolatrous worship of any god other than the one true God is metaphorically straying from a marriage-like covenant with one deity in order to have adulterous relations with another. Certainly Ephrem does not create this scriptural metaphor, but he manipulates the biblical imagery toward his own ends, namely, to justify God's rejection of the Jews. In his *Hymns on Nisibis* Ephrem claims that in the wilderness Moses saw "the idols" of "that People."[46] Again, in his *Homily on Our Lord* Ephrem refers to the Jews wandering from the one God "through their many idols," and he more explicitly links this reference to the golden calf in the subsequent lines: "For the one calf which they made in the wilderness pastured on their lives as on grass in the wilderness. For that idolatry that they concealed in their hearts and brought out from Egypt, when it came out in the open it killed them openly."[47] Condemned in both Testaments,[48] idolatry would have been a highly

44. Ephrem, *Res.* 3.3. For a discussion of Ephrem's imagery of Israel as God's betrothed, see Brock *Luminous*, 115–22. Compare the discussion of the election of the Gentiles in the *Didascalia* 21, 23, 26.

45. See, for example, Ephrem, *Comm. Diat.* 6.10, in which he equates the two. Compare also the biblical prophets, such as Isa 1; Jer 2–3, 13; Ezek 16, 23; Hos 2–4.

46. Ephrem, *CNis.* 43.1. All translations from this series of hymns are from the Syriac text in Edmund Beck, ed., *Des Heiligen Ephraem des Syrers Carmina Nisibena (I)*, CSCO 218, SS 92 (Louvain, 1961); and Edmund Beck, ed., *Des Heiligen Ephraem des Syrers Carmina Nisibena (II)*, CSCO 240, SS 102 (Louvain, 1963).

47. Ephrem, *de Dom. nos.* 6.

48. See, for example, Ex 20:4 (and 20:3), and Lev 19:4, as well as the numerous negative

charged accusation, particularly in Ephrem's context in a city in which paganism was still visible.[49] By emphasizing the idolatry of the ancestors of the Jews (and therefore, Ephrem claims, of all Jews throughout history), Ephrem connects contemporary Jews in his community with idolatrous pagans.[50] Just as Ephrem elsewhere tars "Arian" Christian opponents by connecting them too closely with non-Christian "Jews," here Ephrem tars monotheistic Jews by connecting them too closely with polytheistic pagan "idolaters."

While the charge of idolatry is the most literal that Ephrem makes in retelling Exodus 32, Ephrem, echoing the Prophets, at the same time shifts between the literal idolatrous worship of the calf and the adulterous implications of that idolatry for the Jews' relationship with God. Ephrem describes in detail the metaphorical marriage of Israel to God, as well as her subsequent adultery. He writes,

A pure marriage banquet took place in the desert; and a bridal bed was on Mt. Sinai. The holy one came down, betrothed, and took the daughter of his beloved Abraham. Great are the horrors that happened all at once, because the bride committed adultery in the bridal bed. The negotiator [of the marriage] went up to the bridegroom, and a stranger entered the bridal bed. She came to hate the king and she came to love the calf.[51]

God had betrothed the ancestors of the Jews, but even as Moses was on the mountain negotiating the marriage, with the bridal chamber and wedding feast prepared below, the adulterous crowd broke its marriage vow and committed adultery with the golden calf in the very bridal bed itself at the foot of Mt. Sinai.

The "Testament of Moses" is as explicit in condemning adultery as it is idolatry[52] and even describes a test that a woman who is accused of adultery might undergo so that God might make manifest her guilt or innocence, a

---

references to idols and idolatry in the accusations of the Prophets; and Acts 17; 1 Cor 5:11, 10:7; 1 John 5:21.

49. As discussed in chapter 1, paganism in various forms seems to have been a visible presence in both Nisibis and Edessa during Ephrem's lifetime, and Ephrem condemns idolatry as the antithesis of Christian (and Jewish) monotheism.

50. Compare also Eusebius of Emesa, *Hom.* 19, in which he attributes the destruction of the Temple to the Jews' idolatry, and uses the Old Testament to support his claim that the Jews are idolaters. See also Ralph Hennings, "Eusebius von Emesa und die Juden," *Journal of Ancient Christianity* 5, no. 2 (2001): 240–60.

51. Ephrem, *Res.* 3.2. Ephrem's use of female imagery to describe the people Israel as an adulteress is as old as the Hebrew Bible itself. See, for example, Jer 2:20–3:10, Hosea, and Ezek 16.

52. Exod 20:14.

test in which the accused woman drinks water from the priest that will harm her if she is guilty and leave her unaffected if she is innocent.[53] Ephrem refers to this trial in his *Homily on our Lord* when he writes, "That synagogue that had committed adultery with the calf, he caused to drink the waters of trial so that the sign of adulteresses might be seen in it."[54] Grounded solidly in the biblical laws that govern the Jews, Ephrem accuses the people at Mt. Sinai of adultery and implies that God found them guilty and so justly punished them for their act.

One of the key points that Ephrem makes to his audience in referring to Exodus 32 is that it is through their own actions that the Jewish people lost their covenant with God. The *Epistle of Barnabas* and the *Didascalia* made this claim before Ephrem, but Ephrem folds this argument into a much more elaborate narrative than either of these two texts, with unique effects within his Syrian liturgical context. Ephrem emphasizes Israel's voluntary decision to make the golden calf throughout his retellings of Exodus 32. He writes, "Great are the horrors that happened all at once [at Sinai], because the *bride committed adultery* in the bridal bed. . . . *She came to hate* the king and *she came to love* the calf. . . . Within the desert *she committed deceit*."[55] Ephrem refers to the People who "*exchanged* the giver of the law for a calf";[56] and his writings are filled with descriptions of Israel as an adulterous woman having an affair with the golden calf, implying that both the choice and the motivation were her own.[57]

One reason it was so crucial for Ephrem to emphasize the voluntary nature of the People's decision to make the golden calf is that Ephrem's ideological narrative holds not only the ancient Israelites who stood before Mt. Sinai, but all Jews everywhere responsible for this adultery. Ephrem's occasional switch from using "the People" to refer collectively to the crowd at Mt. Sinai to the contemporary Syriac word for "synagogue," reinforces this connection

53. Num 5:11–31.

54. Ephrem, *de Dom. nos.* 6. The biblical text of Exodus 32 appears itself to be a complex compilation of stories. (See, for example, Herbert Chanan Brichto, "The Worship of the Golden Calf: A Literary Analysis of a Fable on Idolatry," *Hebrew Union College Annual* 54 [1983]: 1–44.) As such, it contains references to three different punishments for the creation of the golden calf (Ex 32:20; 32:27–28; and 32:35). In his *Homily on Our Lord,* Ephrem highlights the punishment of the suspected adulteress, consistent with his emphasis throughout his writings on Jewish Israel as an unfaithful harlot.

55. Ephrem, *Res.* 3.2–3.

56. Ephrem, *Comm. Ex.* 32.8.

57. See, for example, *Res.* 3, *Cruc.* 1, *de Dom. nos.* 6, and *CNis.* 27.9.

between the crowd in Exodus and fourth-century Syrian Jews. Ephrem wrote that the synagogue "committed adultery with the calf, and the one on high hated her."[58] That Ephrem (and God, too, in Ephrem's opinion) held all Jews accountable for this adultery is clear in his *Hymns on Nisibis:* "Your Father took the hated synagogue [for a wife], she who committed adultery with that calf, and on account of that he hated her offspring."[59] In his *Hymns on the Crucifixion* Ephrem again refers to both Sinai and the crucifixion in order to condemn contemporary Jews. In this description, contemporary Jews are a generation apart from their "mother," the crowd assembled at Mt. Sinai. Although this daughter has committed her own crime, the crucifixion of Jesus, Ephrem believes that the two crimes are the same in essence:

For as her mother, she [the daughter of Zion] had become accustomed to adultery. She surpassed her mother in lying. . . . Cunningly she insulted her fiancé in order that she might serve the adulterers. The reproach [of God] that was her mother's was in her mouth, [her mother] who cunningly made the calf. . . . With the fraud against Moses [her mother] made the poured [calf] through which [her mother] became ashamed. Also the daughter was imprinted with the likeness of that mother who was cunning toward hateful [ends]. . . . She was not ashamed openly to kill and to commit adultery.[60]

Through this comparison, Ephrem convicts not only the biblical crowd of Exodus 32, but traces the crime of adultery from Sinai through the crucifixion to contemporary fourth-century Jews everywhere.

The conflation of idolatry and adultery is certainly not new with Ephrem. Quite the contrary, the language is well established in Scripture itself. By adopting the language of the Jews' own Scripture to support his claims, Ephrem grants validity to his own complaints against the Jews.[61] Ephrem increases the insult to the Jews, however, by not only slandering them with their own texts, but by sharpening the biblical language. The charge of adulterous idolatry points to the religious promiscuity of the people at Mt. Sinai, while at the same time eliciting more slanderous imagery of the contemporary synagogue

---

58. Ephrem, *HdF* 14.6. Compare, *de Dom. nos.* 6, quoted above.

59. Ephrem, *CNis.* 27.9.

60. Ephrem, *Cruc.* 1.3–5, 14.

61. The story in Exodus 32 is far from the only time that the Jews' biblical ancestors fall into the error of idolatry. Time and again throughout the biblical narrative of their history, idolatry is used as symbolic of how far they have fallen away from God and how greatly they are in need of repentance and divine forgiveness. Consequently, the biblical prophets such as Jeremiah, Hosea, and Ezekiel repeatedly bemoan the idolatry of their people, and frequently do so with the language of adultery that Ephrem uses in his own writings.

as a whore who broke, and therefore lost, her marriage covenant with God. Ephrem interprets the creation and adoration of the golden calf as a definitive and voluntary historical moment. Ephrem describes God as saying, "I chose the circumcised, but they have rejected themselves . . . the congregation [of Moses] was made bitter by the molten calf,"[62] and more succinctly, "Moses taught; the People apostasized."[63] While Ephrem is clearly intimately familiar with the entire story of Exodus, which includes God's forgiveness and reacceptance of this same people, Ephrem prefers to focus instead in these hymns on God's initial condemnation as a final judgment.[64] For Ephrem, the story of the golden calf represents not only a long past momentary indiscretion in misdirected celebrating, but instead a fateful decision made by the ancestors of contemporary Jews.[65]

It is not only for a definition of the Jewish people, however, that Ephrem's interpretive narrative would have had meaning. His reconstructions of Exodus 32 in his numerous references to this story in his hymns emphasize a particularly clear distinction between Moses and the rest of the Jewish people.[66] While this distinction is of course found in the biblical text itself, for Ephrem Moses' separation from the Jewish people takes on the utmost significance and emphasizes Ephrem's accusation of idolatry against all the people with the sole exception of Moses, who was in the presence of God on Mt. Sinai when the calf was made. From this historical moment on, there is for Ephrem, as there was for the author of the *Epistle of Barnabas,* a permanent distinction between Moses and the rest of "the People," and this allows Ephrem to retell not only the history of Jews, but the history of "Christians," symbolized by Moses, as well. As Ephrem summarizes, "Moses taught; the People apostasized."[67]

Ephrem furthermore emphasizes that this is not an arbitrary distinction,

62. Ephrem, *Virg.* 44.8,15.

63. Ephrem, *Virg.* 49.1.

64. Ephrem makes a similar rhetorical maneuver with his use of the biblical prophets, as discussed below.

65. Compare *Ep. Barn.* 4.6–8, 14.1–4.

66. With respect to this story, Ephrem stays closer to the biblical text in his commentary, so does not emphasize the distinction between Moses and "the People" as sharply there as he does in his hymns. While it is interesting to note such differences between genres, for the purposes of this discussion what is most significant is not so much that Ephrem's commentary follows the biblical text, but rather that there are other texts in which Ephrem chooses to play with the biblical narrative in order to strengthen a particular rhetorical point.

67. Ephrem, *Virg.* 49.13. Compare *Ep.Barn.* 4, 14.

but rather that it highlights the innate character of each, namely, the goodness and purity of Moses and the blindness and impurity of the People. This
is perhaps most explicit in Ephrem's *Hymns on Fasting* in which he describes,
"While Moses was supplicating on the mountain, that blind People was indulging itself. For Moses, a fast of atonement, and for the People, the luxury
of idolatry. Moses with the one on high; the People with the calf. The Spirit
within Moses, and Legion within the People."[68] Ephrem here describes Moses and the people as opposites to one another, emphasizing the goodness of
the former in sharp contrast to the idolatry of the latter. For Ephrem there is
no question that Moses' separation at Mt. Sinai reflects a fundamental difference in character between him and the general crowd, between Moses who
"sweetened the water with wood" and the people who "was made bitter by
the molten calf,"[69] between Moses who "separated himself from his wife"
and the daughter of Abraham who "went whoring with the calf."[70] Ephrem
thus defines two lines of ancestry for Israel (and for his own community): the
descendents of the good and spiritually pure Moses, and the descendents of
the rejected and defiled Jewish people.

The fact that Ephrem equates the negative aspects attributed to those
who created the golden calf with all Jews, including those alive during Jesus'
time and also those contemporary with Ephrem himself, is clear throughout his writings. As demonstrated in greater detail below, Ephrem also condemns the New Testament Pharisees during Jesus' lifetime as the direct descendents of the congregation in Exodus 32, and therefore as tainted through
this heredity. Discussing Simon the Pharisee of Luke 7, Ephrem claims that
Jesus acted as he did "so that the rebellious thought might be formed in the
Pharisee like the rebellious calf that his ancestors formed."[71] As a "son of Israel," Simon the Pharisee's "fraudulence resembles that of Israel; for paganism is shut up in the mind of the People."[72] That this fatal connection with
those who created the golden calf continues even up to the Jews of Ephrem's
own day is explicit in Ephrem's *Hymns against Julian:* "The People raved and
raged and sounded the trumpet [for Julian]. . . . The circumcised saw the im-

---

68. Ephrem, *Ieiun.* 10.4.   69. Ephrem, *Virg.* 44.15.

70. Ephrem, *Nat.* 14.19.

71. Ephrem, *de Dom. nos.* 19. For further discussion of Ephrem's typological comparison of
these two passages, see Angela Kim, "Signs of Ephrem's Exegetical Techniques in his *Homily on
Our Lord,*" *Hugoye: Journal of Syriac Studies* 3, no. 1 (2000) [online journal], available from http://
syrcom.cua.edu/hugoye/Vol3No1/HV3N1Kim.html (accessed 1/15/05).

72. Ephrem, *de Dom. nos.* 43.

age that all at once was a bull. On his coins they saw the shameful bull, and they began feasting . . . because they saw in that bull their ancient calf. . . . The Jews were overjoyed that [the bull] was [with Julian] . . . as a likeness of that calf of the wilderness."[73] Ephrem thus uses the episode of the golden calf both as a prooftext for the malfeasance of the Jews and also as a reason behind their later ignominious conduct.

While Ephrem, like the *Epistle of Barnabas,* includes contemporary Jews as descendents of the congregation at Mt. Sinai, he also traces another thread through the history of Israel—not through the disobedient crowd, but through Moses himself. While Ephrem attributes to the first group all the negative connotations of those rejected by God, through the second he traces the history of those who remained faithful to God, the heroes of Jewish tradition whom Christians claim as their own ancestors. Ephrem understands that it is from this faithful line that Jesus the Jew comes.

That Ephrem identifies a line of faithful Jews who rose above the rest of the Jewish people is clear from his frequent references to certain pillars within the tradition of Israel, such as Noah, Abraham, Moses, and David, whom Ephrem consistently raises up as positive models for Christian behavior.[74] The harsh language with which Ephrem refers to the Jewish people as a whole emphasizes that these heroes stand in stark contrast to the rest of the Jews throughout history. Ephrem makes this distinction explicit in describing the birth of Jesus in the third of his *Sermons on Faith:* God "kept the [Jewish] flock because of something that was within it. The something that was hidden in it went out and became a shepherd of humankind. In a contemptible flock that prince of shepherds was hidden. He left behind the foolish flock because the Gentiles became his pasture."[75] This split within humanity

73. Ephrem, *CJ* 1.16–19.

74. For example, in *Eccl.* 11.1–4, Ephrem lists as righteous Abel, Enoch, Noah, Shem, Melchizedek, Abraham, Isaac, Jacob, Joseph, Moses, Joshua, Aaron, David, Samuel, Elijah, Isaiah, Jeremiah, Ezekiel, and Daniel. The refrain to this hymn is, "Glory be to the Just One who wrote their names in the book of life." Although Ephrem emphasizes in his anti-Jewish rhetoric the role of Exodus 32, in which it was Aaron who made the golden calf at the crowd's demand, Ephrem nonetheless participates in a Jewish and Christian recuperation of Aaron as a righteous follower of God. For some background on Aaron's conflicting biblical roles, and on writers like Ephrem redeeming him despite the golden calf incident, see Aberbach and Smolar ("Aaron").

75. Ephrem, *SdF* 3.251–258. In this passage, Ephrem consistently uses the Syriac word *gzrâ* to refer to the (Jewish) flock. Ephrem uses others of the various Syriac words for "flock" elsewhere in his writings, such as his more common choice of "ʿnā" (see, for example, *Virg.* 8.14; *Nat.* 4.55, 7.6; *SdF* 3.244, 6.16), as well as the less frequent "mrʾithā" (see, for example, *Virg.* 8.14; *Nat.* 4.55). It is worth noting that in this passage Ephrem chooses the less common word that

was clear to Ephrem, and for him it is Jesus' spiritual descendents, Christians, who are the rightful inheritors of God's divine covenant with Israel.

Ephrem associates the good line of Israel with Christians in a variety of ways. First, the language with which Ephrem describes Moses emphasizes that Moses remains pure and in God's favor, as Ephrem describes true Christians throughout his writings.[76] Furthermore, the distinction between Moses and the people in Exodus 32 is paralleled for Ephrem by the contemporary distinction between the pure Christian church and the defiled Jewish synagogue.[77] Ephrem also more explicitly claims Moses for Christianity in his *Homily on our Lord*: "Therefore even though Moses' eyes were bodily, like Paul's, his inner eyes were Christian."[78] Through such descriptions, Ephrem reiterates the distinction between the adulterous congregation of Jews and Moses (and his Christian spiritual descendents). For Ephrem, God's covenant has always been valid, but Jews forfeited that covenant. In the time between Sinai and Jesus, the pure covenant was preserved among a faithful few as a secret good hidden among the "contemptible" People. This reconstruction allows Ephrem to praise prominent Jewish ancestors and to claim Jewish Scripture, as well as to explain how it was that Jesus could have been born a Jew, and yet why there is no valid Judaism after Jesus. After the crucifixion, God removed forever the divine covenant that was still intertwined with Jewish history, leaving a distinct division between Jews, the descendents of the idolaters at Sinai, and Christians, the descendents of Moses, and heirs of God's covenant with Israel.

The ubiquity of the references to Exodus 32 in Ephrem's hymns and his *Homily on Our Lord* suggests that this story is crucial to his understanding of Christianity, Jews, and Judaism. This elaborate metaphor plays a significant role in Ephrem's project of Christian self-definition as it provides him with a key tool with which to assert the community boundaries and the authority of Christianity against a wide variety of opponents, including idolatrous pagans, divinely rejected Jews, and also his Christian opponents who, according to Ephrem, just like the Jews at Mt. Sinai go astray by searching after God inappropriately. Ephrem's construction of Exodus 32 is a rhetorical foundation that undergirds his pro-Nicene arguments, in that his understanding of the

---

also happens to be a homonym for the Syriac word for "circumcised," undoubtedly emphasizing for Ephrem's audience the connection of this "flock" with the circumcised Jews.

76. See, for example, Ephrem, *Ieiun.* 10; *de Dom. nos.* 31–32; *Nat.* 14.

77. See, for example, *Res.* 3, 4; *Cruc.* 1; *Virg.* 35.

78. Ephrem, *de Dom. nos.* 32.

history of God's covenant with Israel allows him to identify (Nicene) Christians as God's covenanted people, and contemporary Jews (and Christian heretics whom he associates with the Jews) as the adulterous descendents of that fateful congregation that went "whoring with the calf."[79]

Ephrem's Use of the Prophets

Ephrem further supports the scriptural-historical framework that he constructs through his exegesis of the story of the golden calf by marshalling the biblical prophets to his defense. Both through references to specific biblical passages and through an invocation of "the Prophets" more generally, Ephrem uses them to echo his own accusations against the Jews and to validate his interpretations of Scripture. Since the Prophets themselves frequently lament the behavior of Jewish Israel, Ephrem, like other Christian authors, found in the Prophets a vocabulary and a support system that were already authoritative to contemporary Jews and Christians alike.[80] These prophets thus served as another scriptural voice through which early Christians such as Ephrem created an image of "the People" that did not rely on the physical presence or behavior of contemporary "Jews," and so could therefore work equally effectively against the Christian opponents whom Ephrem conflates with "the Jews."

Ephrem's specific rhetorical uses of the biblical prophets against the Jews appear in several different contexts. To begin with, there are occasions in his writings when Ephrem refers either to "the Prophets" generally without necessarily referring to particular biblical passages or else to a particular prophet and scriptural narrative in order to support his own condemnation of the Jews. For example, in his *Hymns on the Church* Ephrem uses the land of Judah as a representative for the Jewish people, and compares the land to a scorpion, silent about the praise of God, and dangerous, so that "the prophets trampled her; the apostles shattered her; the Spirit scattered her."[81] In this instance, Ephrem groups the prophets as those who "trampled" the land of Judah, the Jewish people. Ephrem claims that the Jews' own prophets chastised and rightfully accused the Jewish people just as Christian apostles later did.

---

79. Ephrem, *Nat.* 14.19.

80. Compare, for example, Justin Martyr's *Dial.* and *First Apology;* Origen (e.g., *Commentary on Lamentations* 116); and Eusebius of Caesarea, *DE* 3–10.

81. Ephrem, *Eccl.* 41.12. Note that Syriac has the same word for "wind" and "spirit," so this passage could also be translated, "the wind scattered her."

This rhetoric further implies that the Christian apostles, and even Ephrem himself, are justified in their critique of the Jews, and that in their very criticism they participate in a long prophetic tradition within the history of Israel.

One of the most frequent prophetic passages to which Ephrem refers to support and validate his own arguments against the Jews is Jeremiah 8:7, which is part of a prophecy lamenting that time after time the Jewish people turn away from God, in striking contrast to numerous examples of nature consistently doing God's will. Jeremiah 8:4–7 says,

> You shall say to them, thus says the Lord: When people fall, do they not get up again? If they go astray, do they not turn back? Why then has this people turned away in perpetual backsliding? They have held fast to deceit, they have refused to return. I have given heed and listened, but they do not speak honestly; no one repents of wickedness, saying, "What have I done!" All of them turn to their own course, like a horse plunging headlong into battle. Even the stork in the heavens knows its times; and the turtledove, swallow, and crane observe the time of their coming; but my people know not the ordinance of the Lord.[82]

This passage as a whole castigates the Jewish people for continually turning away from God in ways that the author implies is not only unnatural to humans ("when people fall, do they not get up again?"), but is even unnatural to simple animals such as storks and other birds.

Through these examples, Ephrem understands the Jewish people to be shamed by the simple birds who do what God expects of them when the Jews do not. Thus Ephrem writes, "Through a stork and a swallow he reproached that People."[83] Ephrem echoes this accusation against the Jews elsewhere,[84] and perhaps most explicitly uses this particular passage of Old Testament prophecy to demonstrate that God has repeatedly accused the Jews—those of earlier times as well as those contemporary with Ephrem—when he writes, "You reproached the foolish synagogue, my Lord, many times with a stork and a swallow who keep in order [their] times. So that he might shame [his people] . . . he praised the bird[s]."[85] Time and time again Ephrem echoes the Prophets in saying that the "foolish" Jews turned away from God and that as a result, according to Ephrem's presentation of history, God left the Jewish people for another flock, the Christians, who would re-

---

82. Jer 8:4–7. All biblical quotations are from the NRSV.
83. Ephrem, *CH* 15.3.   84. See, for example, *HdF* 84.6.
85. Ephrem, *CNis.* 28.14.

main faithful, a portrayal of history that also purportedly describes his own context in fourth-century Syria.[86]

Jeremiah 8:7 is not by any means the only prophetic text that Ephrem cites in order to support his accusations against the Jews. Ephrem also, like other early Christian authors,[87] condemns the fasts of contemporary Jews through a reference to Isaiah 58, a passage that includes Isaiah's accusations against God's people for fasting impiously and condemnations for their transgressions against God.[88] In addition, however, Ephrem frequently admonishes the Jews for failing to recognize and for even killing the Messiah whom their own prophets had foretold: "their voices attest that the People killed their Lord."[89] In another hymn Ephrem echoes this accusation: "The [Jewish] People have erred in their reading of the Prophets, and they maintained that You were not You. . . . The scribes killed the Son of the King."[90] As with the examples above, these further uses of the biblical prophets provide additional support for Ephrem's own charges against the Jews, and validate his interpretation of Scripture as leading up to Christian "truth."

Ephrem also uses the Jews' blindness in failing to recognize the alleged fulfillment of prophecies from the "Testament of Moses" to help support his charges against the Jews. Throughout his writings, Ephrem emphasizes that Jesus fulfilled the Jews' own prophecies, that the biblical prophets foretold his coming, death, and identity as God's Son. The eighth of Ephrem's *Hymns on Virginity* is entirely devoted to demonstrating these foreshadowings. Ephrem writes, "In Scripture [the Lord] is written. . . . His diadem is portrayed by kings, and by prophets his truth, his atonement by priests. . . . The Prophets have his likeness," and the refrain for this hymn is "Blessed is the one whom the Prophets portrayed."[91] Ephrem condemns the Jews for

---

86. See, for example, *Nat.* 24.22, and the discussion in chapter 2.

87. See, for example, Justin Martyr, *Dial.* 15.

88. For Ephrem's use of Isaiah and reference to Isaiah 58 in the context of condemning Jewish fasting, see *Ieiun.* 2.1. Note that Ephrem here adopts the practice in late antiquity of referring to a larger biblical passage by quoting only one line.

Compare also the entire text about Jonah and the Ninevites that uses the language and narrative of Jonah in order to reiterate the numerous downfalls of the Jews (Ephrem, *Sermon* I in Edmund Beck, ed., *Des Heiligen Ephraem des Syrers, Sermones II* CSCO SS 311/134 [Louvain, 1970]). Although this text has been attributed to Ephrem and shares many concerns in common with Ephrem's writings, its authenticity is not certain (Edmund Beck, trans., *Des Heiligen Ephraem des Syrers, Sermones II* CSCO SS 312/135 [Louvain, 1970], vi–vii).

89. Ephrem, *Cruc.* 8.7.   90. Ephrem, *Virg.* 28.5–7.

91. Ephrem, *Virg.* 8.3–4. Compare also *Cruc.* 2, and *SdF* 6.75–76: "The prophets whom he gave to us cried out that everything is completed by him."

what is in his eyes a rejection of and turning away from God, God's prophets, and their Lord. Ephrem writes, "Put to shame is the People that holds the prophets to be true, for if our Savior had not come, their words would have become lies."[92] The Prophets told the Jews about their coming savior, but according to Ephrem the Jews did not recognize him when he came.

Because of this alleged blindness, Ephrem believes that the Jews themselves have justly been rejected by God. Arguing that the Old Testament is filled with prophecies about the coming truth that is embodied in the Christian recognition of Jesus as Lord, Ephrem appeals, "The People became like a deaf-mute who withheld praise. . . . Woe to the People that did not perceive you. . . . Moses sounded two [trumpets] so that he might teach them; and David played the harp. Who does this silent People resemble? Mute bells that keep silent about the glory."[93] In a similar vein, Ephrem further argues that despite the Jews' possession and reading of the prophecies, they were blind to Christian truth, which is itself in Ephrem's eyes the fulfillment of Jewish prophecy:

The scribes were reading every day that a star would shine forth from Jacob. The People have the voice and the reading; the peoples have the shining forth and the explanation. They have the books and we have the deeds; they have the branches and we their fruits. The scribes are reading in books; the magi are seeing in actions the flash of that reading. . . . [The People] rejected the trumpet of Isaiah that sounded the pure conception; they stilled the lyre of the psalms that sang about his priesthood; they silenced the kithara of the spirit that sang of his kingship. . . . Behold the fool reads in his Scriptures the promises that were distributed to us! As he boasts in his Scriptures, he reads to us his [own] accusation, and he witnesses our inheritance to us.[94]

Participating in what was by then a long tradition of supersessionist Christian writing, Ephrem here uses the Old Testament prophets to justify his condemnation of the Jews in that the prophets foretold a "Christian" truth, making Ephrem's interpretation of Scripture appear to be in complete harmony with the Prophets' own claims.[95]

With even stronger accusations, Ephrem also, as mentioned in chapter two, warns his audience about the physical harm that the Jews have caused

92. Ephrem, *Nat.* 1.18.

93. Ephrem, *Eccl.* 41.1–5.

94. Ephrem, *Nat.* 24.4, 14, 22. Compare Eusebius of Emesa, *Hom.* 14.4, which includes language quite similar to this quotation from Ephrem's hymn.

95. See, for example, Justin Martyr, *Dial.* 16, 39, 93, 95; and Eusebius of Caesarea, *DE* 3–10.

their prophets, another charge that helps to solidify Ephrem's own position on the side of the righteous but attacked prophets and further condemns the Jews by way of reference to the biblical prophets.[96] According to Ephrem, the prophets foretold Christ's coming, but the Jews whose prophets they were did not understand the prophecies, and even went so far as to kill both Christ and the prophets. Thus, Ephrem presents scriptural history as an ideological narrative that depicts Jewish and Christian communities of his own time as clearly defined and sharply distinct from one another, an image that does not acknowledge the more porous boundaries that he accuses his own audience of crossing.

Ephrem's "Jews" and the New Testament

As he uses the "Testament of Moses" to construct a historical framework for his Nicene Christianity, so too Ephrem uses stories and language from the New Testament to support his descriptions of "Jews" and "Christians," and to strengthen the credibility of the social boundaries that his writings draw. Because of his firm belief in the coherent narrative of Scripture, Ephrem's hymns often seamlessly combine without comment images and stories from both Testaments. As a result, while the following discussion emphasizes Ephrem's use of the New Testament in his anti-Jewish rhetoric, his use of the golden calf and other Old Testament stories nonetheless reappear, offering background to and support for Ephrem's additional New Testament-based conclusions.

The Calf and the Crucifixion: Jews as Crucifiers

For Ephrem, the New Testament equivalent to the Old Testament story of the golden calf, both in its revelation of the blindness of the Jews and also in its detrimental consequences for the Jews' position as God's chosen people, is the crucifixion of Jesus as portrayed in the New Testament Gospels. Ephrem understands the stories of the golden calf and of the crucifixion both to demonstrate the Jews' willful rejection of God and God's covenant. For Ephrem the fracture of the covenant at Mt. Sinai meant a split within the Jewish people into a faithful few, represented by the spiritual descendents of Moses and

96. See, for example, *Virg.* 28.9; and *CNis.* 27.10 and 67.3–12. Ephrem certainly was not the first Christian writer to use this accusation against the Jews. Compare, for example, Justin, *Dial.* 73.6 and Eusebius of Emesa, *Hom.* 19.

the true prophets, and the blind and foolish majority, the descendents of the congregation that had committed idolatry with the golden calf. With this second nodal point, however, Ephrem believes that God's covenant no longer remains with the Jewish people as a hidden goodness within an otherwise infected flock,[97] but rather that at the crucifixion God's covenant was openly removed from the Jewish people and given instead to Christians because they recognized and worshipped their Lord.[98] Like the story of the golden calf, the narratives of Jesus' crucifixion embodied for Ephrem a key turning point in the history of Israel. The crucifixion represents a second moment of rupture in the promise between God and the Jews, a moment in which God permanently removed the covenant from the Jews and instead made a covenant with Gentile Christians, of whom the members of Ephrem's own fourth-century Christian community are the spiritual descendents.

In many instances in his writings, Ephrem explicitly links the crucifixion with the golden calf. One of the most explicit of these comparisons, already mentioned briefly above, is Ephrem's description in the first of his *Hymns on the Crucifixion*. In this hymn Ephrem describes Jewish Israel through the metaphor of mother and daughter: at Sinai it was the mother who "made the poured [calf] through which she became ashamed,"[99] and in Jerusalem it was her daughter who murdered Jesus and "had become accustomed to adultery."[100] Ephrem unequivocally equates these two events in this hymn:

For as her mother, she had become accustomed to adultery. . . . The reproach [of God] that was her mother's was in her mouth, [her mother] who cunningly made the calf. . . . Also the daughter was imprinted with the likeness of that mother who was cunning toward hateful [ends]. . . . She was not ashamed to murder and to commit adultery publicly. She resembled her mother.[101]

Ephrem draws a similar connection between these two events in other hymns.[102] For Ephrem the Jews' crucifixion of Jesus harkened back to the only other comparably significant event in the history of Israel, namely the creation and worship of the golden calf at Mt. Sinai.

In Ephrem's writings, these two moments in scriptural history not only

---

97. See Ephrem, *SdF* 3.241–258.

98. As discussed in chapter 2, Ephrem consistently implies that Christians are Gentiles, frequently highlighting the Gentile magi rather than Jesus' Jewish apostles as Christians' forebearers.

99. Ephrem, *Cruc.* 1.4.   100. Ephrem, *Cruc.* 1.3.

101. Ephrem, *Cruc.* 1.3, 4, 5, 14.

102. Compare, for example, Ephrem, *Res.* 3, *de Dom. nos.* 6, and *Comm. Diat.* 11.8.

resemble each other in that Ephrem accuses both mother and daughter of defiling their promised marriage covenant with God, but also each represents a significant turning point in the history of Israel. Just like with Israel's worship of the golden calf, Ephrem understood the crucifixion to mark a radical change in the definition of Israel. Ephrem's historical narratives conclude that with the coming of Jesus, whom the Prophets had foretold, the faithful among Israel were finally and forcefully split apart from the unfaithful majority of Jews. Those who became Christian recognized and worshipped Jesus as their Lord, and inherited God's covenant. As a result those, including the majority of Jews, who did not, were rejected by God and no longer remained among God's chosen people. Ephrem frequently emphasizes that the act of crucifying Jesus changed forever the Jews' relationship with God. Ephrem writes, "Praise be to Christ through whose body the unleavened bread of the People became frail, together with the People."[103] Such accusations about the power of that moment in the fate of the Jews are scattered throughout Ephrem's texts: "Jerusalem found very guilty the accursed ones and crucifiers who dared to enter to build the desolate place desolated by their sins."[104] In other words, the Jews of the fourth century who would go to Jerusalem to rebuild the Temple under the Emperor Julian are still "crucifiers" guilty of the crucifixion of Jesus. The importance of the crucifixion in the history of the Jews from Ephrem's Christian point of view is quite clear, as are the consequences of their actions, which continue to Ephrem's time, and the Jews' responsibility for them.[105]

In Ephrem's presentation of history, the most significant result of the Jews' participation in Jesus' crucifixion was God's consequent rejection of the Jews as God's chosen people, and the transfer of that divine election from the Jewish people to (Gentile) Christians.[106] As at Mt. Sinai, the Jews' rejection of God through the crucifixion of Jesus resulted in the annulment of a

---

103. Ephrem, *Azym.* 19, refrain.   104. Ephrem, *CJ* 4.18.

105. This is true despite the fact that Ephrem also occasionally distributes some of the blame for the crucifixion onto Satan, as discussed in more detail in chapter 4. Likewise, it is Ephrem's blame of the Jews for Jesus' crucifixion that is relevant, despite the fact that the New Testament Gospels narrate that it was the Roman governor who gave the order for Jesus' crucifixion and the soldiers of the governor who mocked (and, in John, stabbed) Jesus.

106. It is noteworthy, however, that in his *Commentary on the Diatessaron,* Ephrem comments that even before the crucifixion the Jews had already forfeited their divine covenant because they did not believe that Jesus was the Messiah (Ephrem, *Comm. Diat.* 20.3). The Jews' rejection of Jesus culminated, however, in his crucifixion, and it is that final event that Ephrem most frequently uses to identify the end of the second of his three epochs.

marriage-like covenant with God. Unlike at Mt. Sinai, however, with the crucifixion God withdrew from the Jews entirely, the terms of God's covenant
were redrawn, and the covenant itself became the inheritance of the Christian church. After narrating Jesus' trial scene in his *Hymns on the Crucifixion,*
Ephrem writes that these details of Jesus' trial and crucifixion "showed the
symbol of the fall of the People."[107] Also in this hymn cycle, Ephrem explains that "through the crucifixion" the Jewish people were washed away
and the Gentiles were chosen in their place.[108] Ephrem similarly describes
the Gentiles' inheritance of the Jews' divine promise in numerous other places: "Hope came to the People. The People cut off their hope and threw it to
the peoples and became without hope. The peoples hurried to clothe themselves in the hope that these had sent."[109] With these lines, Ephrem narrates
the transfer of God's covenant from Jews to Christians. Ephrem leaves no
doubt in his recounting of history, which is specifically the Scripture-based
history of Israel, that it was the Jews who were responsible for the murder of
Jesus, and that the result of that crucifixion was that the Jewish people forfeited their position as God's chosen people, a divine covenant that was then
granted instead to Gentiles in the form of Christianity. This ideological narrative that Ephrem presents thus supports his own particular interpretation
of his social context, and its history, an interpretation that he presents to his
audience as natural and necessarily true.

Jesus as a Jew to the Jews

While the crucifixion is rhetorically the focal point of Ephrem's discussions about the New Testament Jews' rejection of God and by God, Ephrem
understands the crucifixion to be the culmination of numerous other events
in which the Jews secured their fate through their freely chosen actions.[110]
First and foremost for Ephrem, the crucifixion was the epitome of the Jews'

---

107. Ephrem, *Cruc.* 4.10.

108. Ephrem, *Cruc.* 5.3, 5, 8.

109. Ephrem, *Azym.* 2.13. Compare also, for example, Ephrem, *Virg.* 20 and 26; *CJ* 4.25; *CH* 39; *HdF* 44; *HdF* 87.

110. Ephrem's emphasis on the Jews' participation in their own rejection by God is consistent with his overall emphasis on the free will that is inherent in human nature. In fact, in
his *Prose Refutations* Ephrem argues (against Mani, Marcion, and Bardaisan) that what it meant
for Adam (and therefore humankind) to be created in the image of God (Gen 1:26) was that
Adam was created with free will (e.g., *First Discourse to Hypatius*). See also T. Bou Mansour, "La
défense éphrémienne de la liberté contre les doctrines marcionite, bardésanite et manichéenne," *OCP* 50 (1984): 331–46.

earlier persistent failures to recognize, and insistent rejection of, Jesus as God's Son and the Jews' Lord. The Jews' folly in this blindness was complete for Ephrem particularly because Jesus came specifically to the Jews, as a Jew, and fulfilling the Jews' own prophecies. For Ephrem, Jesus' Jewishness supports Christians' belief that after the crucifixion God's covenant left the Jews because of the Jews' own stubborn and blind behavior. At the same time, it also offers a clear explanation for Ephrem's Christian community of how it was that Jesus could have been a Jew, been circumcised on the eighth day and come specifically for the Jews,[111] and yet why after his death Judaism and the laws specific to it were obsolete and Gentile Christians were his true followers and the new heirs of God's promises to Israel.[112]

Ephrem's references to the Jews' rejection of Jesus in spite of Jesus' appearance as a Jew and his fulfillment of the Jews' messianic prophecies appear in Ephrem's writings embedded both in general comments about Jesus fulfilling Scripture,[113] and in more specific comments that allow Ephrem to praise the Gentiles over the Jews for recognizing their Lord, and that simultaneously explain Jesus' Jewishness within Christian history. Among these latter comments are several in which Ephrem emphasizes Jesus' validity as the Jewish Messiah in order to heighten the Jews' culpability in not recognizing and in rejecting him, and to praise Gentile Christians for the reverse.

One of Ephrem's more elaborate examples of this rhetoric is in his *Homily on Our Lord*. In this homily Ephrem reads into Simeon's presentation of Jesus at the Temple the legitimate bestowal of Jewish priesthood and prophecy onto Jesus:[114] "The Son came to the servant [Simeon] not to be presented by the servant but so that, through the Son, the servant might present to his Lord the priesthood and prophecy that had been entrusted to his keeping."[115] Ephrem argues that as a Jewish priest, Simeon was the legitimate

111. Luke 2:21 mentions Jesus' circumcision.

112. As discussed, Ephrem understood there to be three generations, and each generation had some laws that remained the same over time and other specific laws that were only relevant to that particular generation (*SdF* 3). Compare also Eusebius of Caesarea's justification of Jesus' Jewishness, and his emphasis that this gave the Jews no excuse for not recognizing their Messiah (*DE* 1). Paula Fredriksen describes Augustine's different approach to this issue in her discussion of Augustine's position against Faustus (*Augustine and the Jews: The Story of Christianity's Great Theologian and His Defense of Judaism* [New York: Doubleday, forthcoming]).

113. See, for example, Ephrem, *Virg.* 9, 10; *Nat.* 1.

114. Luke 2:22–35. Of course, Ephrem portrays this bestowal not as necessary for the perfection of God's Son, but rather as Jesus' "legitimate" reception of these gifts according to the traditions of the Jews, removing any possible reason for the Jews to reject his legitimacy.

115. Ephrem, *de Dom. nos.* 53. Compare also Ephrem, *Comm. Diat.* 2.16.

heir of Jewish prophecy and priesthood, and as such he passed them to the baby Jesus:

Prophecy and priesthood, which had been given through Moses, were both passed down and came to rest on Simeon. . . . Simeon presented our Lord, and in him he presented the two gifts he had so that what had been given to Moses in the desert was passed on by Simeon in the Temple. Because our Lord is the vessel in which all fullness dwells, when Simeon presented him to God, he poured out both of these upon him: the priesthood from his hands, and prophecy from his lips. The priesthood had always been on Simeon's hands, because of purifications. Prophecy, in fact, dwelt on his lips because of revelations. When both of these saw the Lord of both of these, both of them were combined and were poured into the vessel that could accommodate them both, in order to contain priesthood, kingship, and prophecy. That infant who was wrapped in swaddling clothes by virtue of his goodness was dressed in priesthood and prophecy by virtue of his majesty. Simeon dressed him in these, and gave him to the one who had dressed him in swaddling clothes. As he returned him to his mother, he returned the priesthood with him. And when he prophesied to her about him . . . he gave her prophecy with him as well.[116]

Thus when Mary received her baby back from Simeon, according to Ephrem the infant had received these gifts from a source that should legitimate him in the eyes of Jews and through the traditions of Judaism, thus making illegitimate any Jews' denial of his priesthood and his prophecies:

So Mary took her firstborn and left. Although he was visibly wrapped in swaddling clothes, he was invisibly clothed with prophecy and priesthood. Thus, what Moses had been given was received from Simeon, and it remained and continued with the Lord of these two [gifts]. The former steward and the final treasurer handed over the keys of priesthood and prophecy to the one in authority over the treasury of both of these.[117]

Ephrem elsewhere names Melchizedek rather than Simeon as the important figure through whom Jesus' received his right to the priesthood. In his *Hymns on the Resurrection* Ephrem writes, "From God [comes] his deity . . . from Melchizedek, his priesthood; and from the House of David, his kingdom."[118] Nonetheless, in his *Homily on Our Lord* he emphasizes Simeon in order to legitimate Jesus as the heir and endpoint of the Jewish priesthood,

---

116. Ephrem, *de Dom. nos.* 53–54.

117. Ephrem, *de Dom. nos.* 54.

118. Ephrem, *Res.* 1.12. Compare also Ephrem, *Nat.* 9.3. Of course Melchizedek played an important role in Christian narratives, since according to Genesis 14:18–24 he was a priest of "God Most High" who blessed Abram. The New Testament Epistle to the Hebrews claims that God pronounced Jesus to be "a priest forever, according to the order of Melchizedek"

Jewish prophecy and the Davidic kingship. In a fourth-century context in which he chastises some members of his church for inappropriately honoring Jewish traditions and festivals, Ephrem here harnesses Jewish texts and traditions to support Christianity, showing how they culminate in their fulfillment in Jesus.

Having established to his satisfaction that Jesus legitimately inherited Jewish prophecy and priesthood, Ephrem continues in his *Homily on Our Lord* by explaining that Jesus also received the gift of baptism and the forgiveness of sins from John at the Jordan:

Because John also was the treasurer of baptism, the Lord of stewardship came to him to take the keys of the house of forgiveness from him. John had been whitening the stains of debt with common water, so that bodies would be fit for the robe of the Spirit imparted by our Lord. Therefore, since the Spirit was with the Son, he came to receive baptism from John to mix the Spirit, which cannot be seen, with water, which can be seen, so that those whose bodies feel the wetness of the water should be aware of the gift of the Spirit in their souls, and that as the outside of the body becomes aware of water flowing over it, the inside of the soul should become aware of the Spirit flowing over it. So when our Lord plunged down into baptism, he clothed himself with baptism and drew it out with him, just as he had put on prophecy and priesthood when he was presented in the Temple, and he left bearing the purity of the priesthood on his pure limbs, and the words of prophecy in his innocent ears.[119]

In order not to compromise the Messiah's power, Ephrem explains Jesus' submission to baptism by John as necessary in order to receive legitimately the gift of baptism as his own to give to others, and also in order to make manifest the Spirit that secretly dwelled within him. Since for Ephrem Scripture tells one coherent narrative, he weaves together the New Testament with the Old in order to present Jesus as the legitimate fulfillment of Jewish traditions and prophecies. From the contemporary guardian of each tradition, Jesus gathers prophecy, priesthood, kingship, and the rite of baptism, so that he might be the rightful inheritor of each, even as he brings some to an end through their completion in him.

Summarizing all that Jesus legitimately inherited through these Jewish predecessors, Ephrem concludes,

---

(Heb 5:6). This epistle then contains an extended excursus on the significance of Melchizedek, and all that he foreshadowed about Jesus, and in turn about the temporary state of Jewish Levitical law, and of the subsequent rise of Christianity.

119. Ephrem, *de Dom. nos.* 55. Compare also Ephrem, *Comm. Diat.* 4.1–3.

Every one of the gifts that had been laid aside for the Son, he picked from its proper tree. He took baptism from the Jordan even though John baptized again after him. He took priesthood from the Temple, even though the high priest Annas exercised it. And he also took prophecy, which had been handed down by the righteous, even though Caiaphas used it once to weave our Lord a crown. And he took kingship from the house of David, even though Herod kept the position and functioned in it.[120]

Undaunted by the apparent continuation of Jewish priesthood, baptism, and kingship apart from Jesus, Ephrem insists that Jesus was legitimate even by the Jews' own "rules," thereby heightening their culpability and blindness in their rejection of Jesus.

In addition to emphasizing Jesus' inheritance of these accoutrements that help him to fulfill Old Testament prophecies, Ephrem also occasionally refers more generally to the Jewishness of Jesus, emphasizing Jesus' legitimacy for the Jews not only in his inheritance of these titular roles, but also in his own personal abidance by Jewish law. For Ephrem and others in antiquity, one of the clear markers of Judaism was male circumcision.[121] Ephrem could therefore easily mark Jesus' Jewishness by referring to Jesus' circumcision as recorded in the New Testament,[122] as he does in his *Hymns on the Nativity:*

Let the eighth day that circumcised the Hebrews confess him who commanded his namesake Joshua to circumcise with flint the People whose body was circumcised but whose heart was unbelieving from within [Joshua 5:2–7]. Behold on the eighth day as a babe the circumciser of all came to circumcision [Luke 2:21]. Although the sign of Abraham was on his flesh, the blind daughter of Zion has disfigured it. . . . The first-born, purifier of all, on the day of his purifying purified the purification of the first-born and was offered.[123]

Far from skirting the issue of Jesus' Judaism, Ephrem here touts it in the very process of defining Judaism's end in Jesus' legitimate fulfillment of it. Ephrem elsewhere further reminds his audience of Jesus' Jewishness in debating with other Jewish scholars: "With the scribes our Lord debated. Clothed in their Scripture, he cast [them] down in controversy. . . . he was victorious, whose

---

120. Ephrem, *de Dom. nos.* 56. Even as Ephrem shows Jesus ending Jewish priesthood and kingship, he also accounts for the fact that the Jews continued to follow Annas, Caiaphas, and Herod in these offices.

121. Ephrem, *SdF* 3. (Compare, for example, Sallustius, *De deis et mundo,* 9.5; Justin, *Dial.* 16.2.)

122. Luke 2:21.

123. Ephrem, *Nat.* 26.11, 13.

shield was the Torah and Isaiah his sword and spear and the Prophets his arrows."[124] Ephrem argues that Jesus came as the legitimate fulfillment of Jewish prophecies, and that yet even so the Jews rejected and crucified him. Through these descriptions, Ephrem appeals to those in his audience who may respect the Jewish history and traditions of Christianity through historical "facts" that happen in this case to support his own plea that his audience distinguish between outdated Judaism and the fulfillment of God's promises to Israel in Christianity.

Not surprisingly, Ephrem's emphasis on Jesus' Jewishness and fulfillment of Jewish Scripture and prophecy goes hand in hand with Ephrem's conclusions about the results of the fulfillment of those prophecies. Namely, Ephrem argues that as a consequence of the Jews' blindness, God rejected the Jews entirely in favor of (Gentile) Christians. As demonstrated above, these all crystallized for Ephrem at the moment of crucifixion, although the crucifixion was not a sudden aberration in history from Ephrem's point of view, but rather the foreshadowed culmination of the history of the Jewish people's troubled relationship with God. Therefore in his *Homily on Our Lord* Ephrem writes,

In your own flesh you [Jesus] received the external sign of circumcision, according to which the uncircumcised who were yours were not considered to be yours. Then you conferred your sign, circumcision of the heart, by which the circumcised were recognized as not being yours. For you came to your own, but your own did not accept you. And it is by this fact that they are recognized as not being yours. But those to whom you did not come in your love cry out after you to fill them with the crumbs that fall from the children's table.[125]

Ephrem thus charges the Jews with neglecting the one who was himself circumcised in order to come legitimately to the circumcised Jews. Ephrem echoes this also in his *Hymns on the Crucifixion,*

The crucifiers were shamed. . . . With his crucifixion he abolished the graven images of that People. And he also removed the crucifiers from the peoples. . . . Woe to the circumcised who were not ashamed to mock the Lord of the circumcised. If he had been uncircumcised, then there would have been a cause for his death. . . . He fulfilled the Law, and the People became insufficient. The commandments were fulfilled, and the proud were spilled away [as water].[126]

---

124. Ephrem, *Virg.* 37.7.
126. Ephrem, *Cruc.* 5.1, 3, 5.

125. Ephrem, *de Dom. nos.* 7.

Jesus came as a Jew to the Jews, but when the Jews rejected him he went instead to the Gentiles who recognized him when the Jews themselves did not.

For Ephrem, this history teaches that as a result of the crucifixion any semblance of the legitimacy either of Judaism or of the Jews as God's chosen people has come to an end. The entire eighth hymn of Ephrem's *Hymns on Virginity* addresses this theme:[127]

In Scripture he is written. . . . The prophets have his likeness. . . . By his sacrifice, he abolished sacrifices, and libations by his incense, and the lambs by his slaughter, the unleavened by his bread, and the bitter by his passion. By his healthy meal he weaned [and] took away the milk. By his baptism were abolished the bathing and sprinkling that the elders of the People taught. By his food refused were food tithes. . . . He set a limit and restrained the prophets, and he called and sent apostles. He dismissed and put to rest the former, and put to work and wearied the latter. . . . Brought to an end are the temporal priests. . . . By you the apostles became priests so that the Levites were brought to an end by you.[128]

For Ephrem, Jesus not only marked the fulfillment of Jewish prophecy, but also brought an end to Jewish prophecy and to the Jews' traditions of priesthood and kingship. Jesus' very Jewishness, as evidenced in scriptural history, supports, Ephrem argues, Christians' interpretation of the history of Israel as the Jews' voluntary forfeiting of their divine covenant, epitomized in the crucifixion of their own Lord. In fourth-century Syria, this particular presentation of the history of Israel offers Ephrem several political benefits. Ephrem's particular use and narration of scriptural history in his writings allow him to validate his Christian claims to the texts and traditions of Israel while concurrently severing that history from Jews, whom he is then able to condemn, using the language examined in chapter two, without fear that his slander will tar (orthodox) Christians or Christianity in any way.

Conclusion

Through his discussions of the role that the Jewish people play in the New Testament crucifixion stories, despite the very Jewishness of Jesus that should have legitimated him in their eyes, Ephrem paints a clear picture of the moment in which the Jews finally and permanently lost all connection with God's covenant. As with the story of the golden calf and with the la-

127. Ephrem, *Virg.* 8.
128. Ephrem, *Virg.* 8.3, 4, 9–11, 13, 18, 21.

ments of the prophets of Israel, Ephrem uses these New Testament narratives to construct a history of Israel that legitimates his own Christian authority and Christians' covenant with God, while portraying the Jews as a divinely rejected "other." In so doing, Ephrem shapes a particular ideological framework upon which he maps contemporary social and religious "realities," in fact creating and maintaining those alleged realities through his insistent descriptions of them.

The community boundaries and histories of contemporary Judaism and Christianity that Ephrem's grand narrative purports only to describe, with reference to the authoritative texts of Scripture, are in fact called into being in the very act of Ephrem's particular organization and presentation of biblical and contemporary characters and events. The resulting narrative, as outlined above, is the Jews' irrevocable loss of God's covenant, and the transfer of that covenant from the Jews to (true) Christians, the legitimate (spiritual) descendents of those throughout Israel's history who remained faithful to God. The social and religious implications of this historical narrative that are most significant for fourth-century Syria stem primarily from placing Ephrem's negative descriptions of Jews, as dangerous, defiled, adulterous, blind, foolish, and divinely rejected, into his historical narrative. Ephrem's ideological framework thereby not only creates a sharp distinction between Judaism and Christianity, but concurrently invalidates Judaism after the crucifixion, and presents Ephrem's Christianity as the legitimate heir of Israel's Scripture, traditions, and covenant with God. Ephrem has thus defined a description of Jews and Judaism that relies so heavily on Christian Scripture that it becomes a template that he can detach from living Jews and apply metaphorically to the teachings and behavior of both Judaizing and "Arian" Christian opponents. Anti-"Jewish" language thus becomes a surprisingly useful tool for Ephrem in his two-pronged mission to close the definition of "Christianity" tightly around the Council of Nicaea's injunctions. Quite simply, in Ephrem's rhetoric "Arians" and Judaizers become too "Jewish" to be "Christian."

CHAPTER FOUR

ℒℭ

Ephrem, Athanasius, and
the "Arian" Threat

Ephrem's intimately related narratives of Scripture and history produce an ideological framework through which he constructs the social boundaries of his fourth-century community. The anti-Jewish language of his hymns would have been a powerful tool, however, not only against Jews and Judaizers, as seen above, but also against "Arian" Christians. Sidney Griffith has clearly demonstrated Ephrem's explicit presentation of himself and his church as part of an empire-wide Nicene Christian community.[1] Like the more well-known figure Athanasius, Ephrem was an active and vocal participant in pro-

1. Ephrem's interest in and engagement with the empire as "empire" can be seen throughout his writings, but is particularly clear in *Hymns on Faith* 87, his *Hymns against Julian,* and his *Hymns on Nisibis.* See the following works by Sidney Griffith: "Ephraem, the Deacon of Edessa, and the Church of the Empire," in *Diakonia: Studies in Honor of Robert T. Meyer,* eds. Thomas Halton and Joseph Williman (Washington, D.C.: The Catholic University of America Press, 1986), 22–52; "Setting Right the Church of Syria: Saint Ephraem's *Hymns against Heresies,*" in *The Limits of Ancient Christianity: Essays on Late Antique Thought and Culture in Honor of R. A. Markus,* eds. William Klingshirn and Mark Vessey (Ann Arbor: University of Michigan, 1999), 97–114; "The Marks of the 'True Church' According to Ephraem's *Hymns against Heresies,*" in *After Bardaisan: Studies on Continuity and Change in Syriac Christianity in Honour of Professor Han J. W. Drijvers,* eds. G. J. Reinink and A. C. Klugkist, *Orientalia Lovaniensia Analecta* 89 (Louvain: Peeters, 1999), 125–40. Other scholars have also begun to integrate Syriac studies into the study of Greek-writing Christians. See, for example, Sebastian Brock, *The Luminous Eye: The Spiritual World Vision of Saint Ephrem* (Kalamazoo, Mich.: Cistercian Publications, 1985), 143–57; Paul S. Russell, *St. Ephraem the Syrian and St. Gregory the Theologian Confront the Arians* (Kerala, India: SEERI, 1994); David Taylor, "St. Ephraim's Influence on the Greeks," *Hugoye: Journal of Syriac Studies* 1.2 (1998) [online journal], available from http://syrcom.cua.edu/hugoye/Vol1No2/HV1N2Taylor.html (accessed 5/2/05); and most recently Lewis Ayres, *Nicaea and Its Legacy: An Approach*

Nicene Christians' struggle against subordinationist Christian theology, and his anti-Jewish rhetoric competes in a fourth-century context of political and religious turmoil surrounding questions about the nature of God's Son.[2] The anti-Jewish and anti-Judaizing polemics of both Ephrem and Athanasius define particular religious and social boundaries that serve to legitimate the truth and authority of Nicene Christianity within a context of political hostility. Just as Ephrem shapes the categories "Jew" and "Christian" out of his more complex context, by insistently conflating "Jews" and "Arians," he and Athanasius also create definitions of (Nicene) Christian orthodoxy that exclude their "Arian" Christian opponents. Scholars of Syriac Christianity repeatedly call for an end to the isolation of Ephrem "the Syrian," and of Syriac Christianity itself, from broader conversations about the Roman Empire in late antiquity. This chapter will show the ways in which pro-Nicene leaders Ephrem and Athanasius deployed anti-Jewish and anti-Judaizing language in similar ways against their "Arian" opponents in their efforts to make Nicene Christianity become Roman "orthodoxy."

Ephrem and Athanasius in Context

Ephrem and Athanasius were born within a decade of each other as the fourth century began and they both died in 373 CE. Both grew up in the eastern Roman Empire and became active pro-Nicene supporters of an imperial Christian orthodoxy despite eastern imperial antagonism toward pro-Nicene leaders during much of their adult lives. Likewise, they both lived in cities with significant Jewish populations, and used harsh anti-Jewish rhetoric in their struggle to define the boundaries of Christian orthodoxy. Although Athanasius's political and ecclesiastical career was more prominent in the

---

to Fourth-Century Trinitarian Theology (Oxford: Oxford University Press, 2004). Although Russell does not address anti-Jewish or anti-Judaizing rhetoric in his comparison of these two authors, his study is nonetheless an important part of this same discussion and likewise brings Ephrem into conversation with his Greek-speaking contemporaries.

2. As noted in chapter 2, scholars have slowly begun to recognize Ephrem's participation in these religious and imperial politics. For a recent addition to this conversation, see Ayres, Nicaea. See also these fundamental works: Griffith: "Ephraem, the Deacon of Edessa, and the Church of the Empire"; Griffith, "The Marks of the 'True Church' according to Ephraem's Hymns against Heresies"; Griffith, "Setting Right the Church of Syria: Saint Ephraem's Hymns against Heresies." While these articles note Ephrem's participation in imperial Christian controversy, they do not focus on his anti-Jewish rhetoric and its role in this struggle.

empire than was Ephrem's, both were prolific authors who profoundly influenced Christian history.

Athanasius and Alexandria

In a context of religious and political upheaval, Athanasius constructed the category of "Arianism" in ways that allowed both him and Ephrem to employ anti-Jewish and anti-Judaizing language in their fight against "Arians." Born around the year 299 CE, Athanasius grew up, like Ephrem, as a Christian acutely aware of the possibility of imperial persecution.[3] Already by 325 CE when he accompanied his bishop, Alexander, to the Council of Nicaea, there were growing rifts within the churches in the East, and among Christians in Athanasius's home of Alexandria itself, between those who supported and those who denounced the teachings of Arius.[4] Even as a deacon, Athanasius was in the midst of this political turmoil, and when Alexander died in 328 CE, Athanasius hurried home and was rather surreptitiously, according to early accounts, ordained as the new bishop of Alexandria.[5] Athanasius's struggle against Arius and those whom Athanasius later polemically termed "Arians" (and "Ariomaniacs") lasted almost fifty years, from before his episcopal ordination until his death. After the Council of Nicaea's condemnation of Arius and some of the views attributed to him, and after Alexander's death and Athanasius's own ordination as bishop, Athanasius launched

---

3. While the date of Athanasius's birth is not conclusively known, Barnes convincingly speculates that he was born in 299, based on references to his age at his ordination in other ancient sources (Barnes, *Athanasius*, 10). See Barnes for more detail on Athanasius's history, and the primary sources that record it. Of course, without our modern concept of adolescence as a pre-adult stage of life, at the time of Constantine's edict in 313 Athanasius would have been beginning to enter more fully into the adult world and, as a Christian in Alexandria, would have been surrounded by reverberations from this toleration of Christianity.

4. Because Athanasius is better known in western scholarship than Ephrem is, I have provided only the more directly relevant information about him for this study, along with references to further information. For a brief introduction to the vast literature on Athanasius, see the discussion and bibliography in Charles Kannengiesser, *Athanase d'Alexandrie évêque et écrivain: Une lecture des traités "Contre les Ariens"* (Paris: Beauchesne, 1983); Timothy D. Barnes, *Athanasius and Constantius: Theology and Politics in the Constantinian Empire* (Cambridge, Mass.: Harvard University Press, 1993); David Brakke, *Athanasius and Asceticism* (Baltimore: Johns Hopkins University Press, 1995). See also Alvyn Pettersen, *Athanasius and the Human Body* (Bristol: Bristol Press, 1990); Duane Wade-Hampton Arnold, *The Early Episcopal Career of Athanasius of Alexandria* (Notre Dame: University of Notre Dame Press, 1991); James D. Ernest, *The Bible in Athanasius of Alexandria* (Boston: Brill, 2004).

5. See Sozomen, *HE* 2.17.4, 25.6; as well as Barnes, *Athanasius*, 18, 247n.

himself wholeheartedly into a heated polemical and political war against Arius and his supporters. Not only did the nature of Christian doctrine come to be at stake in the following decades, but so too did Athanasius's episcopal title and at times even his life itself.

The Christian conflict that played out over the following decades pulled the empire this way and that under different emperors. As the bishop of Alexandria and an outspoken pro-Nicene leader, Athanasius was an important figure in those decades of struggle. Present at the Council of Nicaea, granted audience with emperors, and actively supported by Julius, the bishop of Rome, Athanasius was both well connected in imperial politics as well as dangerously embroiled in the vicissitudes of this controversy. He conducted his episcopacy of more than forty years from all over the empire as he lived through multiple exiles and traveled to church councils and imperial courts in his attempt to secure the political authority of his pro-Nicene teachings.[6]

As an important part of his high-profile career, Athanasius's writings, such as his *Orations against the Arians, Defense against the Arians, Defense of the Nicene Council*, and *History of the Arians*, represent a powerful tool in his pro-Nicene struggle. Although his *Defense against the Arians*, composed around 349, was not distributed widely during his lifetime, the other three works were circulated publicly in the 340s and 350s and had a strong influence on shaping the terms of the intra-Christian controversy.[7] These texts all clearly denounce Athanasius's "Arian" opponents and also compare them to Jews in ways similar to some of Ephrem's texts.[8] In addition, many of his other writings, particularly his *Festal Letters*, contain anti-Jewish language and refer, even if less explicitly, to the same intra-Christian dispute. Athanasius thus used anti-Jewish language in order to reify particular social categories and to argue against his "Arian" opponents.

6. Athanasius was exiled from his Alexandrian see in the mid-330s, the early 340s, and the late 350s.

7. I have relied on Barnes, *Athanasius*, for the dating of Athanasius's texts. For a discussion of publication in late antiquity, see Harry Gamble, *Books and Readers in the Early Church: A History of Early Christian Texts* (New Haven: Yale University Press, 1995).

8. As Brakke has clearly demonstrated, many of Athanasius's other texts, particularly his *Life of Antony*, also played a significant role in Athanasius's struggle against Arian opponents (Brakke, *Athanasius*, especially 129–41). See also Alvyn Pettersen, "The Arian Context of Athanasius of Alexandria's *Tomus ad Antiochenos* VII," *JEH* 41, no. 2 (1990): 183–98. I have, however, focused on his more explicitly anti-Arian texts here in order to demonstrate the connection there with his anti-Jewish language.

Although Athanasius's anti-Judaism in these texts relies primarily on Christian Scripture for its portrayal of Jews, the troubled history of Judaism within Alexandria also provides the backdrop for his rhetoric. Alexandria had been the home of an active Jewish diaspora community since the city's early days.[9] As soldiers, immigrants, and slaves, Jews filtered into the Ptolemaic city, and by the time of the Roman takeover of Egypt in 30 BCE Alexandrian Jews were a strong minority within the city,[10] and the Jews' history in Alexandria was periodically one of great conflict. Philo, himself an Alexandrian Jew, records that in 38 CE the tetrarch (and later king of Judea) Agrippa's visit to Alexandria set into motion a series of events that led to the murder of many local Jews by a non-Jewish mob.[11] Likewise, in 66 CE there was more local violence against Alexandrian Jews,[12] and between 115 and 117 CE under the emperor Trajan there was a full-scale Jewish revolt in Alexandria.[13] The Jews in Alexandria thus had a history of tumultuous relations with their city's non-Jewish inhabitants even before Christianity became a dominant influence within the city.[14] Thus, like Ephrem's cities of Nisibis and Edessa, Athanasius's Alexandria had a significant Jewish population that provided a backdrop for the fourth-century intra-Christian conflicts. These authors' decision to use anti-Jewish rhetoric against their Christian opponents, and the sharpness of that rhetoric, cannot have been unaffected by this context, nor can it fail to have affected continuing Christian-Jewish relations in these cities. Nonetheless, in the anti-Jewish rhetoric that Athanasius uses against Christian opponents, he relies primarily on scriptural depictions of Jews, which do not require the knowledge or presence of contemporary Jews in order to be persuasive to a Christian audience. Although Ephrem, by contrast, never

9. Elias J. Bickerman, *The Jews in the Greek Age* (Cambridge, Mass.: Harvard University Press, 1988), 87–90. For the history of and bibliography on Alexandria, see especially Christopher Haas, *Alexandria in Late Antiquity: Topography and Social Conflict* (Baltimore: Johns Hopkins University Press, 1997).

10. See, for example, Haas, *Alexandria*, 91–127; John Barclay, *Jews in the Mediterranean Diaspora: From Alexander to Trajan (323 BCE–117 CE)* (Edinburgh: T&T Clark, 1996); Mary Smallwood, *The Jews under Roman Rule: From Pompey to Diocletian* (Leiden: Brill, 1976). See also Josephus, *Antiq.* 14.7 and *Wars* 2.18.

11. Philo, *In Flaccum*, and *Legatio ad Gaium* 18–20. Compare also Josephus, *Antiq.* 18.8. This violence appears to have begun in response to the Jews' celebration of Agrippa's visit.

12. See again Haas, *Alexandria*, 91–127; and Barclay, *Diaspora*, chapter 3; as well as Josephus, *Wars* 2.18. These attacks came as the Romans were laying siege to Jerusalem in the war that destroyed the Temple.

13. See Timothy D. Barnes, "Trajan and the Jews," *JJS* 40 (1989): 145–62. The Jews revolted in Alexandria (and Cyprus) as Trajan fought in the East against Adiabene and Persia.

14. See Haas, *Alexandria*, especially 91–127.

became bishop of one of the most influential sees in the empire as Athanasius did, Ephrem nevertheless also turned some of his anti-Jewish language against subordinationist Christian opponents.

Contextualizing Ephrem's Terminology: Nisibis and Edessa

Like Athanasius, Ephrem lived in the eastern Roman Empire between the years 306 and 373 CE and thus wrote most of his texts under the pressure of political hostility and the imminent threat of the success of so-called "Arian" Christianity. By the beginning of the fourth century, Christianity had spread widely within the Roman Empire, and in 313 CE, during Ephrem's childhood, the emperors Constantine and Licinius dramatically improved Christianity's political standing within the empire.[15] Along with political toleration, however, came a pressing need for further Christian self-definition in order to ensure that only "true" Christians gained power and that "heretical" Christians could be punished. As described above, this situation led to decades of intra-Christian conflict across the empire. Ephrem's language about his Christian opponents sheds light on both the identity of these opponents as well as the power that his anti-Jewish language would have had in his religious and political context. As Ephrem's poetic language only occasionally uses the name "Arian," however, it is first necessary to examine what terminology he uses to describe his ecclesiastical opponents.

When Constantine convened the Council of Nicaea shortly after gaining control over the eastern part of the Roman Empire, he established a precedent for imperial participation in the establishment of Christian doctrine.[16] Although those who opposed Arius prevailed at the 325 CE council, upon Constantine's death in 337 CE, control of the empire was split among his sons, and pro-Nicene Christians experienced different fortunes in different parts of the empire. Although in the West Constans followed Julius and other western bishops in supporting Athanasius, in the East Constantius exiled Athanasius and supported Athanasius's "Arian" opponents.[17] Following the brief reigns of Julian "the Apostate" and Jovian, Valens, another emper-

15. For a record of this decree, see Lactantius *On the Deaths of the Persecutors* 48.2–12. Eusebius also recounts his version of this history and of the legal ordinances in *HE* 10.5.

16. Of course, in the Roman world *religio* was inherently connected with political leadership, as demonstrated, for example, by the Roman emperor's position as *pontifex maximus*. For an in-depth discussion of, and bibliography on, this topic, see Mary Beard, John North, and Simon Price, *Religions of Rome*, vol. 1, *A History* (New York: Cambridge University Press, 1998).

17. Again, recall the discussion above regarding Athanasius' construction of the term "Arians" in the decades following the Council of Nicaea.

or who supported subordinationist Christianity, controlled the East, the final emperor Ephrem was to know before his own death in 373 CE.[18] The majority of Ephrem's writings thus support Nicene Christianity in a time when the emperor who governed Syria did not. Nonetheless, Ephrem remained unflagging in his polemic against non-Nicene Christians, an adamant proponent of Nicene Christianity in an empire ruled by those who opposed it.

As detailed above, Ephrem spent most of his life in Nisibis, and then in 363 CE moved to Edessa. Both of these cities were diverse commercial centers and home to Jews, followers of Mani, Marcion, and Bardaisan, and the cults of Bêl and Nebo. In addition, however, in this religiously diverse culture, Ephrem also recognized the danger of other Christians who threatened the very identity of pro-Nicene Christians and their claim to represent "true" Christianity. Needless to say, in a struggle for the title "Christian," community designations are both subjective and of the utmost importance, and Ephrem's rhetoric claims that during his lifetime pro-Nicene Christians were not the clear winners in a struggle for the appropriation of the name "Christian."[19]

Within this richness of religious alternatives, Ephrem lived under the political control of pro-Homoian emperors for most of his adult life. The more pressure a group feels from opposing parties, particularly parties who wield some political, social, and legal power over the group, the more strident the threatened group's polemic against the dominant group is likely to become. It is clear that Ephrem's sharp polemic comes out of a political context in which a form of Christianity to which he was opposed appeared to be "winning," and most certainly had the benefit of political support.

Due to Jacob of Nisibis's participation in the Council of Nicaea, Ephrem would have known early about the concept of an imperial orthodoxy, and also of pro-Nicene Christians' claim that there was a threat to it that was associated with Arius and recognizable by the misidentification of the Son as a "creature." Ephrem's Nisibene writings attest to his familiarity with Arius, in that he names Arius as a heretic "of our own day" and refers to the trou-

18. The varieties of subordinationist Christianity are significant for the discussion in chapter 5, but Ephrem's language distinguishes primarily the larger categories of those who support Nicene Christianity and those who adhere to a more subordinationist theology. Ayres argues that Ephrem's later language reflects "an anti-Homoian and possible anti-Heterousian theology" (Ayres, *Nicaea*, 229).

19. Recall the discussion above of Ephrem's complaint that instead of "Christians," orthodox Christians in his region were called Palûtians after their early leader Palût (Ephrem, *CH* 22.5).

ble caused by "Arians and Aetians."[20] In his *Hymns against Heresies,* Ephrem mentions Mani, Marcion, and Bardaisan much more frequently than he does Arius, and focuses more on the problems caused by the former than by the latter. Ephrem's *Sermons on Faith,* however, also from his Nisibene period, focus instead on these "Arian" Christians, whom he does not explicitly name in these homilies, but whom he describes as those who "diminish the First-born" by treating him "like a Creature."[21] Thus when Ephrem wrote his *Sermons on Faith,* this concern seems to have been pressing to his Nisibene community.

It is not clear exactly when Ephrem first began to face the threat of subordinationist teachings in Nisibis itself, but his *Sermons on Faith* reveal that Ephrem eventually felt compelled to inoculate his congregation against the danger posed by what he saw as a heresy that was tearing apart an empire that should have been united in (Nicene) Christian orthodoxy. Lewis Ayres identifies in Ephrem's arguments for pro-Nicene theology similarities to the language of some of his Greek neighbors whose context and opponents are more precisely known. Thus, Ayres suggests that Ephrem is countering not only "Heterousian" theology broadly speaking, but he identifies Ephrem's language more specifically as "anti-Homoian," against "the Homoian theology promoted by Valens."[22] The fact that Ephrem includes "Aetians" in his *Hymns against Heresies* is important both for dating the hymns and also for learning more about who his opponents might have been.[23] The strongly subordinationist language with which Aetius and his student Eunomius described the Son caused Gregory of Nyssa to claim that they had not only in-

20. Ephrem, *CH* 24.19, 22.4. Ephrem refers to "Arians" in *CH* 22.4, 22.20, 24.12, and 24.16; and to "Arius" in *CH* 24.19, 21. (See also "Arian" in *Comm. Diat.* 12.9.)

21. Ephrem, *SdF* 2.339–40, 326. It is interesting to note that Ephrem does not seem as invested in applying the name "Arian" to his opponents as Athanasius did, even while both authors use complex rhetorical maneuvers to describe their opponents as outside the bounds of Christian orthodoxy.

22. Ayres, *Nicaea,* 229–30.

23. Aetius was not a distinct figure in imperial politics until his return to Antioch around 350, and the name "Aetians" does not appear in extant texts before the late 350s. (I am grateful to Lewis Ayres for his helpful conversations about these matters. Compare also Ayres, *Nicaea,* 230–35.) If Sidney Griffith's assessment that Ephrem wrote his *Hymns against Heresies* in Nisibis is correct, then the fact that Ephrem mentions "Aetians" as a group that is distinct from "Arians" suggests that he wrote these hymns between the late 350s and 363 (Griffith "Deacon," 37). It is likely, however, that these hymns span a period of time. If so, the reference to the Aetians could come from one of his later hymns in this series. That Aetius returned to Antioch in Syria soon before 350 makes this influence entirely plausible due to his geographical proximity to Ephrem.

herited the heresy of Arius but had twisted it even further from Christian truth.[24] The specific arguments with which Ephrem condemns these opponents in his *Hymns against Heresies* and his *Sermons on Faith* (and also in his later Edessene *Hymns on Faith*), namely their insistent intellectual inquiry, further supports this conclusion that in these later texts Ephrem was reacting to a particular local strand of subordinationist Christianity that had been influenced by the teachings of Aetius.

It is clear that it is these same subordinationist opponents whom Ephrem attacks in his *Sermons on Faith*, despite the fact that he does not name them as "Arians" or "Aetians" in these writings.[25] Instead, he identifies them as those whose challenging inquiry, which he associates with Greek education, has led them inappropriately to define the Son as a "Creature." In Sermon 2 Ephrem simultaneously identifies his opponents as Christians who treat the Son as a "Creature" and identifies their inappropriate inquiry as the root of this error: "The one who *investigates* is greater than that which can be investigated. You call him 'Creator,' and [yet] you *search* him like a Creature. . . . Through *investigation* you are diminishing the First-born."[26] In Sermon 6, he further explains the limits of appropriate investigation into the nature of the Son: "If you seek [to know] about the existence of the Son, you learn in the blink of an eye. But if you seek about *how* it is, that is a question until he comes."[27] Pro-Nicene leaders frequently criticized Aetius, and later Eunomius, for their use of technical human logic to try to define the Son and the Son's relationship with the Father.[28] These sermons show that Ephrem, too, used these criticisms to attack his Christian opponents, perhaps even while he was still in Nisibis before 363.[29]

---

24. Grg. Nyss., *Eun.* 1.37, 45–46.

25. This claim is not new, and has been adequately established by others, even though they rely on the term "Arian" to describe these Christians whereas I prefer to avoid this problematic label. In addition to Ayres, *Nicaea*, see Beck, *Theologie des heilige Ephraem*, 62–80; Beck, *Ephraems Reden*, 111–18; Griffith, "Deacon"; Peter Bruns, "Arius hellenizans?—Ephräm der Syrer und die neoarianischen Kontroversen seiner Zeit," *Zeitschrift für Kirchengeschichte* 101 (1990): 21–57; Russell, *St. Ephraem the Syrian and St. Gregory the Theologian Confront the Arians;* Paul Russell, "An Anti-Neo-Arian Interpolation in Ephraem of Nisibis' Hymn 46 *On Faith*," in *Studia Patristica XXXIII*, ed. Elizabeth Livingstone (Louvain: Peeters, 1997), 568–72. See also Lienhard, "The 'Arian' Controversy"; Slusser, "Traditional Views"; and Lyman, "Topography of Heresy."

26. Ephrem, *SdF* 2.323–26, 339–40.

27. Ephrem, *SdF* 6.297–300.

28. See, for example, Grg. Naz., *Or.* 29.17–19. Richard Vaggione refers to this as "a theme used by almost every Nicene author who ever attacked Aetius or Eunomius" (Vaggione, *Eunomius*, 91).

29. Ephrem has particular criticisms that he uses to characterize each of his various oppo-

By the time that Ephrem moved to Edessa, he had become even more vocal about lamenting the state of the Roman Empire, which was being torn apart through internal Christian conflict that he blamed on errant Christian leaders.[30] In his *Hymns on Faith*, he accuses these "disputers" of creating this turmoil through their insistence on naming the Son a creature.[31] Instead of branding these Christians as "Arians" or "Aetians," however, Ephrem identifies them by highlighting their inappropriate methods of seeking knowledge about God. As Sidney Griffith has already noted, Hymn 7 includes a comprehensive excursus on the behavior that Ephrem condemns about those who teach subordinationist doctrines:

Come, let us wonder at the people who saw the king in a humble state and did not *investigate*, nor *seek*. No one of them *disputed*; pure faith shone there in silence. When he was humble, the magi did not dare to *search* him. How do we dare to *search* him, now that he went up and dwells at the right hand on high?[32]

Ephrem explains that true Christians do not investigate, seek, dispute, or search, verbs that appear throughout Ephrem's writings as negative references to these errant Christians who make the Son a creature. For Ephrem, human language is insufficient to contain God, and efforts to define God unsuccessfully try to place limits on what is limitless.[33] Ephrem thus most

---

nents. For example, he highlights that Manichaeans idolatrously worship the sun and moon; he repeatedly connects the Jews with unbelief and the crucifixion of God's Son; and he continually accuses Christians with a subordinationist theology of inappropriate searching and seeking. In his writings, these epithets do not change their referent in each text, but rather each becomes synonymous with its respective heretical group.

30. See, for example, Ephrem, *HdF* 53.2. Undoubtedly the religious and political makeup of Edessa was different from that of Nisibis, but Ephrem's move also coincided with a significant shift in imperial power as well as a geographical move closer to Antioch and Constantinople, all of which also affected his context, and in turn his rhetoric.

31. Ephrem, *HdF* 53.3, 9–14. In this hymn, Ephrem witnesses to his opponents' use of Prov 8:22 to support their use of "Creature" to describe the Son (Ephrem, *HdF* 53.10). Proverbs 8:22 is a passage that was frequently cited by "Arian" Christians to support their view that the Son was God's first creation. See, for example, Arius, *Ep. Eus.* 5; Eusebius of Nicomedia, *Ep. Paulin.* 4; Athanasius, *Ar.* 1.53, 2.1, 18, 72, 3.1; *Decr.* 13, 26; *Dion.* 10, 11; *Ep. Aeg. Lib.* 17; *Ep. Serap.* 2.7, 9; *Syn.* 26; Eunomius, *Apol.* 26.15–16, 28.23–24; Epiphanius, *Panarion.* 69.12.1, 14.1 (see Richard Vaggione, *Eunomius of Cyzicus and the Nicene Revolution* [Oxford: Oxford University Press, 2000], 385–86).

32. Ephrem, *HdF* 7.6. Ephrem's descriptions of the Son humbling himself and then going up to dwell with God are reminiscent of the language in the Gospel of John and in Phil 2:6–11.

33. See, for example, Ephrem, *SdF* 1.1–40, 3.11–26; David Bundy, "Ephrem's Critique of Mani: The Limits of Knowledge and the Nature of Language," in *Gnosticisme et monde hellénistique*, ed. Julien Ries (Louvain-la-Neuve: The Catholic University of Louvain, 1982), 289–98; Pierre Yousif, "Foi et raison dans l'apologétique de Saint Ephrem de Nisibe," *PdO* 12 (1984/1985): 133–51; Griffith "Deacon," 43–45; David Bundy, "Language and the Knowledge of God in Ephrem Syrus,"

frequently alludes to Christians who teach subordinationist doctrine not by naming them "Arians" but by naming their association with these forms of intellectual inquiry that he condemns as contrary to right Christian faith.[34]

Ephrem strongly condemns these "searching" Christian opponents not only, however, by challenging their faith and their use of their rational intellects, but also by using anti-Jewish language to describe them as clearly un-Christian. While Ephrem's anti-Jewish rhetoric has traditionally been read only as complaints against real local Jews, the combination of a predominantly anti-Homoian (or at least anti-Heteroousian) agenda with this anti-Jewish language makes his *Hymns on Faith* and *Sermons on Faith* key texts for investigating how Ephrem sometimes manipulates anti-Jewish narratives of history and Scripture in order to legitimate Nicene Christianity within a struggle against Homoian opponents. Early scholars had difficulty reconciling the anti-Jewish language of the third of Ephrem's *Sermons on Faith* with its apparently anti-"Arian" agenda. J. B. Morris found the two subjects at such odds with each other that he wrote about Sermon 3, "After a long digression upon the Jews . . . St. Ephrem returns . . . to his old [anti-Arian] subject. But this digression is so long as to seem almost to have been foisted in here from some other Homily."[35] Beck, too, explained Ephrem's language by describing that Ephrem wrote the *Sermons on Faith* against two separate threats to his community: Arians and actively proselytizing Jews.[36] Beck thus assumes that the anti-Jewish language serves as polemic against a literal Jewish threat to Ephrem's community, separate from the "Arian" conflict. Reading the anti-Jewish language in light of, not as separate from, the contemporary intra-Christian struggle, however, requires less manipulation of the text and of its context.

Ephrem was certainly not unique in comparing subordinationist theology and Judaism.[37] In fact, these Christians were particularly vulnerable to this

---

Dialogue and Alliance 1 (1988): 56–64; T. Koonammakkal, "Ephrem's Imagery of Chasm," in *Symposium Syriacum VII, 1996*, OCA 256 (Rome, 1998), 175–83; Paul Russell, "Ephraem the Syrian on the Utility of Language and the Place of Silence," *JECS* 8, no. 1 (2000): 21–37.

34. Ephrem writes, for example, "*Investigating* is the opposite of belief. . . . If there is *searching,* there is not believing" (SdF 2.501–4). Compare also, "The one who believes does not *search;* but if he *searches,* he does not believe" (Ephrem, SdF 3.69–70).

35. J. B. Morris, *Select Works of St. Ephrem the Syrian* (Oxford, 1847), 396n.

36. Beck, *Ephraems Reden*, 111, 118–20.

37. No discussion of this topic can begin, of course, without mention of Rudolf Lorenz's seminal work, *Arius judaizans: Untersuchungen zur dogmengeschichtlichen Einordnung des Arius* (Göttingen: Vandenhoeck & Ruprecht, 1979). Nonetheless, this current discussion is not so

comparison because pro-Nicene leaders could accuse them of denying the full divinity of the Son, like the Jews did, in their insistence that the Son was a creature, God's first creation.[38] Nonetheless, Ephrem approaches his comparison from a slightly different angle, emphasizing more the similarity that he sees between the probing searching of his Christian opponents and the challenging questions of the New Testament Pharisees. Conflating Jews and subordinationist Christians, Ephrem constructs a clear and unified enemy of "true" Christians, weaving a narrative of history that calls new social boundaries into being in his world. Ephrem crafts his rhetoric in order to legitimate and clearly define a united Nicene Christianity and to cut off his opponents from the Christian community by conflating them with the "rejected" and "hateful" Jews.

This interpretation suggests that while both Jewish and Christian communities lived in Nisibis and Edessa during Ephrem's lifetime, the immediate context for *some* of his anti-Jewish language was primarily the intra-Christian Trinitarian debate that followed the Council of Nicaea, rather than the behavior of local Jews or "Christians" who were attending "Jewish" festivals. In these anti-"Arian" writings, Ephrem presents a narrative of local community boundaries that is not a transparent window onto his community's dynamics, but rather works to present a particular picture that offers Ephrem social and political advantages. Contrary to conclusions of previous scholars, Ephrem's rhetoric in these texts can be read as consistently employed in a literary campaign in support of Nicene Christianity. This conclusion argues against the necessity of believing that Jews were persistently proselytizing among, or posed a serious threat to, local Christians, and points rather to the role of anti-Jewish language in Ephrem's efforts to promote Nicene Christianity against the subordinationist teachings of his "Christian" opponents.

---

much concerned, as Lorenz was, with whether or not Arians were Judaizing in literal ways, as it is concerned with how their opponents portrayed them. It is worth noting, however, that for all his similarities to Athanasius in some respects, Ephrem highlights his opponents' Pharisee-like searching instead of elaborating at length on the "Jewish" details of "Arian" teachings about the Son in the ways that Athanasius and the Cappadocians do.

38. See the discussion in chapter 5, as well as the exploration of this theme in Lorenz, *Arius judaizans? Untersuchungen zur dogmengeschichtlichen Einordnung des Arius.* This connection has long been noted in scholarship. See John Henry Newman, *The Arians of the Fourth Century* (New York: Longmans, Green and Co., 1919).

Redefining Christians and Jews

In the middle of the fourth century, both Ephrem and Athanasius used anti-Jewish and anti-Judaizing language against "Arians," a category that Athanasius had recently constructed. Beck dates the *Sermons on Faith* to Ephrem's time in Nisibis, earlier than his Edessene *Hymns on Faith,* and the hymns contain more focused and explicit language, a difference that may reflect the clearer definition of the concept of "Arianism" by authors such as Athanasius only in the second half of the fourth century, as well as Ephrem's growing personal familiarity with the problem as it spread around the empire. Given the political climate in the East during Ephrem's time in Edessa, his strident language comes as little surprise. While largely less vitriolic than Ephrem's most ad hominem anti-Jewish attacks against the "stench of the stinking Jews,"[39] Ephrem's rhetoric in his *Hymns on Faith* and *Sermons on Faith* offers striking examples of his use of anti-Jewish polemic to combat more than only Judaizing Christian opponents. In these writings, Ephrem's ideological narratives negotiate his contemporary power struggle, as he explicitly and repeatedly connects his contemporary Christian opponents with Jews by mapping the would-be Christians onto caricatures of the blind, misled, and murderous Jews of Christian Scripture in order to legitimate and naturalize Nicene Christianity. Comparing Ephrem's and Athanasius's rhetoric reveals that both authors used similar rhetorical strategies to compare their "Arian" opponents to "Jews." In particular, there are striking similarities in their comparisons of their Christian opponents to New Testament Jews as well as their rhetorical use of violence that they both attribute to Jews throughout history. Examining these rhetorical themes shows not only that Ephrem's anti-Jewish language is sometimes anti-"Arian," but also demonstrates the similarities of the rhetorical and social projects in which Ephrem and Athanasius were engaged, thus uniting Ephrem more firmly with the Greek-speaking Romans to his west.

Christian Opponents as New Testament "Jews"

Since the time of their writing, the New Testament Gospels provided Christians with easy fodder for anti-Jewish claims and stereotypes. Those leaders who debated with Jesus in the Gospel narratives quickly became ex-

---

39. Ephrem, *CH* 56.8 (Edmund Beck, ed., *Des Heiligen Ephraem des Syrers Hymnen contra Haereses,* CSCO 169, SS 76 [Louvain, 1957]).

amples for Christian writers of all Jews' rejection of Jesus, and Gospel passages such as Matthew 27:25 allowed Christians to misrepresent Jews—as a people—as responsible for the violent murder of the Christian Messiah, or even of God. Ephrem and Athanasius use both of these scripturally based anti-Jewish claims to help strengthen their anti-"Arian" arguments.

Around 340, soon after the beginning of his second exile, Athanasius wrote his *Orations against the Arians,* a series of orations that work to create the category "Arian" and at the same time deny "Arians" the right to call themselves Christian. In these orations, Athanasius argues that the "Jewish" beliefs and behavior of the Arians prove that they are, in fact, Jews.[40] For example, Athanasius elaborates on his frequent references to his "Ariomaniac"[41] opponents by calling them "new Jews."[42] In the first oration, Athanasius specifically compares his opponents to the New Testament Pharisees: "[Arius] fell into the error of the Pharisees . . . So too [like the Pharisees] . . . Arius pretends to speak of God, introducing the language of Scripture, but is on all sides recognized as godless Arius, denying the Son and reckoning him among the creatures."[43] Here Athanasius argues that Arius denies the Son just as the New Testament Pharisees did, thereby connecting Arius with the Jewish antagonists of Christian Scripture.[44] Through this anti-Jewish rhetoric, supported by the texts of

40. See Brakke, "Jewish Flesh." See also Uta Heil, *Athanasius von Alexandrien: De Sententia Dionysii,* Patristische Texte und Studien 52 (Berlin: de Gruyter, 1999).

41. See, for example, Athanasius, *Ar.* 1.4, 2.17, 3.1, 3.27, 3.58. All quotations from Athanasius's *Orations against the Arians* are based on the Greek text in PG 26, with reference to the English translation, *Select Writings and Letters of Athanasius, Bishop of Alexandria,* ed. Archibald Robertson (NPNF, 2nd ser. 4; repr. Edinburgh, 1987), referred to from now on as *Ath.* NPNF. Charles Kannengiesser has called into question the authenticity of the third Oration (see Kannengiesser, *Athanase d'Alexandrie*). While in his recent study E. P. Meijering acknowledges that we do not know the authorship of this text with absolute certainty, he concludes that the language of the third *Oration* is consistent with Athanasius's other writings and so supports Athanasian authorship (E. P. Meijering, *Athanasius: Die dritte Rede gegen die Arianer, t. 1, 1–25* [Amsterdam: J. C. Gieben, 1996], 23). I have therefore tentatively used this third *Oration* as further supporting evidence of Athanasius's rhetoric, but have not relied on it when it does not echo other places in Athanasius's writings.

42. See, for example, Athanasius, *Decr.* 27 and also *H. Ar.* 61. All quotations from Athanasius's *History of the Arians* in this text are from *Ath.* NPNF, with my own changes to the translation based on the Greek text in Opitz, *Werke.* Compare also "the current Jews" in *Ar.* 3.8.

43. Athanasius, *Ar.* 1.4.

44. Athanasius makes a connection of a different sort between Arians and Jews in his *Encyclical Letter* when he writes that "for the sake of the mad Arians" his Nicene Christians and churches are being persecuted "by Gentiles and Jews" (*Ep. encyc.* 7). (All quotations from Athanasius's *Encyclical Letter* are my own translation based on the Greek text in Opitz, *Werke.*) Haas uses this reference to bolster his claim that "during the Arian controversy, portions of the Jewish community gave considerable support to the Arians in their efforts to stamp out

Christian Scripture, Athanasius reinforces an image of Judaism as the antithesis of Christian truth and "Arians" as linked with Jews. In the midst of the fourth-century intra-Christian conflict, such rhetoric would have earned significant political capital in his efforts to dissuade his audience from granting Arius's followers the title of Christian orthodoxy.

In his *Defense of Dionysius*, Athanasius makes a similar comparison, again connecting his Christian opponents' alleged denial of the Son to the disbelief of the New Testament Jewish leaders. In this letter, Athanasius argues against his "Arian" opponents for the (Nicene) "orthodoxy" of Dionysius, a third-century bishop of Alexandria (233–265). Athanasius claims that Arians are "new Jews" who attempt to adopt the support of this respected "orthodox" bishop in the same way, and as unsuccessfully, as the Jews who killed "Christ" once appealed to Abraham.[45] Athanasius first observes, "But perhaps [the Arians] do not wish ever to depart from this wickedness of theirs; for they emulate this from those around Caiaphas, just as they have learned from them to deny Christ."[46] Athanasius then gives the specifics of how it is that the Arians mimic the Jews: "For [the Jews] too, when the Lord had done so many works, by which he showed himself to be the Christ, the Son of the living God, and being convicted by him . . . and unable for a moment to face the proofs against themselves, escaped to the patriarch with the words, 'We have Abraham as our father' [Matthew 3:9; Luke 3:8; John 8:33], thus thinking to cloak their own unreasonableness."[47] Athanasius continues, however, to argue that just as the Jews did not convince Jesus in their appeal to Abraham, neither are the "Arians" of Athanasius's time convincing in their appeal to Dionysius:

Homoousian Christianity within [Alexandria]. Often, this support took the form of an alliance with the other major group opposed to the Christians—the pagans" (Haas, *Alexandria,* 126). While this is an interesting claim that might lead to deeper insight about Athanasius's choice to link the Jews and Arians in his rhetoric, and the persuasiveness of this rhetoric, Haas's claim is overstated, based on the evidence that he cites. Nonetheless, this quotation from Athanasius does offer more evidence for his connection of the Arians with the Jews, and calls into question whether the two groups may occasionally have found themselves on the same side of an argument against Nicene Christians, and whether in turn that connection might have helped to strengthen Athanasius's rhetorical association. It is certainly possible that the specific persecution that Athanasius mentions in his letter was not prompted by Arians, but was to the Jews' advantage nonetheless.

45. John 8:33 (cf. Matt 3:9; Luke 3:8).

46. Athanasius, *Dion.* 3. All quotations from Athanasius's *Defense of Dionysius* in this text are from *Ath.* NPNF, along with my own changes based on the Greek text in Opitz, *Werke.*

47. Athanasius, *Dion.* 3.

But neither did they gain anything by these words, nor will these people, by speaking of Dionysius, be able to escape the guilt of the others. For the Lord convicted the latter of their wicked deeds by the words, "This Abraham did not do" [John 8:40], while the same truth again shall convict these impious and false people. For the Bishop Dionysius did not agree with Arius, nor was he ignorant of the truth.[48]

Just as Abraham did not support the guilty Jews, Athanasius argues, Dionysius does not support the guilty "Arians." He summarizes, "On the contrary, both the Jews then and the new ones now inherited their mad fight against Christ from their father the devil [cf. John 8:44]. . . . And indeed this would suffice for the entire refutation of the new Jews, who both deny the Lord and slander the fathers and attempt to deceive all Christians."[49] Athanasius thus not only confutes his opponents' attempt to appropriate a local Christian hero, but at the same time slanders his contemporary opponents by conflating them with the New Testament Jewish leaders who confronted and killed Jesus, and by calling them, along with the Jews, children of the devil.

Just as Athanasius refers to the Jewish leaders as "those around Caiaphas" in his *Defense of Dionysius* in order to attack the denial of the Son's true nature, in his *Orations against the Arians* he compares his Christian opponents to Caiaphas, this time emphasizing their similar unbelief. In his third *Oration*, Athanasius writes,

These then are what the irreligious allege. . . . they might speak, along with Caiaphas, even more Judaically, saying, "Why at all did Christ, being a man, make himself God?" [cf. John 10:33], for these things and things like them the Jews then murmured when they saw, and now the Ariomaniacs disbelieve when they read, and have fallen away into blasphemies. If then one should carefully parallel the words of these and those, one will of a certainty find them both arriving at the same unbelief, and the daring of their irreligion equal, and their dispute with us a common one.[50]

Through this rhetoric, Athanasius explicitly connects Arians with Jesus' (Jewish) New Testament antagonists, rhetorically distancing his contemporary opponents from being true Christian believers.[51]

In his numerous hymns, Ephrem makes similar comparisons, although he adds to the criticism of Jewish and Arian unbelief the positive model of

---

48. Athanasius, *Dion.* 3.

49. Athanasius, *Dion.* 3–4. The anti-Judaism of the Gospel of John is particularly sharp. As a result it appears frequently in these pro-Nicene writings.

50. Athanasius, *Ar.* 3.27. Compare also *Ar.* 3.58, 67.

51. Compare also *Decr.* 27.

the Gentile magi from the Gospel of Matthew as role models that Christians should imitate.[52] Ephrem makes similar comparisons between his Christian opponents and New Testament Jews in several of his sermons and hymns *de fide*. Citing the New Testament for support, in *Hymns on Faith* 44 Ephrem chastises those who inappropriately search after the nature of God: "Be reproved, bold ones, and be restrained, searchers! . . . It was thus that the People strove with [Christ] through their questions: 'Who [is he], and whose son [is he], and how did he come and [how] is he here?' And they thought that it was hard [to believe] that a virgin gave birth, and the elders and the scribes reviled [him] on account of this."[53] Thus, Ephrem chastises "searching" Christians through negative comparisons to the New Testament Jewish opponents of Jesus.

Likewise, in *HdF* 7 Ephrem again condemns "all these who *investigated*,"[54] connecting his contemporary Christian opponents with traditional Jewish antagonists of the Gospel narratives. In this hymn Ephrem elaborates by comparing the investigating Christians to Herod, to the unrepentant thief crucified with Jesus,[55] and to the Gospel scribes and Pharisees:

The [thief] of the left, he *disputed* [Luke 23]. His *disputing* cut off his hope. The scribes *disputed*. They fell with Herod who *questioned* him [Luke 23]. . . . To all these who *investigated,* Christ did not give himself. . . . The Pharisees *disputed,* "who is this, and whose son?" As *searchers* of truth, they fell from the truth. As *seekers* of verity, in *seeking* it, they destroyed it.[56]

For Ephrem these negative examples are in direct contrast to the Gospel forerunners of proper Christians, those who are "innocent" and to whom Christ *did* give himself,[57] those who follow the examples of the magi in Matthew's Gospel who "did not dare to *search*,"[58] and of the other thief in Luke's Gospel who "did not *dispute;* he believed without *searching*."[59] In this

52. Ephrem, *SdF* 6, *HdF* 7, *Nat.* 21.
53. Ephrem *HdF* 44.6, 9. Compare Matt 21:10, 23; 22:42; Mark 11:28; Luke 5:21, 7:49; John 1:19, 6:42, 8:25.
54. Ephrem, *HdF* 7.7.
55. Luke 23:32–33, 39–43 (cf. Matt 27:38, 44; John 19:17–18).
56. Ephrem, *HdF* 7.7, 9.
57. Ephrem, *HdF* 7.7.
58. Ephrem, *HdF* 7.7 (cf. Matt 2). This distinction is interesting, since of course the magi did search for the baby Jesus (Matt 2). Ephrem emphasizes, however, that the magi followed the star on faith, whereas the Pharisees and Jewish leaders probed for proof of Jesus' divinity through intellectual argument.
59. Ephrem, *HdF* 7.7 (cf. Luke 23:39–43).

hymn, Ephrem uses the verbs for searching and disputing in order to liken his Christian adversaries to the New Testament villains Herod, the scribes, and the Pharisees, and to distance them from the Gentile magi, the forerunners of "true" Christians.[60]

The example of the magi in Matthew's gospel provides Ephrem with a particularly useful way to code appropriate and inappropriate behavior as "Christian" and "Jewish," respectively. Conveniently, by focusing on the behavior, rather than the heritage or identity, of scriptural characters, Ephrem constructs a general caricature of "good" and "bad" behavior that he can then transfer from Jewish characters to his Christian opponents. Ephrem includes in *Sermons on Faith* 6 a general statement that he believes applies both to the situation in the Gospels as well as to his contemporary situation: "The finding of the Son is with unlearned people, and *seeking* him is with the learned. Those who were far away came and became disciples. Foreigners entered and partook. Those from without wondered at those within, that they still were *seeking*."[61] He follows this immediately with an explicit observation that he is, in fact, making a direct comparison between the time of Jesus and his own time: "This final situation resembles that which was from the beginning."[62]

In Sermon 6 Ephrem elaborates by describing how his initial comments relate to Jews in the time of Jesus. He writes,

The magi from afar perceived the king that was born in Bethlehem [Matthew 2]. The simple magi indeed reflected upon the scribes and the Hebrews, that upon their hands was borne the king's Son who was born there. Those [magi] from afar came and found what those [Pharisees] who were near did not perceive. The king was standing among them, and they were harassing [him] with *questions*. The king was born just as he was born, and these were *investigating* about his birth. The foreigners wondered that until now they are still *seeking* [about] his birth in the book. The pledge of him was with those without, and the *investigating* of him was with those within. . . . For the magi [there was] revealed truth; for the Pharisees, [only] *questions*.[63]

---

60. In *Hymns on the Nativity* 21 Ephrem again compares Christians to the New Testament magi who came and worshipped God's Son, and his Christian opponents to the negative examples of the New Testament Jews who did not recognize the Son (Ephrem, *Nat.* 21.24–25). True Christians, Ephrem claims, are those who like the magi worship instead of investigating.

61. Ephrem, *SdF* 6.82–88. Recall the earlier discussion regarding Ephrem's relation to Greek and Greek learning.

62. Ephrem, *SdF* 6.89–90.

63. Ephrem, *SdF* 6.91–114. It would perhaps be more surprising to see the magi represented

In this passage, the antagonists are clearly "the scribes and the Hebrews," and particularly "the Pharisees" in the Gospel stories. Not only did these Jews not recognize the message that God sent to them in God's Son, Ephrem argues, but the Pharisees, stereotypical biblical Jews for Ephrem, were consumed by questioning and challenging the details of Jesus' birth. Conversely, the Gentile magi "from afar," representing true Christians in Ephrem's scripturally based metaphor, found truth where those who inappropriately investigated found nothing but questions. This description offers Ephrem a convenient segue into his contemporary intra-Christian controversy, as he makes clear in the passage that follows.

Once Ephrem has placed the Christian Gospels, which both he and his Christian opponents respected as sacred Scripture, into this particular framework, he then makes the promised connection between that earlier time and his present time. In this way he uses the New Testament stories with their established heroes and villains to create a pattern against which he can line up the narrative of his contemporary Christian conflict, clearly delineating in the process where he and his Christian opponents fall with respect to the scriptural reference points. Immediately following the discussion of magi and Pharisees, Ephrem explains,

You also, O learners, do not be troubled about this, that your teachers are still *seeking* the truth. Just as he was found in Bethlehem by the magi who investigated concerning him, he is found in the true church by the one who seeks him properly. . . . Do not let this time, which resembles the former time, distress you. . . . For the *questions* of the learned were troubled by that coming [of the Son], [and] similarly now the *questions* are troubled before his [second] coming.[64]

Just as the New Testament Pharisees blindly questioned concerning God's Son and challenged his birth and his relation to the Father, Ephrem argues that so, too, his contemporary Christian opponents challenge God's Son through similar inappropriate questions and inquiries. It could not be lost on Ephrem's audience that like the Pharisees to whom they are compared, these "searching" Christians also challenged the details about the nature of the Son. This explicit comparison between the Gospel Pharisees and Ephrem's

---

as "simple" instead of wise, were it not for the details of Ephrem's metaphor, which rely on the magi representing simple and unquestioning faith in God's Son in opposition to the intellectual inquiry of the learned Pharisees.

64. Ephrem, *SdF* 6.115–38. Note that for Ephrem these verbs of searching are not inherently bad, but rather they must be exercised on appropriate subjects, and in appropriate measure, in order to avoid the follies of the Pharisees. See, for example, *SdF* 2.127–44.

contemporary Christian opponents leaves no question that the Christians' inappropriate searching places them on the wrong side of this equation, playing Pharisees to the metaphorical magi of Ephrem's pro-Nicene Christians.

In fact, in Sermon 6 Ephrem implies that not only are his opponents the equivalent of those Jews who denied God's Son, but that the heretics are actually worse than these Jews and all manner of non-Christians. Ephrem writes,

The [pagan] priests felt the Truth. . . . The magicians also felt it. . . . The Chaldeans also felt it. . . . The diviners also felt it. . . . The possessed felt it. . . . Those [pagans] who erred perceived that with its divinity it destroyed the graven images. The Truth cried out in creation and the *disputers seek,* "where is it?" Those who hated the Son perceived [the Truth], and those who preach him are *seeking* it. Although the People denied him, they knew who had uprooted them.[65]

Even those who do not follow God's Son, even Jews themselves, Ephrem argues, perceived "the truth," unlike Ephrem's contemporary Christian opponents who persist in still seeking it (and will never find it through their reasoned investigating). In this way, then, even though Ephrem identifies his opponents as "those who preach [the Son]," they are even worse than pagans and Jews.

One of the most elaborate and explicit comparisons of Jews with Christians whose teachings subordinate the Son in Ephrem's writings is in the final verses of number 87 of his *Hymns on Faith.*[66] In these verses, Ephrem compares the behavior of his contemporary Christian opponents point by point with the New Testament Gospel narratives of Jesus' trial and crucifixion at the hands of "the Jews."[67] In this hymn, Ephrem directly compares Jews and "searching" Christians, describing the latter as the contemporary equivalent to the Jews of Jesus' time who, in Ephrem's New Testament-based description, harassed and eventually murdered God's Son. Through language such as this, Ephrem rhetorically takes "Christianity" away from his opponents and reserves it solely for pro-Nicene Christians.

---

65. Ephrem, *SdF* 6.51–68.

66. Some of this discussion on *HdF* 87 also appears in Christine Shepardson, "'Exchanging Reed for Reed': Mapping Contemporary Heretics onto Biblical Jews in Ephrem's *Hymns on Faith,*" *Hugoye: Journal of Syriac Studies* 5, no. 1 (2002) [online journal], available from http://syrcom.cua.edu/hugoye/Vol5No1/HV5N1Shepardson.html. This article also contains a full translation of *HdF* 87.

67. Compare the similar language in Gregory of Nyssa's later text against Eunomius: Grg. Nyss., *Eun.* 1.264–66 (NPNF 1.21).

That Ephrem addresses subordinationist Christianity in these hymns is clear from the language that he uses to describe his opponents in Hymn 87, as "disputants" who wanted to reach "the Son, who is more subtle than the mind."[68] He calls his opponents "searchers" and "disputants" from within the Christian "household," echoing the verbs of inquiry that he associates with subordinationist Christianity, and he condemns these Christians' "investigating . . . searching . . . seeking."[69] Most explicitly of all, Ephrem claims that through these searchers Satan clothes the Son "with various names . . . either that of 'creature' or that of 'made thing,' while he is the Maker."[70] This reference specifically to calling the Son a "creature" leaves no doubt that Ephrem is writing against a version of the Trinitarian teaching of Arius that was condemned at Nicaea.

Throughout his writings, Ephrem vacillates about where the blame lies for the Jews' actions and for their rejection of and by God, sometimes making the Jews themselves solely responsible for their actions (as described in both the Old and New Testaments), and other times blaming Satan for manipulating history in such a way as to use the blind and foolish Jews as unwitting minions to carry out his plans of corruption. In Hymn 87 Ephrem places the blame not on the Jews, or the Christian heretics he associates with Jews, but principally on the figure of Satan, who in this reconstruction of history orchestrates both the Jews' and the Christians' reprehensible actions. While this in some way alleviates, by removing their agency, the condemnation that Ephrem elsewhere pours directly onto the Jews, he does not exempt them from the punishing consequences of their actions. He describes that as a result the Jews, "the crucifiers," were "despised and expelled as strangers."[71] Even though he portrays Satan as the ultimate agent behind the harmful (as Ephrem sees them) actions of both the Jews and these so-called Christians,[72] this historical reconstruction merely makes them sinister lackeys, passive (and ultimately passé) pawns in a Satanic drama that is being played out on the stage of human history.[73]

According to this hymn, Satan originally harbored himself among the Jews, as was clear from the history of their destructive and ungodly behavior, culminating with Jesus' passion and what Ephrem describes elsewhere as their murder of God's own Son.[74] In Hymn 87, however, Ephrem claims that after

68. Ephrem, HdF 87.1–2.   69. Ephrem, HdF 87.10, 17, 20.
70. Ephrem, HdF 87.14.   71. Ephrem, HdF 87.10.
72. Ephrem, HdF 87.9.   73. Compare John 8:44.
74. See, for example, HdF 87. This accusation of murder is frequent in Ephrem's writings.

they had committed such a heinous crime, the Jews were no longer a viable means through which Satan could secretly influence the world, because they could no longer conceal their partnership with Satan. Ephrem writes, "Satan saw that he had been exposed in the former things, for the spitting had been revealed, [as had] the vinegar and thorns, nails and wood, garments and reed, and the spear that struck him. And they were hated and revealed, and [Satan] changed his deceits."[75] The world's alleged open recognition of the Jews' partnership with Satan then forced Satan to find new pawns through whom he could continue to influence history and attack God (and God's Son). According to Ephrem, the "searching" Christians served as Satan's new tool after the Jews had worn out their usefulness in this capacity. Ephrem writes, "The former scribes Satan disrobed; he clothed the later ones. The People that had grown old, the moth and the louse gnawed it and ate it, and they released and let it go. The moth came to the new garment of the new peoples."[76] Satan has moved on from the Jews to these misled Christians. He "began with the People, and he came to the peoples in order that he might finish."[77] Ephrem understands that Satan has recently changed players in his ongoing effort to corrupt, destroy, and fight against God. For Ephrem, it is these errant Christians who are the "new garment," and in that respect the new Jews through whom Satan continues to harass God and God's people.

In several of his *Sermons* and *Hymns on Faith,* Ephrem identifies and describes his Christian opponents as the replacement for the Jews through a direct comparison between contemporary "searchers" and many of the negative (Jewish) characters in the Gospel scenes of Jesus' trial and crucifixion. In Hymn 87 one by one Ephrem maps the concrete, literal actions of the New Testament Jewish leaders onto a figurative characterization of the "heretical" Christians' behavior. Ephrem thus demonstrates to his audience that not only do both these false Christians and the Jews of Jesus' time pose a threat to true followers of Christ, but both groups in fact present precisely the same threat. Through his rhetoric, Ephrem conflates these Christians with the Jews blamed for Jesus' death, "proving" to his audience that although the

---

For only a small portion of the numerous examples, see *de Dom. nos.* 5, 6; *Cruc.* 1, 5; *Azym.* 1, 18; and *CNis.* 67. In *Hymns on Fasting* 5.6, Ephrem even accuses the Jews of killing God, not just God's Son, on the cross, a charge that is first extant in Melito of Sardis's *Peri Pascha* (Edmund Beck, ed., *Des Heiligen Ephraem des Syrers Hymnen de Ieiunio,* CSCO 246, SS 106 [Louvain, 1964]).

75. Ephrem, *HdF* 87.16.

76. Ephrem, *HdF* 87.9. Compare Matt 9:16–17; Mark 2:21–22; Luke 5:36–39.

77. Ephrem, *HdF* 87.12.

Christians' blows may be less literal than the physical blows with which the Jews allegedly struck Jesus, these Christians are in fact through their rebellious thoughts causing a second passion. Ephrem writes of the Christians' metaphorical mimicry of the New Testament narrative, "A second passion did Satan want to reinstate."[78] Unsatisfied merely with Jesus' physical death, Satan continues his attack upon Christians and God, figuratively reenacting Christ's passion through his attacks upon the nature of the Son as well as upon Nicene Christians.

Ephrem begins by comparing the reed with which the Jews allegedly mocked and struck Jesus to the reed stylus with which these Christians record their "heretical" inquiries into God.[79] Ephrem, emphasizing the subordinationist nature of his opponents' teachings, writes, "Instead of that reed that the former People gave the Son to hold [Matthew 27:29], [there are] later ones who dared in their tracts to write with a reed that he even is [only] human."[80] Instead of physically striking Jesus with a reed, these Christians, Ephrem claims, deal comparable blows against the Son through the tracts that they write with their reed pens. Ephrem bemoans, "Reed for reed the evil one exchanged against our savior."[81] Whereas Satan could at one time openly strike at his enemy through the Jews' attacks, he must now act more subtly, striking through the strife and falsehood espoused in the subordinationist writings.[82] Ephrem argues that through their disputes and searching these Christians harm the Son in a duplication of the actions of the Jews at the crucifixion.

Likewise, Ephrem compares the "garments of various colors" with which

---

78. Ephrem, *HdF* 87.19.

79. The details of who mocks Jesus, and whether or not they strike him with a reed vary in different texts of the New Testament Gospels as well as the Diatessaron, which Ephrem had available to him. In his *Commentary on the Diatessaron* Ephrem attributes all the mocking and harassment of the passion to the Jews (*Comm. Diat.* 20–21).

80. Ephrem, *HdF* 87.13 (cf., Ephrem, *Comm. Diat.* 20.17). In *Hymns on Crucifixion* 5 and 8 Ephrem also compares a reed from the Passion Narratives to reed styli, but he does so in different ways. In his *Hymns on Crucifixion,* he primarily compares the reed with which the crucified Jesus was offered a drink to the reeds with which prophets, kings, and scribes of Israel (especially King David as author of the Psalms) wrote against the behavior of Jesus' crucifiers. For example, Ephrem writes, "David wrote with a straight staff in order that he might shame that People who disgraced [Jesus] with that reed" (*Cruc.* 8.4). Likewise, Ephrem notes, "Instead of the one reed with which they beat [Jesus], the [many] reeds of the scribes beat them. . . . A thicket of reeds are the books of the writers; they beat the crucifiers with their books" (*Cruc.* 5.14).

81. Ephrem, *HdF* 87.13.

82. Ephrem, *HdF* 87.16.

he claims Jesus was clothed to the "various names" with which these Christians clothe the Son: "And instead of garments of various colors in which [Satan] clothed him [cf. Mark 15:17; John 19:2], he painted a designation deceitfully. With various names indeed he clothes him, either that of 'creature' or that of 'made thing,' while he is the Maker."[83] In Ephrem's depiction, through the Christians' subordinationist inquiries Satan reenacts the passion that took place at the hands of the Jews. Ephrem describes a direct comparison for every detail of the Passion Narrative, identifying his Christian opponents through their inappropriate searching:

He changed the cross; *dispute* became a hidden cross. And instead of nails [John 20:25; cf. *Comm. Diat.* 20.28], *questions* entered. And instead of Sheol, [there was] denial . . . Instead of the sponge that dripped with vinegar [Matthew 27:48; Mark 15:36; John 19:29; cf. *Comm. Diat.* 20.27], he gave arrows, [that is,] *searching,* all of which dripped with death. The gall that they gave to him, our Lord refused [Matthew 27:34; cf. *Comm. Diat.* 20:27]. Fraudulent *seeking* that the bitter one gave, to fools is sweet.[84]

More than merely participants in a struggle to claim the title "Christian" for themselves, Ephrem's opponents emerge from these texts as assailants and abusers of God's Son, alike in every detail to the New Testament Jews whom Ephrem blames for mocking and abusing "the Lord."

In Hymn 87 Ephrem also portrays the intra-Christian conflict as itself the direct outcome of Satan's actions, just as the Jews' murder of God's Son was in Jesus' lifetime, and he describes this fourth-century strife as also comparable to the passion. Ephrem writes about Satan,

He brought in confusion instead of that blow with which our Lord was struck [Matthew 27:30; Mark 15:19]; and instead of spitting [Matthew 27:30; Mark 15:19; cf. *Comm. Diat.* 20.17], *investigating* came. And instead of garments [Matthew 27:35; John 19:23; cf. *Comm. Diat.* 20.27], secret divisions. And instead of a reed [Matthew 27:29; Mark 15:19; cf. *Comm.Diat.* 20.17], contention came so that he might slap all. Haughtiness cried out to fury its sister, and envy and rage and pride and guile answered and came. They took counsel against our savior, as on that day that they took counsel when he suffered [i.e. "that day . . . of his passion"].[85]

Through this rhetoric Ephrem thus attempts to construct a historical reality in which these Christians, like the Jews before them, become the unquestioned enemy both of God and of true Christians.

---

83. Ephrem, *HdF* 87.14. Compare Ephrem, *Comm. Diat.* 20.17.
84. Ephrem, *HdF* 87.19–20.   85. Ephrem, *HdF* 87.17–18.

While this rhetoric is not as vituperatively anti-Jewish as some of Ephrem's other writings, its repeated references to the Jews' participation in the crucifixion do insistently call to mind the negative portrayals of Jesus' Jewish opponents in the New Testament Gospels. In this last section of Hymn 87, Ephrem defines a sharp dichotomy between Jews and Christian Gentiles that he portrays as historically significant and imbued with opposing values. Not only does Ephrem refer to the first group as "the crucifiers,"[86] clearly identifying them as those who were responsible for killing Jesus, but the narrative of the hymn continues with an elaborate retelling of "the People" mocking Jesus at his crucifixion, reemphasizing for Ephrem's audience their inescapable identification with this particular moment in scriptural history. Furthermore, with his association of these New Testament Jews with the more ontological category of "Jews," Ephrem categorically conflates, as he so frequently does in his writings, Jews of all times and places with the specific negative portrayal of the Jews that he is describing, in this case Jewish characters in the Gospel Passion Narratives. For Ephrem, it was not a discrete collection of individual Jews who mocked and crucified Jesus, and who were, as a result, responsible for the death of the Son; rather it was the entire Jewish "People" who participated and who share the guilt of this crime, and it is this negative image of Jews that he equates with his Christian opponents in this hymn.

Ephrem uses the connections that he draws between fourth-century events and Jesus' passion in order to emphasize not the depravity of the Jews themselves so much as that of his more immediate Christian opponents whose image Ephrem tars by rhetorically connecting them with "the crucifiers." By portraying these Christians as the modern equivalent to, and in fact Satan's replacement for, "the People" who murdered God's Son, Ephrem attempts firmly to establish that they are both theologically and perhaps even physically dangerous to God as well as to true (Nicene) Christians. In Hymn 87 Ephrem manipulates Christian depictions and fear of the Jews, rooted in (among other things) the New Testament Gospel stories' portrayals of the Jews who were hostile to Jesus, in order to present a grand historical narrative that discredits his Christian opponents. Ephrem goes to great lengths to describe these Christians searching for the natures of God and the Son, as well as their claims of the Son's subordination to God, as the figurative equivalent to the Jews' more

86. Ephrem, *HdF* 87.10.

literal mocking and murder of Jesus. Comparing these verbal attacks with the abuse portrayed in the Gospel Passion Narratives, Ephrem is able rhetorically to connect his contemporary Christian opponents with what he portrays as the universally despised people of the Jews.

Through such rhetoric, some Christians found themselves in the perhaps surprising position of being portrayed as the contemporary equivalent to those (Jews) who did not recognize Jesus as the Messiah. Recognizing the boundary lines that Ephrem's rhetoric attempts to define and police within Christianity demonstrates the power of his narrative within a Syrian Christian community torn by the "Nicene-Arian" struggle. In these sermons and hymns, Ephrem rhetorically redraws social and religious boundaries in such a way as to crystallize a sharp distinction between two Christianities, furthering his own intensely political cause while "masking" his language in the robe of divine truth.[87] Like the anti-Jewish rhetoric that Athanasius uses to denounce his Arian opponents, Ephrem's polemic likewise uses the negative portrayals of Jewish leaders in Christian Scripture to criticize not only contemporary Jews but also Christian opponents whom he associates with these scriptural Jews. By describing subordinationist Christianity as the contemporary equivalent of, and in fact replacement for, the Jewish enemies of Christian lore, Ephrem and Athanasius replace a blurred line between two Christian groups with what they present as the unmistakable distinction between Christians and Jews, rhetorically expelling those "Arian" Christians from the Christian community and leaving them firmly on the side of the Jews.

Blind and Dangerous Like "the Jews"

In addition to using biblical stories, Ephrem and Athanasius also draw comparisons between their Christian opponents and "Jews" by using the same negative adjectives to describe both groups, thereby implying their correlation. We have already seen the wealth of anti-Jewish rhetoric available to Ephrem, but Athanasius's writings, too, contain specific negative descriptions of Jews and Judaism that help make the "Arians" appear un-Christian through Athanasius's association of them with Judaism. David Brakke's discussion of Athanasius's anti-Jewish language points to Athanasius's critical description of Judaism as fleshly and local, in direct contrast to the more highly valued

---

87. Here I return to Eagleton's language for the ways in which ideological rhetoric typically functions (Eagleton, *Ideology,* 202).

spiritual and universal nature of Christianity.[88] Furthermore, Athanasius repeatedly criticizes "the unbelief of the Jews,"[89] "Jewish malignity,"[90] and "the deceit of the Jews,"[91] and he calls the Jews "errant"[92] and "weak in perception."[93] Writing against Christian opponents, both authors clearly highlight the violence of "the Jews" and "Arians"—and the consequent danger that they pose to "true" Christians—in order to strengthen their claims to represent Christian orthodoxy.

Ephrem reiterates throughout his *Hymns on Faith* his description of Jews and his Christian opponents as "blind." In Hymn 8 Ephrem refers to the Jews at Mt. Sinai as "the blind People,"[94] and in Hymn 9 he compares "the blind People" of the Jews to "you blind ones" among the Christians he accuses.[95] Hymn 27 also linguistically links the two by referring to his Christian opponents as a "blind assembly of disputers."[96] In this case, not only are his disputing (Christian) opponents again blind, but Ephrem uses the Syriac word for "assembly" that derives from the same root as the word that he consistently uses to refer to a Jewish synagogue, as opposed to the synonym that he typically uses for Christians. Through common traits such as blindness, Ephrem rhetorically links his searching opponents with the negatively-coded errors, history, and people of the Jews.

Ephrem likewise recalls the linked charges of adultery and idolatry discussed above. For example, in Hymn 44 he argues that through their intellectual inquiry, these non-Nicene Christians commit both adultery and idolatry. By attributing adultery and idolatry to these Christians, Ephrem simulta-

---

88. For this well-argued discussion, as well as further bibliography, see David Brakke, "Jewish Flesh and Christian Spirit in Athanasius of Alexandria," *JECS* 9, no. 4 (2001): 453–81. See also Daniel Boyarin, *Carnal Israel: Reading Sex in Talmudic Culture* (Berkeley: University of California Press, 1993).

89. Athanasius, *Inc.* 33. I have translated this phrase from the Greek text in Athanasius, *Contra Gentes and De Incarnatione,* ed. and trans. R. W. Thomson (Oxford: Oxford University Press, 1971).

90. Athanasius, *Decr.* 1. Quotations from Athanasius's *Defense of the Nicene Council* are my own translation from the Greek in Opitz, *Athanasius Werke,* vol. 2, part 1 (Berlin: de Gruyter, 1935).

91. Athanasius, *Ep. fest.* (Syr) 11.13. All quotations from the Syriac remnants of Athanasius's *Festal Letters* are from William Cureton, ed., *The Festal Letters of Athanasius* (Piscataway, N.J.: Gorgias Press, 2003), with reference to *Ath.* NPNF.

92. Athanasius, *Ep. fest.* (Syr) 5.4.   93. Athanasius, *Ep. fest.* (Syr) 7.4.

94. Ephrem, *HdF* 8.5.

95. Ephrem, *HdF* 9.13. Compare also Ephrem, *SdF* 6.67; *SdF* 6.150, 156.

96. Ephrem, *HdF* 27.4.

neously maligns their character and rhetorically links them with the Jews, against whom Ephrem frequently levels the same charges. Ephrem writes to his own church congregation,

Rebuke your thought! Do not commit adultery and bear for us a Messiah that does not exist, and [do not] deny the one that exists. Be on guard! Do not make an idol in your *investigating*. Be on guard! Do not depict with your intellect a divination of your mind and an offspring of your thought. . . . *Searching* belongs to an adulteress; *seeking,* to a harlot. She committed adultery in her *investigating* and conceived and bore for us a Messiah of constructions. . . . For the fabrication of their intellect the Jews wait; the divination of their wisdom the children of error worship.[97]

For Ephrem, inappropriate intellectual searching is one of the most offensive acts that his Christian adversaries commit, and one that helps define them in contrast to pro-Nicene Christians (whom Ephrem describes as accepting God through faith, rather than based on rational proof, explanation, or investigation). In this case, Ephrem describes their searching and investigating as adultery, as attempts to penetrate and know what is forbidden to them. This adultery, in turn, results in what Ephrem describes as an idol of their intellectual construction. Their investigating into the nature of the Son creates, Ephrem claims, "a Messiah that does not exist," a false image of the Son that they have constructed for themselves to worship. This "idol" is the product of human intellect, not the true image of the Son that, according to Ephrem, is known through simple faith. Here again the charges of adultery and idolatry go hand in hand. As demonstrated above, however, the dual charge of adultery and idolatry is primarily one that Ephrem links with the worship of the golden calf at Mt. Sinai. For an audience familiar with Ephrem's hymns and homilies, the language of adultery and idolatry is heavily connected with the Jews in this way, so that leveling similar charges against these Christian opponents rhetorically links them with the Jews.[98]

Ephrem's writings against non-Nicene Christians also recall the anti-

97. Ephrem, *HdF* 44.10–11. Note the allusions to the worship of the golden calf, discussed above.

98. Unlike the story of the golden calf, however, in Hymn 44 Ephrem describes the construction of the idol as a result of the adultery, rather than describing the adulterous relations as being with the idol itself as it was with the golden calf. Whereas in Exodus 32 the idol, the golden calf, was the object of lust and worship with which the Hebrews committed adultery, in Hymn 44 the idol is instead the progeny of the adulterous relationship; the false Messiah that they construct through their investigating is the offspring of the adulterous relationship.

Jewish charges of the danger that his opponents pose to true Christians, and in this way he again echoes similar accusations leveled against Arians by Athanasius. The sentences that follow Athanasius's comparison with Caiaphas in his third *Oration* compare Johannine sayings of Jesus' Jewish interlocutors with alleged "Arian" sayings, hoping to demonstrate further the similarities in their views of the Son.[99] In this text Athanasius compounds his accusations by comparing not only the questions but even the murderous actions of the New Testament Jewish leaders, as Ephrem also does:

Next, while the Jews were seeking to kill the Lord . . . the Arians themselves also learned to say that neither is he equal to God, nor is God the own and natural Father of the Word. But also those who think these things seek to kill. . . . For both these groups deny the eternity and Godhead of the Word because of those human attributes that the savior took on account of that flesh that he bore.[100]

Athanasius emphasizes both groups' denial of Christ's full divinity and accuses them of "seeking to kill." Through such rhetoric, Athanasius highlights the similarities that he sees between Jews and "Arians" at the same time that he warns about the dangers they pose. As for Ephrem, one result of this rhetoric is to increase the gap between Arians and "Christians" while narrowing that between Arians and Jews, which in turn allows Athanasius's own (Nicene) Christianity to claim the title of Christian truth.

Athanasius's accusation that Arians mimic Jews by murdering is even more adamant in his *History of the Arians,* in which he comments, "Thus the new Jewish heresy not only denies the Lord, but also has learned to murder."[101] The immediacy of his accusations in this text results from the context in which he wrote it. In 353 when Constantius gained control over the West as well as the East, he supported the appointment of Athanasius's opponents to more of the empire's episcopal sees. It is scarcely surprising, then, that several of Athanasius's writings from this period compare the violence and force used by Arians against Nicene leaders and churches to the violence of the New Testament Jewish leaders against Jesus. This connection is most explicit in his *History of the Arians,* which dates to the time of Athanasius's third exile, which began in 356. In this text Athanasius notes his Christian opponents' violence against Nicene churches, their persecution of himself and

---

99. Athanasius, *Ar.* 3.27.
100. Athanasius, *Ar.* 3.27. Compare Ephrem, *HdF* 87, *SdF* 3.
101. Athanasius, *H. Ar.* 19.

other Nicene leaders, and the emperor Constantius's role in these events.[102] He then accuses this "new Jewish heresy" of murder.[103] Describing further outrages against his church, he again compares Arians with Jews: "But the Arians were not even yet touched with shame, but, like the Jews when they saw the miracles, were faithless and did not believe."[104] Continuing the comparison, Athanasius comments that the "Arians" inherit their violence and impiety from the Jews and all the heretics who preceded them:

And this indeed also these present Jews learned from the Jews of old, who . . . accused the Lord. . . . The Jews, leaving behind the divine Scriptures, now, as the apostle [Paul] said, contend about "myths and endless genealogies" [1 Timothy 1:4]; and the Manichees and Valentinians with them, and others, corrupting the divine Scriptures, put forth myths of their own inventions. But the Arians are bolder than the other heresies, and have shown the others to be their younger sisters, whom, as I have said, they surpass in impiety, emulating them all, and especially the Jews in their wickedness. For as those [Jews] . . . immediately led [Paul] to the chief captain and the governor, thus these even more than those think to use the sole power of the judges, and if anyone so much as speaks against them, he is dragged before the governor or the general.[105]

As these quotations show, Athanasius faults the actions of his contemporary Christian opponents, and denounces them by comparing them to the Jews described so negatively in Christian Scripture. His references to contemporary politics, and to the imperial persecution of pro-Nicene leaders, reveal the immediacy as well as the purchase of his religious rhetoric.

Becoming even more explicit about his complaints against contemporary imperial politics, as well as his comparison between "Arians" and the New Testament Jews, Athanasius continues,

This heresy . . . has enlisted that enemy of Christ, Constantius, as it were the anti-Christ himself, to be its leader in impiety. . . . It happened that when the [Nicene] bishops were condemned to banishment, certain other persons also received their sentence on charges of murder or sedition or theft . . . [Constantius] released these people after a few months, as Pilate did Barabbas. . . . Is it not therefore clear to all that the Jews then who were demanding Barabbas and crucifying the Lord are these very people who now fight against Christ with Constantius?[106]

102. See, for example, Athanasius, *H. Ar.* 45, 66.

103. Athanasius, *H. Ar.* 19.   104. Athanasius, *H. Ar.* 58.

105. Athanasius, *H. Ar.* 61, 66. See Virginia Burrus's discussion on Athanasius *"Begotten, Not Made": Conceiving Manhood in Late Antiquity* (Stanford: Stanford University Press, 2000), 36–79.

106. Athanasius, *H. Ar.* 67–68. It is interesting to note that despite many similarities in the

In his *History of the Arians,* then, Athanasius uses the calumnious images of the Jewish leaders who accuse Jesus in the Gospels in order to condemn his own fourth-century "Arian" opponents as the "very people" of the New Testament Jews. Through these comparisons of his Christian opponents and New Testament Jews, Athanasius conflates the two so that they appear to be the very same threatening enemy.

As Athanasius does in these examples, Ephrem also appeals to Jews and Judaism as a rhetorical foil with which to frighten and to chastise his church audience. He employs anti-Jewish rhetoric to make the non-Nicene Christians both victims whom he is attempting to rescue, and potentially dangerous enemies from whom he needs to protect "orthodox" Christians. Ephrem warns his congregation to beware of those who would mislead them: wandering Christians will be easy prey for the Jews who stand poised to deceive and even murder those who stray from Christian orthodoxy.[107] According to Ephrem's rhetoric, the Jews were and remained an active threat to all Christians. He warns that it is not possible to keep the Jewish people from killing; he describes the Jews as a group: "having tasted much blood, it was not able to stop killing. Then it killed openly; now it kills secretly."[108] Ephrem implies that by straying beyond the safety of his own Nicene "orthodox" community, Christians increase the chance that they will be seized by the Jews, who "did not fear while leading you [Christian] astray."[109] Ephrem further portrays the Jews as bloodthirsty murderers who, having taken upon themselves even the blood of God, now attack Christians: "Flee from [the Jewish people], weak one! Your death and your blood are nothing to it. It took the blood of God; will it be frightened away from your own blood?"[110] Through such grisly descriptions, Ephrem warns those church-attendees who hear him of the dangers that await them should they continue to separate themselves from Christian orthodoxy.

---

rhetoric of Ephrem and Athanasius, Ephrem's language does not blame the emperor for the persecutions of pro-Nicene Christians, but rather blames instead the impious bishops who lead the emperor astray. See, for example, Ephrem, *HdF* 87.21–23. See also Griffith, "Deacon."

107. Ephrem, *SdF* 3.397–402. I presented a portion of this section at the XIII International Conference on Patristic Studies in Oxford in August 1999, and that paper was subsequently published: Christine Shepardson, "Anti-Jewish Rhetoric and Intra-Christian Conflict in the Sermons of Ephrem Syrus," in *Studia Patristica,* Vol. XXXV, XIII International Conference on Patristic Studies (Louvain: Peeters, 2001), 502–7.

108. Ephrem, *SdF* 3.329–32.   109. Ephrem, *SdF* 3.353.

110. Ephrem, *SdF* 3.349–52. Compare similar language in Gregory of Nazianzus's later writings from Constantinople (e.g., Grg. Naz., *Orat.* 21.14).

Yet Ephrem not only describes the Jews as an immediate (and deadly) threat to the misled Christians, he also conflates these Christians with the Jews, condemning them through guilt by association. Methodically magnifying his opponents' distance from Christian orthodoxy, Ephrem implies that they are the Gentile equivalent of the Jews who murdered God's Son and who pose a threat to true Christians. Ephrem draws a direct correspondence between the crucifying Jews and the Christians who inappropriately search out the mysteries of God: "If the unbeliever is a crucifier, and if the worshipper is a *searcher*, there is great weeping. . . . [God] went to the seed of Abraham; the heirs became murderers. He went to the Gentiles who were simple; the innocent ones became *searchers*."[111] Through this rhetoric, Ephrem weakens his opponents' relationship to Christian orthodoxy, and his antagonists become dangerously linked to the Jews, whom he describes elsewhere in this sermon as sickly, violent, mad, and accursed, a "contemptible" and "foolish flock" of "murderers."[112]

While Ephrem's rhetoric comparing the searching Christians to the Jews who crucified Christ maligns the Christians he claims have gone astray, it also places them in the position of threatening Nicene Christians, just as the Jews do. Although he maintains a grammatical distinction between "you," the Christians, and "them," "the [Jewish] People," it is from the orthodox Christians rather than from the Jews that Ephrem separates the "searchers" through his rhetoric. By emphasizing the distance between Nicene and Heteroousian, or Homoian, Christians, Ephrem heightens the immediacy of the danger posed to the latter by the Jews, emphasizing both the Jewish threat to the dissenting Christians, and the threat that they themselves, like the Jews, pose to "true" (Nicene) Christians.

111. Ephrem, *SdF* 3.387–94. Beck compares this to Ephrem's later description in *HdF* 87.13–22 of "Arianism" as a second (literary rather than physical) crucifixion (Edmund Beck, trans., *Des Heiligen Ephraem des Syrers Sermones de Fide,* CSCO 213, SS 89 [Louvain, 1961], 229n). In both treatises Ephrem draws a direct comparison between the Jews who crucified Christ and Ephrem's Christian opponents who search the nature of God.

Similarly, in *HdF* 23 Ephrem refers to the Jews as "deniers" and to errant Christians as those who "dare to search" when he writes, "Akin to the deniers is whoever dares to search. . . . Draw these comparisons discriminately, for the one denied his divinity and the other searched to diminish God" (*HdF* 23.2–3). In this concise criticism, Ephrem ties these Christians to the Jews through a specific critique of their teachings, and the connection that Ephrem sees with the teachings of the Jews. Ephrem argues that just as the Jews deny or never recognized Jesus' divinity, so too these Christians seek to define the nature of the Son in such a way that they, too, "diminish" God.

112. Ephrem, *SdF* 3.291, 250, 250, 367, 255, 257, 392.

The rhetorical connection of Ephrem's contemporary opponents with the archetypal anti-Christian, the Jews, serves to depict Nicene Christianity as a safe haven from the dangers of the strife and spiritual threats posed by the Christian schism. Ephrem elaborates specifically on this point, attempting to delineate the boundaries of the true church, and to define who will and will not enter into the heavenly kingdom. Ephrem warns his audience against the dangers to their souls if Christians should pry and dispute on earth, as he has already accused his Christian opponents of doing:

And if you should *search* this there, indeed, your suffering [would be] in the kingdom, when everyone rejoices in the Messiah and you are suffering in *seeking* him. . . . And if you should thus *dispute* there, the kingdom would not receive you, lest you enter and impose division in the place that is full of concord. But that kingdom will seek the vengeance of the holy church, lest the troublesome ones who caused trouble here enter that kingdom.[113]

Ephrem then continues by drawing an explicit connection between the true church on earth and the eternal kingdom of God: "An image of that kingdom is this true church."[114] Therefore, not only are those who dispute, as the "searchers" do, endangering their chance of entering the kingdom, but Ephrem also denies them access to the true church while on earth. He argues, "For just as it is right that there be concord in the kingdom, thus it is right that there be agreement in the holy church. If there is not disputing there, why is there searching here? And if in that [kingdom] there is calm and peace, why is there conflict in this [place]?"[115] The true church is one that mirrors the kingdom, a place free of strife and contention, and also a place into which those who seek and pry may not enter, and to which they do not belong. Ephrem thus attempts to unify Christians under Nicene control, while expelling from the community those with whom he disagrees so as to sanction and maintain Nicene authority within Christianity in Nisibis and, in fact, the Roman Empire.

Having laid this framework, Ephrem then addresses directly the conflict within his contemporary community. Having described the Jews and errant Christians as intellectuals who try to reach through reason what "true" Christians know to accept on faith, Ephrem appeals to his audience, "Do not be troubled, hearer, if the learned goes awry. Do not grow weak, O learner,

113. Ephrem, *SdF* 6.307–22.   114. Ephrem, *SdF* 6.325–26.
115. Ephrem, *SdF* 6.327–34.

if the *disputer* wanders."[116] Ephrem then adds to these warnings the threat to Christianity as a whole that he claims this internal fighting causes. Like Athanasius, Ephrem bemoans the turmoil and strife that afflicts the Christian Empire. He laments the "priests who stabbed one another . . . brothers persecuted one another . . . we are divided in dispute . . . we are divided in seeking . . . we are divided one against another . . . indeed, there is great fighting among us."[117] Beyond matters of personal salvation, Ephrem argues that the internal strife of the Christian community is in fact bringing about the fall of Christianity itself, affecting all Christians regardless of their beliefs, while the paganism around them thrives and prospers, even feeding on the Christians' weaknesses. Not only does Ephrem present Christian division as a threat to the well-being of individuals, and cause for exclusion both from the true earthly church and from the heavenly kingdom, but he also portrays the contemporary turmoil itself as a threat to the continued existence of Christianity of any sort.

At the end of *Sermons on Faith* 6, Ephrem turns from the fighting back to the specifics of his internal Christian opponents. Picking up the military imagery with which he outlined the pagan military threat that has come upon the Christians through their own fractious behavior, Ephrem returns to his earlier accusations that his opponents have caused this strife: "The just one brought evils, so that with them he might quiet our evils. . . . He threw at us visible arrows so that he might quiet the hidden arrows. . . . If he brought unsheathed swords, it was that they might quiet unsheathed tongues."[118] The ultimate thrust, then, is Ephrem's attempt to weave a narrative in which he clearly delineates the error, and in fact threat, of his Christian opponents. The contemporary military threats to Nisibis when Ephrem wrote would have been clearly apparent to Ephrem's audience.[119] By blaming these political hardships on intra-Christian strife, Ephrem creates an urgent incentive for Christians to expel the dissent from their community and end the intra-Christian conflict. Through his comparisons of these Christians and the Jews, Ephrem leaves no room for doubt that it is the "searching" Christians who are to blame for the fighting. Ephrem offers the hope that these Christians will mend their errant ways and unite the Christian community under

116. Ephrem, *SdF* 6.163–66.
117. Ephrem, *SdF* 6.353, 357, 393–405, 478.
118. Ephrem, *SdF* 6.487–98 (cf. John 18:11).
119. See the references in chapter 2 to Shapur II's sieges of Nisibis during Ephrem's lifetime.

Nicene authority "so that we may oppress on all sides wars hidden and visible."[120]

What Ephrem presents as an objective description of his world leads his
audience rhetorically to the inevitable conclusion that if only the Jew-like
Christian "searchers" would cease their harmful quarreling, not only would
they reach God's kingdom, but intra-Christian fighting in the Roman Empire
would end, which would in turn stop the Persians from conquering Roman
forts, and would even (with the unification and consequent strengthening
of Christianity) earn the respect of their non-Christian neighbors. Ideology
"has the function of producing an *obvious* 'reality' that social subjects can as-
sume and accept, precisely as if it had not been socially produced and did not
need to be 'known' at all."[121] Ephrem's narrative explains the political unrest
on the Roman and Persian border where Nisibis lies, as well as the fourth-
century intra-Christian strife in the Roman Empire, and places it all within a
framework that extols Nicene Christianity as the solution to both conflicts.
Thus, through the judicious use of anti-Jewish language, Ephrem musters a
forceful argument against subordinationist Christianity for the legitimation,
and in fact necessity, of the unchallenged authority of Nicene Christianity.

Ephrem presents the Jews as particularly hostile in order to portray the
situation of the errant Christians as one of dire and imminent danger. Described as misled by their own curiosity and actively threatened by malicious
Jews, "investigating" Christians are presented with only one viable solution,
to espouse Ephrem's Nicene Christianity. To do otherwise, Ephrem suggests,
would only be to persist in pain and error and to risk death at the hands of
the Jews (and perhaps also the Persians). Ephrem's careful construction of
Jews and Judaism in this treatise therefore supports a distorted picture of the
relationship among Nicene Christians, Arian Christians and Jews. The "insider" nature of Ephrem's Christian audience contradicts the image that he
portrays of the close proximity of these "searching" Christians to the Jews
and their alleged distance from Nicene Christians. It is ultimately, though,
the threat of the Jews, Ephrem implies in this sermon, that will convince
these Christians to rescue themselves from imminent danger, ceasing to be

---

120. Ephrem, *SdF* 6.507–8 (cf. Ephrem, *CNis.* 28).

121. James H. Kavanagh, "Ideology," in *Critical Terms for Literary Study,* eds. Frank Lentricchia and Thomas M. Laughlin (Chicago: University of Chicago Press, 1990), 311. Compare Louis Althusser, "Ideology and Ideological State Apparatuses (Notes towards an Investigation)," in
Lenin and Philosophy and other Essays, trans. Ben Brewster (London: New Left Books, 1971).

a threat either to themselves or to orthodox Christians, so that all Christians will be united in true (Nicene) Christianity.

In his *Orations against the Arians* Athanasius echoes some of these same concerns, and explicitly argues that "Arians" cannot rightfully claim the name "Christian." Whereas Ephrem makes this argument implicitly, Athanasius explicitly supports his claim by expounding alleged proofs that his opponents are not Christians and by emphasizing again their connection with Jews, arguing that the Arians are in fact Jews. Athanasius begins by arguing that because his opponents are named "Arians" after Arius rather than "Christians" after Christ, they are not Christians. In the first of these orations, Athanasius writes,

The Arian [heresy] . . . pretends to cloak herself in the language of Scripture, like her father the devil [cf. John 8:44], and forces her way back into the Church's paradise, in order that with the pretence of Christianity, she . . . might deceive people into wrong thoughts about Christ. . . . I have thought it necessary . . . to show . . . that those who call these people Christians go astray very much. . . . For with them in place of Christ is Arius. . . . [Arius and those with him] are named Arians in place of Christians, having this badge of their irreligion. . . . For never at any time did Christian people take their name from the bishops among them, but rather from the Lord. . . . But for those who derive the faith which they profess from others, it is right that they should have the name of the one whose property they have become.[122]

Athanasius continues this argument at some length, noting that the "heretical" followers of Marcion, Valentinus, Basilides, Mani, Simon Magus, Novatus, and Meletius are named after their leader instead of after Christ. Athanasius concludes with the observation, "Thus when Alexander of blessed memory had cast out Arius, those who remained with Alexander remained Christians, but those who went out with Arius left the Savior's name to us who were with Alexander and those [who left] were from then on named Arians."[123] As he concisely summarizes, "being Arians, they are not Christians."[124] Of course Athanasius's very rhetoric is itself calling into being that which he claims is true. It is not that his opponents claim for themselves the name "Arian," but that through such rhetoric Athanasius insistently places that title upon them in his continued effort to assert the authority and validity of his own Nicene Christianity. Through this rhetoric, Athanasius denies his opponents the contested name of "Christian."

122. Athanasius, *Ar.* 1.1–2.   123. Athanasius, *Ar.* 1.3.
124. Athanasius, *Ar.* 1.10.

Not only excluding Arians from "Christianity," Athanasius returns to criticizing their alleged resemblance to the Jews, and even exhorts them to follow their Jewishness through to its end and be Jews, rather than pretending to be Christians while adopting the beliefs of the Jews: "Being Judaic, . . . either let them openly confess themselves to be disciples of Caiaphas and Herod instead of hiding Judaism with the name of Christianity, and let them deny outright as we have said before the Savior's appearance in the flesh, for this is the same mind as their heresy. Or if they fear to Judaize openly and to be circumcised, on account of pleasing Constantius . . . then let them not say the things of the Jews."[125] Giving his opponents two clear choices, Judaism or (Nicene) Christianity, Athanasius describes his opponents' similarities to Jews, and calls upon them to claim the name "Jew" for themselves instead of misleadingly calling themselves "Christian": "For it is right if they decline the name [of the Jews], also to turn from [the Jews'] thoughts. . . . If then you wish to become Christians, put off the madness of Arius and cleanse with the words of religion those ears of yours which blaspheming has defiled, knowing that, by ceasing to be Arians you will cease also from the malevolence of the present Jews."[126] Athanasius conflates his Christian opponents with Jews, thereby forcing them by default in the bipolar world of his rhetoric into the realm of Judaism. Athanasius supports the accuracy of this placement by highlighting the similarities he sees between the two groups' emphasis on the humanity of Jesus (in the case of the Jews) and of the Son (in the case of the Arians).

Athanasius goes even further in his first *Oration* and extrapolates from the conflation of the "Arians" with Jews, wondering why the "Arians," since they resemble Jews, do not also follow Jewish law. He argues about Arius' views, "But this is not of the church. . . . Why then, if they think these things, do they not also circumcise as the Jews? But rather they pretend Christianity while they fight against it."[127] Athanasius does not plead that his opponents should become fully Jews for their own betterment, but rather that they should stop deceiving others and should either display their Judaism outwardly in their actions as in their beliefs, or else they should live up to their claim to be Christian by adopting the beliefs of Christian "orthodoxy."

125. Athanasius, *Ar.* 3.28.

126. Athanasius, *Ar.* 3.28. Compare also Athanasius, *Ep. Max.* As noted above, Athanasius also writes that based on his teachings Arius should join either pagans or Jews, offering three possible categories instead of two (Athanasius, *Ep. Adelph.*).

127. Athanasius, *Ar.* 1.38.

Living in the eastern empire in these decades of intra-Christian conflict, Ephrem and Athanasius both used anti-Jewish and anti-Judaizing rhetoric to argue against their subordinationist Christian opponents. Both authors combine anti-Jewish rhetoric with anti-"Arian" charges of Judaizing in order to conflate the "Arians" with the Jews of Christian Scripture. By so doing, they malign their Christian opponents even as they distance them from "Christianity" itself. Anti-Jewish rhetoric thus serves a very practical purpose for Ephrem and Athanasius in the midst of a struggle to claim the title "Christian" for supporters of Nicene orthodoxy. In the earlier years of this intra-Christian conflict, in a context with a significant Jewish population, and in the process of defining the very category "Arian," sharp anti-Jewish language and comparisons with Jews seem to have been particularly useful rhetorical tools with which both to define and to stigmatize "Arian" Christians as non-Christian "Jews."

The Cappadocians against Eunomius

As subordinationist Christianity and pro-Nicene Christianity became two recognizably distinct alternatives in the later fourth century, pro-Nicene Cappadocian leaders, instead of conflating "Jews" and "Arians," primarily charged Eunomius and his followers with an inconsistency between behavior and belief that positioned Eunomians as an untenable third alternative to Christians and Jews. Still comparing subordinationist Christian theology with Judaism, but more explicitly acknowledging the Christian identity of their opponents, the pro-Nicene Cappadocian writers emphasized not so much that Arians *were* Jews, but that they were *not* Christians, and that they should either consistently practice Jewish behaviors along with their "Jewish" beliefs or else accept right Christian thinking along with their claims to be "Christian." With less pointed anti-Judaism than Ephrem and Athanasius, these Cappadocian authors used the Jews primarily as a shaming device, declaring their Christian opponents to be even worse than Jews. The anti-Eunomian writings of Basil of Caesarea, Gregory of Nazianzus, and Gregory of Nyssa demonstrate the continuation and evolution of pro-Nicene leaders' use of anti-Judaizing language against subordinationist Christian opponents.[128] Thus, their rhetoric witnesses to the significance of anti-Jewish language in the intra-Christian

128. For a fuller discussion of this topic, see Christine Shepardson, "Defining the Boundaries of Orthodoxy: Eunomius in the Anti-Jewish Polemic of His Cappadocian Opponents," *CH* 76, no. 4 (2007): 699–723.

conflicts of the fourth century in which Ephrem and Athanasius participated and in which they deployed similar rhetoric, as we have seen.

By the middle of the fourth century, pro-Nicene Cappadocian leaders were entering the limelight of this Trinitarian controversy. Basil of Caesarea,[129] his classmate Gregory of Nazianzus,[130] Basil's younger brother Gregory of Nyssa,[131] and Aetius's student Eunomius of Cyzicus, whom pro-Nicene leaders accused of dangerously adapting the (already "heretical") teachings of Arius, all came from Cappadocia and gained ecclesiastical positions there in the later fourth century. It is, therefore, not just geographical and chronological differences that distinguish Basil and the two Gregories from Ephrem and Athanasius; these Cappadocians also wrote against a different stripe of subordinationist Christian theology, primarily that advocated by Eunomius, a follower of Aetius who was exiled in 358 and again in 360 for his strongly subordinationist teachings. These later pro-Nicene leaders still used anti-Jewish

129. For more on Basil, his life, and his writings, see P. J. Fedwick, *The Church and the Charisma of Leadership in Basil of Caesarea* (Toronto: Pontifical Institute of Mediaeval Studies, 1979); Paul Jonathan Fedwick, ed., *Basil of Caesarea: Christian, Humanist, Ascetic,* 2 vols. (Toronto: Pontifical Institute of Mediaeval Studies, 1981); B. Gain, *L'église de Cappadoce au IVe siècle d'après la correspondance de Basile de Césarée,* OCA 225 (Rome: Pontifical Institute, 1985); Philip Rousseau, *Basil of Caesarea* (Berkeley: University of California Press, 1994); Anthony Meredith, *The Cappadocians* (Crestwood, N.Y.: St. Vladimir's Seminary Press, 1995); V. H. Drecoll, *Die Entwicklung der Trinitätslehre des Basilius von Cäsarea: Sein Weg vom Homöusianer zum Neonizäner* (Göttingen: Vandenhoeck & Ruprecht, 1996); Thomas Böhm, "Basil of Caesarea, *Adversus Eunomium* I–III and Ps. Basil, *Adversus Eunomium* IV–V," in *Studia Patristica XXXVII* (Louvain: Peeters, 2001), 20–26; Raymond Van Dam, *Families and Friends in Late Roman Cappadocia* (Philadelphia: University of Pennsylvania Press, 2003); Andrea Sterk, *Renouncing the World, Yet Leading the Church: The Monk-Bishop in Late Antiquity* (Cambridge, Mass.: Harvard University Press, 2004).

130. For information and bibliography about the life of Gregory of Nazianzus, see Paul Gallay, *Grégoire de Nazianze* (Paris: Éditions ouvrières, 1959); Rosemary Radford Ruether, *Gregory of Nazianzus: Rhetor and Philosoper* (Oxford: Oxford University Press, 1969); McGuckin, *Gregory,* as well as Bernardi, *Grégoire;* Norris, "Introduction"; Leslie Brubaker, *Vision and Meaning in Ninth-Century Byzantium: Image as Exegesis in the Homilies of Gregory of Nazianzus* (New York: Cambridge University Press, 1999); Meredith, *Cappadocians;* Van Dam, *Friends;* Anne Richard, *Cosmologie et théologie chez Grégoire de Nazianze* (Paris: Institut d'études augustiniennes, 2003); Sterk, *Renouncing.* See Russell, *Ephraem,* for a comparison specifically of Gregory of Nazianzus with Ephrem.

131. For more on Gregory of Nyssa, see Michael Azkoul, *St. Gregory of Nyssa and the Tradition of the Fathers* (New York: Edwin Mellen Press, 1995); Anthony Meredith, *Gregory of Nyssa* (London: Routledge, 1999); Sarah Coakley, ed., "Re-thinking Gregory of Nyssa," *Modern Theology* 18, no. 4 (2002): 431–561; Meredith, *Cappadocians;* Van Dam, *Friends;* Sterk, *Renouncing;* Martin S. Laird, *Gregory of Nyssa and the Grasp of Faith: Union, Knowledge, and Divine Presence* (New York: Oxford University Press, 2004). Specifically regarding Gregory's anti-Jewish language, see Jean Reynard, "L'Antijudaïsme de Grégoire de Nysse et du pseudo-Grégoire de Nysse," in *Studia Patristica XXXVII* (Louvain: Peeters, 2001), 257–76.

rhetoric in emphasizing their opponents' subordinationist theology, but their specific arguments differed from those of Ephrem and Athanasius in addressing the later Cappadocian context.

The intellectual connections among Arius, Aetius, and Eunomius have been well established.[132] Although Aetius and Eunomius do not themselves claim to have adopted (or adapted) the teachings of Arius, their pro-Nicene opponents insistently note connections among their teachings.[133] Arius was most often characterized by his opponents as calling the Son a creature by declaring, "there was when He was not."[134] Arius argued for a theology that preserved above all the uniqueness of God.[135] For Arius, it was of the utmost importance to preserve a distinction between the Son and God the Father. This resulted in his insistence on the distinction of the Son from the Father, which in turn led his opponents to accuse him of subordinating the Son to the status of creature. The pro-Nicene writers who attacked Aetius and Eunomius, on the other hand, complained that these later opponents took the teachings of Arius to an extreme that Arius himself had not articulated. In his teachings, Eunomius emphasized, in contrast to Arius, that some knowledge about God was innate and could be discerned through careful intellectual study.[136] Like Ephrem's criticism of the inappropriate intellectual inquiry of

132. For a recent history of Eunomius, see Richard P. Vaggione, *Eunomius of Cyzicus and the Nicene Revolution* (New York: Oxford, 2000). See also Thomas Kopecek, *A History of Neo-Arianism,* 2 vols. (Cambridge, Mass.: Philadelphia Patristic Foundation, 1970). See also H. M. Gwatkin, *Studies of Arianism,* 2nd ed. (Cambridge, Mass.: Deighton, Bell and Co., 1900; originally 1882; reprint, New York: AMS Press, 1978); H. M. Gwatkin, *The Arian Controversy* (New York: Longmans, Green, and Co., 1914); Robert C. Gregg and Dennis E. Groh, *Early Arianism: A View of Salvation* (Philadelphia: Fortress Press, 1981); Charles Kannengiesser, *Holy Scripture and Hellenistic Hermeneutics in Alexandrian Christology: The Arian Crisis,* Colloquy 41 (Berkeley: Center for Hermeneutical Studies in Hellenistic and Modern Culture, 1982); Charles Kannengiesser, "Arius and the Arians," *JTS* 44 (1983): 456–75; R. C. Gregg, *Arianism: Historical and Theological Reassessments* (Cambridge, Mass.: Philadelphia Patristic Foundation, 1985); R. P. C. Hanson, *The Search for the Doctrine of God: The Arian Controversy 318–381* (Edinburgh: T&T Clark, 1988), 598–636; Rowan Williams, *The Making of Orthodoxy: Essays in Honour of Henry Chadwick* (New York: Cambridge University Press, 1989); Timothy D. Barnes and Rowan Williams, *Arianism after Arius* (Edinburgh: T&T Clark, 1993); Barnes, *Athanasius;* Richard Lim, *Public Disputation, Power, and Social Order in Late Antiquity* (Berkeley: University of California Press, 1995); Maurice Wiles, *Archetypal Heresy: Arianism through the Centuries* (Oxford: Clarendon Press, 1996); L. Ayres and G. Jones, eds., *Christian Origins: Theology, Rhetoric, and Community* (New York: Routledge, 1998); Rowan Williams, *Arius: Heresy and Tradition,* 2nd ed. (London: SCM Press, 2001; originally London: Darton, Longman & Todd, 1987); Ayres, *Nicaea.*

133. See Grg. Nyss., *Eun.* 1.46; Athanasius, *Syn.* 6.1–2.

134. See Athanasius's accusation against Arius in *Ar.* 1.10, 11, 22; *Decr.* 18; *Ep. Afr.* 6.

135. See, for example, the characterization of Arius's views in Philostorgius *HE* 2.3.

136. See, for example, Eunomius, *Apol.* 6.10–17, 7.1–2, 10.8–10.

his opponents, pro-Nicene leaders routinely attacked Aetius and Eunomius as dialecticians and "logic-choppers," referring to their detailed philosophical arguments, their complex theological vocabulary, and their insistence that rational thought could reveal significant knowledge about God.[137] Their opponents also characterized their teachings as emphasizing the generation of the Son in contrast to the ungenerate Father, thereby highlighting the Son's dissimilarity from (and subordination to) the Father.[138] This subordinationist theology differs from that of Arius in that it is not governed by the preservation of an unknowable God, but rather by the more detailed descriptions of the differences between the ungenerate Father and the begotten Son.[139] Despite these significant differences among the teachings of Arius, Aetius, and Eunomius, however, the pro-Nicene writers who confronted them insistently connected them with each other, borrowing condemnations of one to accuse another. After Aetius and Eunomius were condemned at the Council of Seleucia in 359, Eunomius returned to Cyzicus where he wrote his first *Apology* against Nicene Christianity and was ordained bishop. It was Eunomius's *Apology*—a defense of his subordinationist theology—that prompted a heated response from Basil of Caesarea in the form of his *Against Eunomius* (362/3). Years later in 378/9 Eunomius's second apology, *Apology for the Apology*, itself a response to Basil's *Against Eunomius*, likewise sparked active retaliation from Gregory of Nyssa in *Against Eunomius* (early 380s). With the dissemination of his first *Apology* and his new status as bishop, Eunomius entered onto the political and ecclesiastical stage.

In comparison to the writings of Ephrem and Athanasius, the Cappadocians' writings contain relatively few references to Jews, Judaism, and Judaizing.[140] Nonetheless, in his oration *Against the Arians and On His Own Position*, Gregory of Nazianzus does compare his Christian opponents with Jews when he refers to the "new Judaism" of "Arius and those who depend on Arius."[141] In *Against Eunomius*, Gregory of Nyssa likewise refers to the

---

137. See Grg. Naz., *Orat.* 27.2, 29.17–21, 31.18; Grg. Nyss. *Eun.* 2.604.

138. Against Aetius and Eunomius, see Grg. Nyss., *Eun.* 1.46 (NPNF 1.6); Eunomius, *Apology* 7–11, 13–15, 17–28; *Apology for the Apology* i.164, 186, 192–93, 201–2, 216, 271, 332, 334, 337, 362, 364, 367, 373, 382–83, 391, 401; ii.172, 309.

139. See, for example, Eunomius, *Apology for the Apology* 1. See also Vaggione, *Eunomius*, 237–40; Ayres, *Nicaea*, 144–49.

140. This is not to say that others works by Basil do not contain any anti-Jewish rhetoric. See, for example, *Hex.* 9.6 and Runia.

141. Grg. Naz., *Orat.* 33.16. All translations of *Orations* 32–37 are based on the Greek text published in *Discours 32–37* (SC 318), ed. Claudio Moreschini and trans. Paul Gallay (Paris: Editions

subordinationist theology of his opponent Eunomius as "a new Judaism," and explains that he writes his treatise "wishing to show to the listeners the relationship of the doctrine of Eunomius to the thoughts of the Jews."[142] Gregory of Nyssa accuses his Christian opponents of advocating "the Jewish doctrine,"[143] and claims that Eunomius "Judaizes in his doctrine."[144] Like Ephrem and Athanasius, then, the Cappadocians describe the theological Judaizing of their Christian opponents. Unlike the earlier authors, however, they primarily emphasize an alleged inconsistency in their opponents' Christian name and "Jewish" beliefs, rhetorically suggesting that it would be better for them to be either fully Jewish or fully Christian rather than to attempt to maintain their untenable position between the two.

In contrast to Ephrem and Athanasius, the Cappadocian writers generally maintain their opponents' subordinationist Christianity not as conflated with Judaism, but as lying uncomfortably between Christianity and Judaism.[145] Even before Basil became bishop of Caesarea in 370, he actively participated in the ongoing theological struggles of his time. In *Against Eunomius,* he accuses Eunomius of holding Jewish beliefs and then claims that even the Jews' position is more coherent and defensible than that of Eunomius, an argument that both Gregory of Nazianzus and Gregory of Nyssa echo two decades later.[146] All three Cappadocian bishops compare their Christian opponents

---

du Cerf, 1985). Norris argues that although Gregory rarely gives an explicit identity to the opponents of his *Theological Orations,* the charges that Gregory levels against his opponents and the context in which he writes suggests that these "Arians" as Gregory once calls them (*Or.* 31.30) are followers of Eunomius (Frederick W. Norris, *Faith Gives Fullness to Reasoning: The Five Theological Orations of Gregory Nazianzen,* trans. Lionel Wickham, Frederick Williams [New York: Brill, 1991], 53–56).

142. Grg. Nyss., *Eun.* 3.7.8–9 (NPNF 9.1). All quotations of Gregory of Nyssa's *Against Eunomius* are my translations from the Greek text in *Gregorii Nysseni Opera,* vol. I–II: *Contra Eunomium Libri,* ed. Vernerus Jaeger (Berlin: Weidman, 1921), which I cite by Jaeger's notations of book *(Lib.),* volume *(Tom.)* and paragraph number. I have also included in parentheses the book and chapter references to the NPNF English translation because the Jaeger citations are difficult to match to the English translation (*Select Writings and Letters of Gregory, Bishop of Nyssa,* eds. William Moore and Henry Austin Wilson [NPNF, 2nd ser., vol. 5; Eerdmans, 1954]).

143. Grg. Nyss., *Eun.* 1.177 (NPNF 1.15).

144. Grg. Nyss., *Eun.* 3.8.23 (NPNF 10.2).

145. In Basil's arguments against Eunomius, the "Arian" heresies are heretical precisely because of their inappropriate location too close to Judaism and too far from where Christianity ought to be. This is particularly interesting, given that Basil frequently describes Christianity itself as a third category, balanced halfway between Judaism and Hellenism (see David T. Runia, "'Where, Tell Me, Is the Jew . . . ?': Basil, Philo, and Isidore of Pelusium," *VC* 46 [1992]: 172–89).

146. Basil, *Eun.* 1.24; Grg. Naz., *Orat.* 38.15; Grg. Nyss., *Eun.* 3.2.156 (NPNF 4.9); Grg. Nyss., *Eun.* 1.179 (NPNF 1.15).

to the Jewish leaders in the New Testament just as Athanasius and Ephrem did in their writings.[147] Unlike Ephrem and Athanasius, however, who emphasized the similarities of "Arians" and "Jews," tarring their Christian opponents with all the anti-Jewish polemic in their imaginative repertoires, these three Cappadocian writers strictly declare their opponents to be not Jews, but worse than Jews: they are those who falsely claim the name "Christian" but maintain "Jewish" beliefs without (to their detriment) following Jewish traditions such as circumcision.[148] Instead of Ephrem's and Athanasius's threatening rhetorical cry, "Look out—they are Jews!" the Cappadocians instead rhetorically bemoan, "If only they would be Jews!" Just as the earlier authors used comparisons with a clear Jewish community to turn a more nebulous Christian opposition into a clear "Arian" heresy, these later authors use Jews along with this "Arian" category that Athanasius helped to define in order to tar their new opponent Eunomius as heretical. The rhetoric of these three writers shows the continuity of anti-Jewish and anti-Judaizing rhetoric in this dispute, as well as the adaptations that later pro-Nicene authors made to the earlier rhetoric. Briefly comparing the language of Ephrem, Athanasius, and the Cappadocians demonstrates that the Jews served as a common straw figure that pro-Nicene leaders regularly used in their attempts to discredit subordinationist Christian opponents. Within this shared rhetorical strategy, the unique details of each author's polemic undoubtedly reflect the particular context in which, and opponents against whom, he wrote. It is worth noting that while we cannot precisely date Ephrem's texts, his rhetoric in this respect mirrors more closely the earlier Alexandrian language of Athanasius than it does the anti-Eunomian arguments of the Cappadocians.

The writings of John Chrysostom make a significant postscript to the discussion of the use of anti-Jewish and anti-Judaizing language in pro-Nicene writings against opponents with a subordinationist theology. In 386 and 387, John Chrysostom wrote a series of sermons against subordinationist "Anomean" teachings in Antioch, but they do not make such dramatic charges of Judaizing in the ways that either Ephrem and Athanasius or the Cappadocians did.[149] This difference is particularly striking given that Chrysostom interrupted his sermons against the Anomeans in order to present his

147. See, for example, Basil, *Eun.* 1.23; Grg. Nyss., *Eun.* 1.107 (NPNF 1.10).

148. Basil, *Eun.* 1.24.; Grg. Naz., *Orat.* 33.14; Grg. Nyss., *Eun.* 1.179 (NPNF 1.15); Grg. Nyss., *Eun.* 1.262–263 (NPNF 1.21).

149. John Chrysostom, *On the Incomprehensibility of the Nature of God.*

Discourses against Judaizing Christians, which are replete with vitriolic polemic about the errors and dangers posed by Jews and Judaism, as well as with sharp warnings and rebukes against Judaizing Christians. Nonetheless, the anti-Judaizing accusations do not carry over into the anti-Anomean sermons that Chrysostom preached interspersed with these anti-Judaizing sermons. While the concurrent timing of these two sets of sermons provides a tenuous link between them, Chrysostom does not make much of a rhetorical effort to connect the two, aside from one important comment in his *Discourses against Judaizing Christians* that the two subjects are related.[150] Chrysostom, it seems, primarily chastised as too "Jewish" not those who followed a subordinationist Christian theology, but rather "Christians" who participated in "Jewish" practices. Chrysostom's writings certainly did not mark the end of Christian writers using Jews and Judaism to construct a "Jewish" enemy out of another Christian group. Far from it, the connection with Judaism remained a threat that Christians could attach to any opponents who allegedly emphasized, to whatever extent, the humanity over the divinity of the Son, such as Nestorian and Chalcedonian Christians. This charge continues in full force in the later Nestorian controversy, aided by the Nestorian belief that Christ was not born divine (i.e., Mary his mother can not be referred to as "God-bearing"), thus emphasizing his humanity and denying his full (and co-terminus) divinity, as Nestorians' opponents would argue the Jews also do. Likewise, Chalcedonian Christians also sometimes found themselves accused by "Miaphysite" Christians of being too much like Jews.[151] Nonetheless, specifically within the so-called Nicene-Arian conflict, in all of its forms over the decades of the fourth century, Chrysostom's writings reflect a significant shift from the earlier pro-Nicene writings.[152]

---

150. John Chrysostom, *Disc.* 1.1.6.

151. For an introduction to this later use, including examples from primary sources, see Lucas Van Rompay, "A Letter of the Jews to the Emperor Marcian Concerning the Council of Chalcedon," *Orientalia Lovaniensia Periodica* 12 (1981): 215–24.

152. See Paul Harkins's introduction to his translation of Chrysostom's *Discourses against Judaizing Christians* (FC 68). See also J. N. D. Kelly, *Golden Mouth: The Story of John Chrysostom, Ascetic, Preacher, Bishop* (London: Duckworth, 1995), and Sterk, *Renouncing,* for more about Chrysostom's context, and his Anomean opponents. See Fred Allen Grissom, "Chrysostom and the Jews: Studies in Jewish-Christian Relations in Fourth-Century Antioch" (Ph.D. diss., Southern Baptist Theological Seminary, 1978); Robert Wilken, *John Chrysostom and the Jews: Rhetoric and Reality in the Late Fourth Century* (Berkeley: University of California Press, 1983); Klaas A. D. Smelik, "John Chrysostom's Homilies against the Jews: Some Comments," *Nederlands Theologish Tijdschrift* 39 (1985): 194–200; Adolf Martin Ritter, "John Chrysostom and the Jews: A Reconsideration," in *Ancient Christianity in the Caucasus,* ed. Tamila Mgaloblishvili

"Jews" and "Arians" in Syria

Placing Ephrem's rhetoric back into his most immediate context of eastern Syria demonstrates most fully the significance of these discussions for fourth-century Syriac Christianity and the religious make-up of Nisibis and Edessa. Ephrem uses anti-Jewish language to warn his Christian audience away from both "real" Jewish festivals and also from Heteroousian Christians, whom he sometimes paints in the negative images of New Testament Jews. Ephrem thus uses Jews in his writings to refer both to fourth-century people, as well as to rhetorically constructed biblical images with which he threatens his Christian audience. In the vocabulary of Judith Lieu, Ephrem uses the language of "the Jews" to signify "image" as well as "reality."[153] When Ephrem uses "the Jews" to warn his audience against subordinationist Christian teachings, however, we must likewise question whether these "Arians" are any more "real" than "the Jews." This investigation suggests that Ephrem's descriptions of those who promote subordinationist beliefs *are* equally nuanced, fighting against "real" subordinationist teachings that held sway politically in the second half of the fourth century in Syria, and also against a rhetorically imagined opponent, the threat of whom strengthened Ephrem's attempts to pull his community tightly together within his imperial ideal of pro-Nicene Christianity. Ephrem's comments about his Jewish and subordinationist Christian opponents seem to slip elusively between *descriptive* and *prescriptive* language, purporting to describe his local context even as his rhetoric seems to attempt to call into existence the very "reality" he claims to describe. There is, of course, no magical reading grid with which to sift some hypothetically "real" from "rhetorical" descriptions, and Ephrem's poetic traces necessarily lie somewhere between the two. Recognizing his rhetorical sophistication does, however, caution against interpreting his language about "Jews" and "Arians" too simplistically.

(Surrey, England: Curzon, 1998), 141–52, 231–32; Kelly, *Golden Mouth;* and Pieter W. van der Horst, "Jews and Christians in Antioch at the End of the Fourth Century," in *Christian-Jewish Relations through the Centuries,* eds. Stanley E. Porter, Brook W. R. Pearson (Sheffield: Sheffield Academic Press, 2000), 228–38. Smelik, "John Chrysostom's," counters Wilken, *John Chrysostom,* and argues that John Chrysostom's primary opponents in these homilies are Jews rather than Judaizing Christians. While I agree with Smelik that Chrysostom's interest was in separating clearly the church and the synagogue, I agree with Wilken that the immediate provocation for these homilies is church-going "Christians" attending "Jewish" festivals.

153. Judith M. Lieu, *Image and Reality: The Jews in the World of the Christians in the Second Century* (Edinburgh: T&T Clark, 1996).

Ephrem is concerned with making Nicene not only the behavior but also the theology of his Christian congregation. What Ephrem's "real" and "rhetorical" uses of "the Jews" have in common is not only to charge his Judaizing and "Arian" opponents with an inappropriate "Jewishness," but to emphasize that they both threaten the boundaries of Nicene orthodoxy. It is in this guise, as a strident proponent of Nicene orthodoxy that Ephrem connects and attacks these two threats to his Christian flock.

But if "Jews" are not always Jews in Ephrem's rhetoric, we must certainly also question just who and where these "Arian" Christians were, and how "real" they appear to have been to Ephrem. Ephrem's writings attest to his familiarity with Arius and refer to the trouble caused by "Arians and Aetians."[154] The specific language with which Ephrem condemns his subordinationist opponents in his *Hymns against Heresies,* and *Sermons on Faith,* that is, by condemning them for their insistent intellectual inquiry, further supports the conclusion that in these texts Ephrem was reacting not only to subordinationist Christianity generally, but to a particular strand of it that had been influenced by the teachings of Aetius. Although Ephrem's arguments are not as detailed as are contemporary Greek conversations, his language suggests that, like Athanasius and the Cappadocians, by the middle of the fourth century he too is fighting against this politically dominant threat to Nicene Christianity. Ephrem demonstrates his knowledge of the threat of subordinationist teachings, as well as the general content of those teachings, echoing Greek Nicene challenges to the particularly Aetian (and later Eunomian) flavor of these teachings. What is not yet clear, however, is what the nature of this "Arian" or "Aetian" threat was in Nisibis and Edessa.

When Ephrem criticizes those in his "Christian" audience whom he accuses of Judaizing by participating in Jewish festivals, he is clear in his use of pronouns that those in his audience are part of a Christian "we," even though they are dangerously being tempted away by a rhetorically distant Jewish "they."[155] The impression that this language gives is that the synagogue and the church are distinct, and that the Judaizing Christians belong in Ephrem's Christian church congregation, but are being tempted by the physical and ideological "other" of the synagogue of Jews. Although I argue that the ideological separation between church and synagogue is not yet in

154. Ephrem, *CH* 24.19, 22.4. Ephrem refers to "Arians" in *CH* 22.4, 22.20, 24.12, and 24.16; and to "Arius" in *CH* 24.19, 21. (See also "Arian" in *Comm. Diat.* 12.9.)

155. See, for example, *SdF* 3.289.

Ephrem's time as great as his rhetoric implies, his language does imply that "Jews" and "Christians" belong in different places.

This language is notably different from the language that Ephrem uses when he speaks of subordinationist Christian teachings. While the Jews with whom Ephrem compares the errant Christians remain "other," the errant Christians themselves remain part of the Christian community. For example, in *Hymns on Faith* 44 he warns that through their seeking, his opponents turn the Son into a creature whom they then worship idolatrously: "Do not [you, sg.] commit adultery and bear for *us* a Messiah that does not exist, and [do not] deny the one that exists. . . . Do not depict with *your* intellect a divination of your mind and an offspring of *your* thought. . . . [You] committed adultery in *investigating* and conceived and bore for *us* a Messiah of constructions."[156] As much as Ephrem warns the "you" in his audience about the dangers of those who search God inappropriately, they nonetheless remain part of the Christian "we" who worship the Messiah. Ephrem's language implies that he is dealing in his own local context not with a separate congregation of "Arian" Christians, or a particular local "heretical" leader who is physically taking Ephrem's congregants away from his church, but rather with the threat of those teachings infiltrating the Christians in his own congregation, perhaps even without them realizing that these imperially supported teachings are in error according to Ephrem's Nicene boundaries for his congregation.

When Ephrem describes the so-called Nicene-Arian conflict, he describes it as a temporary and painful struggle within the Christian community, not as the necessary separation of two distinct communities such as Christians and Jews. In *Hymns on Faith* 87 and *Sermons on Faith* 6, for example, he hopes for Christian unity under an imperial Nicene Christianity, and even blames "Arian" Christian leaders for misleading the emperor, who should otherwise unite his empire under Nicene Christian "truth."[157] Ephrem emphasizes that although some Christians have been misled in their Christianity; they are all still Christians and ought to heal their intellectual fractures. For Ephrem the synagogue is separate and other, but these Christians stray in their minds even as they remain Christians whom he addresses as part of his own (insistently Nicene) congregation.

---

156. Ephrem, *HdF* 44.10–11.
157. *SdF* 6; *HdF* 87.

In comparison to the rhetoric of Athanasius, Ephrem's poetic polemic against subordinationist teachings, and the Christians who support them, sounds rather general and vague. He does not cite his opponents' writings or spoken claims, except to outline generally their teachings about "the creature" and their mode of intellectual inquiry. As with the problem of Judaizing, so too with this controversy Ephrem criticizes in an effort to make his congregation conform to the boundaries of Nicene orthodoxy. Just as he draws clear boundaries for their behavior with respect to Judaizing and Nicene orthodoxy, so too, he delineates clear lines between orthodox and heretical teachings about God and God's Son, fighting not against a separate Nisibene or Edessene "Arian" church, but against the non-Nicene teachings currently dominating the empire that might infiltrate his community and lead his flock astray. Thus while Ephrem seems to warn against "real" fourth-century teachings, the rhetorical opponents whom his poetry paints are again "image" as well as "reality," a constructed clear threatening and dangerous "other" with which he attempts to frighten his listeners to take shelter behind the safe walls of Nicene orthodoxy.

Conclusion

Fourth-century Christianity in the Roman Empire was consumed by religious leaders' struggles to secure imperial authority, pitting pro-Nicene Christians against opponents with various subordinationist theological views. The status of the different Christian factions vacillated, depending on which Christian leaders had gained the emperor's support at any given time. Although pro-Nicene Christians had support in the West throughout much of the fourth century, this was not the case in the East where emperors routinely exiled bishops who supported the Council of Nicaea and filled their positions with episcopal appointments more in line with a subordinationist theology. Within these intra-Christian controversies, Judaism played a unique and significant role. Because their opponents subordinated the Son to the Father, pro-Nicene leaders such as Ephrem and Athanasius compared their opponents' beliefs to those of the Jews who in the Gospel of John expressed concern that Jesus made himself equal to God.[158] Rudolf Lorenz's in-depth study of early Christians' rhetorical connections between "Arians" and Jews concludes that

158. John 5:18.

there is no reason to suspect that Arius and his followers were "really" any more likely to follow the Jewish Law than any other Christians.[159] This did not, however, prevent their pro-Nicene opponents from leveling Judaizing charges against them in order to condemn the validity of "Arian" Christianity. The precise contemporaries Athanasius and Ephrem, in the process of defining and actively reifying "Arians" as a cohesive (and heretical) group, both used very sharp anti-Jewish and anti-Judaizing language in order more clearly to define and more easily to denigrate their opponents. By conflating their contemporary opponents with Jews, these authors concurrently portrayed them unfavorably and as non-Christians.

Within his specifically Syrian context, Ephrem, writing when the fate of Nicene Christianity was anything but certain, struggles to present his audience with a sharply crystallized social reality. Using Scripture and history, he portrays Christians as the heirs of God's promises to Israel, Jews as divinely rejected and threatening enemies, his Christian opponents as "searchers" who stray dangerously near the Jews, and Nicene Christians as the only true Christians. The rhetoric examined here emphasizes Ephrem's portrayal of the relative positions, connections, and tenets of these various religious communities. Ephrem's rhetoric assumes that Nicene Christianity *is* Christianity. The correlating reverse side of this assumption is Ephrem's belief that any non-Nicene Christianity, such as that of his opponents, is not "Christianity" at all. Like the scriptural historical narratives discussed in chapter three, these assumptions serve a legitimating function for Ephrem through the "universalization" of the desire to be Christian and the "narrativization" of Nicene Christianity as the only legitimate bearer of that title.[160]

Closely aligned with Ephrem's assumption that subordinationist Christianity is, de facto, not true Christianity, are his insistent attempts to conflate its adherents with the Jews. Taken together, Ephrem's presentations of Nicene Christians as "Christians" and his comparisons of his opponents with "Jews" offer strong rhetorical support for his right to claim Christian authority for Nicene Christianity. His unqualified references to Nicene Christianity as "Christianity" veil the fact that Nicene Christianity is one type of Christianity among others, each claiming to be the one true Christianity. Likewise, his association of the "searchers" with the Jews rhetorically denies the distinc-

---

159. Lorenz, *Arius*, esp. 141–79.
160. For more specific definitions of this vocabulary, see Thompson, *Ideology,* 61.

tions that would be clear between these two groups if he referred to them as "Christians" and "Jews," respectively. Through the displacement of categories of contested value, "(true) Nicene Christian" and "(Homoian) 'searching' Christian," onto categories of accepted value, "Christian" and "Jew," "the positive or negative connotations of the term are transferred to the other object,"[161] valuing Ephrem's Nicene Christians highly at the expense of his allegedly Jew-like opponents.

In addition to legitimating Ephrem's claim to Christianity (and concurrently delegitimating the others' ability to make a similar claim), his anti-Jewish rhetoric also plays a critical role in defining the community boundaries of the world that he and his audience inhabit. Ephrem's anti-Jewish rhetoric frequently struggles concurrently to sharpen a distinction between two ambiguous Christianities and to conflate the more clearly distinct communities of Jews and adherents to subordinationist Christianity. To begin with, Ephrem's use of anti-Jewish rhetoric hardens an "us" and "them" distinction between Christians and Jews, concealing differences among Christians by unifying them under the title "Christian." Ephrem's rhetoric thus parallels much ideological language "by constructing, at the symbolic level, a form of unity which embraces individuals in a collective identity, irrespective of the differences and divisions that may separate them."[162] The purchase for Ephrem is that his use of "Christian" as a synonym for "Nicene Christian" forces his opponents to choose between the two monolithic categories of (Nicene) Christianity and Judaism; Ephrem's rhetoric erases subordinationist Christianity, rhetorically denying that the definition of "Christian" is still contested.

At the same time as Ephrem constructs a unified Christianity, however, he simultaneously warns his audience that under his (definitive) definition, his "searching" opponents do not qualify as Christians, so that while in theory Ephrem includes his opponents as part of a Christian "we," the sine qua non of their membership is their acceptance of Nicene tenets. "Christians" who fail to comply with Ephrem's definition find themselves suddenly and violently forced by his rhetoric into the category of "Jews." In the process of describing a binary world with rigid community boundaries, Ephrem portrays these Christians as both threatened by the Jews (who threaten all Christians, but especially those who wander from the safety of orthodoxy) and as

161. Thompson, *Ideology*, 62.
162. Thompson, *Ideology*, 64.

a threat, like the Jews, to true (Nicene) Christians. Ephrem calls for all Christians to unite against the harmful, threatening Jews, and also warns that true (Nicene) Christians must also beware and unite against the imminent "Jewish" threat of subordinationist Christianity.

As we can see throughout Ephrem's writings, though most explicitly in his writings *de fide,* Ephrem frequently and significantly conflates his Christian opponents with Jews. Denying the bitter contemporary struggle for Christian legitimacy, authority, legality, and political support in the fourth-century Roman Empire, Ephrem describes a clearly bounded Christian community, governed by Nicene authority and defined in sharp distinction to the dangerously threatening Jews. Using these rhetorical strategies, Ephrem presents the wayward Christians with a crystal-clear choice: either join God's chosen people in the true church of Nicene Christianity or else doom yourself through your Pharisee-like searching and seeking to subject the Son to a second passion and to call down upon yourselves God's rejection and condemnation. Aside from confirming simply that Ephrem's writings, like those of many other Christian leaders in late antiquity, include an abundance of anti-Jewish language, this demonstrates some of the hitherto unrecognized complexity and nuance of Ephrem's pro-Nicene anti-Judaism. This picture only strengthens the recent academic challenge to earlier depictions of Syriac Christianity as largely isolated from the rest of Roman Christianity. Ephrem emerges from this study as an active and rhetorically astute participant in fourth-century Nicene Christians' struggle to gain authority in the Roman Empire, using anti-Jewish language like his contemporary Athanasius in an effort to define Nicene Christianity as "Christianity," and Christianity as the religious orthodoxy of the Roman Empire.[163]

163. Compare Paul Russell's conclusions (Russell, *Arians,* 4), as well as those of Sidney Griffith ("Deacon"). See also Averil Cameron, *Christianity and the Rhetoric of Empire: The Development of Christian Discourse* (Berkeley: University of California Press, 1991).

ʕ୨ଓʔ

Syria and the Construction of
Christian Orthodoxy

The unique relationship between Judaism and Syriac Christianity has traditionally facilitated eastern Syria's isolation in scholarship on the Roman Empire and early Christian history.[1] Using Ephrem's Syriac texts as a starting point for understanding the role that anti-Jewish language played in the theological controversies of the fourth century not only relocates eastern Syria firmly within political and cultural exchanges of the Roman Empire, but also challenges traditional narratives of early Christian history. Recognizing that early Christianity did not suddenly and radically separate from other forms of Judaism better allows for an understanding of the complex relationship between the synagogue and those whom Ephrem calls Christians in Syria. Rather than a unique datum that stands apart from the rest of early Christian history, in this new narrative Syriac Christianity emerges as a significant part of this history, in active conversation with other Christian leaders.

Fourth-century Christians used both Greek and Syriac anti-Jewish rhetoric to naturalize their construction of an imperial orthodoxy that excluded their Christian opponents. In eastern Syria, in a context of multiple and somewhat fluid religious alternatives, Ephrem's vitriolic anti-Jewish language upheld Nicene expectations in the face of those in his congregation who would literally Judaize, and those Homoian and Heteroousian Christians who, he

1. See Christine Shepardson, "Syria, Syriac, Syrian: Negotiating East and West in Late Antiquity," in *The Blackwell Companion to Late Antiquity*, ed. Philip Rousseau (Blackwell Press, 2008, forthcoming).

claims, theologically Judaize in their treatment of the Son. In the service of promoting Nicene orthodoxy, Ephrem uses liturgical anti-Jewish rhetoric to spread his message about the new Nicene boundaries of his Christian community. Like numerous Christians before him, Ephrem found anti-Jewish rhetoric a particularly useful language with which to define the limits of Christianity, and like Athanasius and the Cappadocians, he deployed it to castigate the subordinationist theology of his Christian opponents. Wielding scriptural narratives as well as contemporary criticisms, Ephrem shaped an ideal community out of his complex context: Jews are a dangerous and divinely rejected people, Christians follow the Council of Nicaea, and there is no middle ground between these two on which Judaizing or theologically errant "Christians" can stand.

Control of eastern Syria shifted back and forth between the Persian and Roman Empires in antiquity. Kathleen McVey notes, "When Jacob was appointed the first bishop of Nisibis in 308/9, it is probable that his appointment was made through the hierarchy within the Roman Empire rather than in Persia—an indirect consequence of the reestablishment of Roman Imperial control in the region."[2] Thus, with the beginning of the fourth century, eastern Syriac Christianity had new political motivation to look west to the Roman Empire, and after 325 Roman Christianity itself had a new political edge with which to impose "orthodoxy" among Christians under Roman control. Jacob and Ephrem oversaw the subjection of Nisibene Christianity to Roman law, and judging from Ephrem's writings they both embraced Nicene Christianity with open arms. It was only after the Council of Nicaea that local church leaders had an imperially supported model against which they could measure their own local church. Fourth-century Syria was not unique in having a Christianity that in the early fourth century was still strongly colored by local beliefs and traditions. Of course, Christianity's diversity continued to flourish after the Council, but at the same time, numerous leaders around the empire struggled to meld the newly imperial model with their own local churches. It is this context, familiar to Christian leaders throughout the empire, in which Ephrem wrote and from which we can most productively interpret him. Recognizing this compels scholars to include Syriac Christianity firmly within scholarship on Christianity in the Roman Empire.

---

2. Kathleen McVey, "Introduction," in *Ephrem the Syrian: Hymns*, ed. and trans. Kathleen McVey (New York: Paulist Press, 1989), 8.

This study implies several adjustments to the traditional picture of Syriac Christianity. Early Syriac Christianity does historically share some connection with local Judaism, but this should neither be uncritically connected with "Jewish-Christianity," nor should scholars use Ephrem's fourth-century rhetoric to justify such a characterization. Recent critical studies demonstrate similarities in exegetical style and content between Jewish traditions and those of Syriac Christian authors such as Ephrem. These shared traditions reflect (and undoubtedly facilitated) some continued permeability and contact between the Syriac church and the synagogue in Ephrem's time, which itself aggravated Ephrem's anti-Jewish rhetoric because of his heightened need to delineate clear new boundaries for his Christian community. Just as he defined "Christianity" in Nisibis and Edessa to include Christians with a Nicene, but not a subordinationist, view of the Son, he also defined the boundaries such that he excluded Christians whose behaviors did not fit the Nicene mold because they were too close to Judaism.

Ephrem's anti-Judaizing charges point beyond the earlier mobility of Scripture between the church and the synagogue in Syria to the additional question of the mobility of fourth-century individuals between the two. Some of Ephrem's anti-Jewish rhetoric does appear to target Judaizing Christians—those who, like the audience Ephrem describes in his *Hymns on Unleavened Bread,* attend his church and also celebrate the Jewish Passover. This does not necessarily confirm either that Ephrem's Syriac church was the object of Jewish proselytizing or that Ephrem's rhetoric is evidence of a prevalent "Jewish-Christianity" that characterizes the fourth-century Syriac church. Scholars have long agreed that John Chrysostom wrote his *Discourses against Judaizing Christians* to address a similar concern, that some of his fourth-century church members were attending Jewish festivals, and yet unlike for Syriac Christianity this has, for good reasons, not led to a scholarly consensus that Antiochene Christianity was particularly Jewish throughout its early history. From the fourth century, Ephrem introduces us to a Syriac Christianity that he is determined to bring into line with the tenets of Nicene orthodoxy.

In addition to redrawing constructions of early connections between Jews and Christians in Syria, this analysis reveals that Ephrem's anti-Jewish language attacks not only Jews and Judaizers but also Christians who subordinate the Son to the Father. In an effort to reify his ideals through his very descriptions of them as reality, Ephrem constructs his contemporary world as well as its history through his careful presentation of Scripture. Through the clearly defined boundaries that Ephrem draws around Christians and Jews, he is able to describe his Christian opponents in such a way that they fall short of his definition of "Christian" and therefore find themselves slipping into the non-Christian category of "Jew." Creating binary oppositions out of the more fluid reality of his fourth-century context, Ephrem defines "Jew" as antithetical to "Christian" and his Christian opponents as non-Christian and like Jews; and then uses the anti-Jewish rhetoric that permeates his hymns in order to attack both of these alleged threats to his Nicene Christian ideal.

Finally, this analysis supplements the recent scholarship, such as the work of Sidney Griffith, that challenges the traditional separation of fourth-century Syriac Christianity and the writings of Ephrem from wider studies of fourth-century Christianity in the Roman Empire. Comparing Ephrem's use of anti-Jewish language with that of some of his Greek-speaking Nicene contemporaries proves fruitful in illuminating the role of anti-Jewish language within the fourth-century controversy over the nature of the Son, as well as in connecting Ephrem's concerns and language with those of his Greek contemporaries. Given Ephrem's own depiction of himself and his congregation as active participants in empire-wide events and controversies, his texts cannot adequately be interpreted outside of this larger imperial context. Far from being a theologically unsophisticated poet on the religious and geographical fringes of imperial Christianity, Ephrem emerges as a vocal Nicene Christian leader struggling to prevail in the topsy-turvy political and religious context of the fourth-century eastern Empire.

We are thus able to refocus our picture of early Syriac Christianity, the parameters of early Christian anti-Jewish language and its role in fourth-century intra-Christian controversies, the connection of fourth-century Syria to the Roman Empire more broadly, and the details of the Christian communities of Nisibis and Edessa under Ephrem's tutelage. Unsettled by what he saw as the unmonitored permeability of the boundaries of his local church communities, Ephrem marshaled his vast poetic and rhetorical skills in an effort to define clearly right from wrong, Christian from non-Christian, and to coerce his audience to remain within his newly Nicene Christian community. With his anti-Jewish scriptural narratives defining their reality, his anti-Jewish imperatives demanding their attention, and his anti-Jewish songs reverberating in their ears, his church attendees did indeed find themselves subject to active religious proselytism, but at the hands of the pro-Nicene deacon of the Christian church. Although the Council of Nicaea did not resolve the intra-Christian conflict of the fourth-century Roman Empire, it did provide a new model of imperial orthodoxy that its proponents were quick to promote. Given the nature of the fourth-century theological controversies, anti-Jewish rhetoric offered pro-Nicene leaders a persuasive tool with which to construct Nicene Christianity as the religious orthodoxy of the empire.

Bibliography

Primary Sources

Ammianus Marcellinus. *Res gestae.* Text and translation in *Ammianus Marcellinus,* 3 vols. Edited by J. C. Rolfe. LCL. Cambridge, Mass.: Harvard University Press, 1963–1964.

Aphrahat. *Demonstrationes.* PS 1.1–2 English translation of *Demonstrations* 11–13, 15–19, 21 and, 23 in Jacob Neusner. *Aphrahat and Judaism: The Christian Anti-Jewish Argument in Fourth-Century Iran.* Leiden: Brill, 1971.

Arius. *Epistula ad Alexandrum Alexandrinum.* Text in *Athanasius Werke,* vol. 3. *Urkunden zur Geschichte des arianischen Streits: 318–328.* Doc. 6. Edited by Hans-Georg Opitz. Berlin: W. de Gruyter, 1936.

———. *Epistula ad Eusebium Nicomediensem.* Text in *Athanasius Werke,* vol. 3. *Urkunden zur Geschichte des arianischen Streits: 318–328.* Doc. 6.3. Edited by Hans-Georg Opitz. Berlin: W. de Gruyter, 1936.

Athanasius. *Ad afros epistola synodica.* PG 26. English translation in Archibald Robertson. *Select Writings and Letters of Athanasius, Bishop of Alexandria.* NPNF, 2nd series, vol. 4. New York: Christian Literature Company, 1892. Reprint, Edinburgh, 1987.

———. *De decretis synodi.* Text in *Athanasius Werke,* vol. 2.1. Edited by Hans-Georg Opitz. Berlin: W. de Gruyter, 1936, 1–45. English translation in Archibald Robertson. *Select Writings and Letters of Athanasius, Bishop of Alexandria.* NPNF, 2nd series, vol. 4. New York: Christian Literature Company, 1892. Reprint, Edinburgh, 1987.

———. *De incarnatione.* Text and English translation in *Contra Gentes and De Incarnatione.* Edited by R. W. Thomson. Oxford Early Christian Texts. Oxford: Oxford University Press, 1971.

———. *De sententia Dionysii.* Text in *Athanasius Werke,* vol. 2.1. Edited by Hans-Georg Opitz. Berlin: W. de Gruyter, 1936. English translation in Archibald Robertson. *Select Writings and Letters of Athanasius, Bishop of Alexandria.* NPNF, 2nd series, vol. 4. New York: Christian Literature Company, 1892. Reprint, Edinburgh, 1987.

———. *De synodis.* Text in *Athanasius Werke,* vol. 2.1. Edited by Hans-Georg Opitz. Berlin: W. de Gruyter, 1936, 231–40. English translation in Archibald Robertson. *Select Writings and Letters of Athanasius, Bishop of Alexandria.* NPNF, 2nd series, vol. 4. New York: Christian Literature Company, 1892. Reprint, Edinburgh, 1987.

———. *Epistulae.* PG 26: 529–648. English translation in Archibald Robertson. *Select Writings and Letters of Athanasius, Bishop of Alexandria.* NPNF, 2nd series, vol. 4. New York: Christian Literature Company, 1892. Reprint, Edinburgh, 1987.

————. *Festal Letters (Syriac)*. Text in *The Festal Letters of Athanasius*. Edited by William Cureton. London: Society for the Publication of Oriental Texts, 1848. English translation in Archibald Robertson. *Select Writings and Letters of Athanasius, Bishop of Alexandria*. NPNF, 2nd series, vol. 4. New York: Christian Literature Company, 1892. Reprint, Edinburgh, 1987.

————. *Historia arianorum ad monachos*. Text in *Athanasius Werke*, vol. 2.1. Edited by Hans-Georg Opitz. Berlin: W. de Gruyter, 1936, 183–230. English translation in Archibald Robertson. *Select Writings and Letters of Athanasius, Bishop of Alexandria*. NPNF, 2nd series, vol. 4. New York: Christian Literature Company, 1892. Reprint, Edinburgh, 1987.

————. *Orationes contra arianos*. PG 26. English translation in Archibald Robertson. *Select Writings and Letters of Athanasius, Bishop of Alexandria*. NPNF, 2nd series, vol. 4. New York: Christian Literature Company, 1892. Reprint, Edinburgh, 1987.

————. *Vita Antonii*. Text and French translation in *Vie d'Antoine*. Edited by G. J. M. Bartelink. SC 400. Paris: Éditions du Cerf, 1994.

Basil. *Contra eunomium*. Text and French translation in *Contre Eunome*. 2 vols. Edited by Bernard Sesboüé, Georges-Matthieu de Durand, and Louis Doutreleau. SC 299, 305. Paris: Éditions du Cerf, 1982, 1983.

————. *Hexameron 1–9*. Text and French translation in *Contre Eunome*. 2 vols. Edited by Stanislas Giet. SC 26. Paris: Éditions du Cerf, 1968.

Chronicle of Edessa. Text in *Chronica minora, I*. Edited by Ignatius Guidi. CSCO 1, SS 1. Louvain: Imprimerie Orientaliste, 1955.

Constitutiones apostolorum. Edited by Franciscus Xaverius Funk. *Didascalia et Constitutiones Apostolorum*. Paderbornae: Ferdinani Schoeningh Library, 1905.

De Dea Syria. Text and English translation in *The Syrian Goddess (De Dea Syria) Attributed to Lucian*. Edited and translated by H. W. Attridge and R. A. Oden. Society of Biblical Literature Texts and Translations, 9. Missoula: SBL, 1976.

Didascalia Apostolorum. Text and English translation in *The Didascalia Apostolorim in Syriac*. 2 vols. Edited by Arthur Vööbus. CSCO 401, SS 175. Louvain: Secretariat of the CSCO, 1979.

Ephrem. *Carmina Nisibena*. Text and German translation in *Des Heiligen Ephraem des Syrers Carmina Nisibena*. 4 vols. Edited by Edmund Beck. CSCO 218–219, 240–241, SS 2–93, 102–103. Louvain: Secretariat of the CSCO, 1961, 1963.

————. *Commentary on the Diatessaron*. Text in *Saint Ephrem: Commentaire de l'Evangile Concordant, Texte Syriaque (Manuscrit Chester Beatty 709)*. Edited by Louis Leloir. Dublin: Hodges, Figgies & Co., 1963. And *Saint Ephrem: Commentaire de l'Evangile Concordant, Texte Syriaque (Manuscrit Chester Beatty 709), Folios Additionnels*. Edited by Louis Leloir. Louvain: Peeters, 1990. English translation in *Saint Ephrem's Commentary on the Diatessaron: An English Translation of Chester Beatty Syriac MS 709 with Introducion and Notes. Journal of Semitic Studies* Supplement 2. Carmel McCarthy. Oxford: Oxford University Press, 1993.

————. *Commentary on Exodus*. Text in *Sancti Ephraem Syri in Genesim et in Exodum Commentarii*. 2 vols. Edited by R. M. Tonneau. CSCO 152–153, SS 71–72. Louvain: Secretariat of the CSCO, 1955. English translation in Edward Mathews and Joseph Amar. *St. Ephrem the Syrian, Selected Prose Works: Commentary on Genesis, Commentary on Exodus, Homily on our Lord, Letter to Publius*. FC 91. Washington, D.C.: The Catholic University of American Press, 1994, 217–65.

———. *Commentary on Genesis.* Text in *Sancti Ephraem Syri in Genesim et in Exodum Commentarii.* 2 vols. Edited by R. M. Tonneau. CSCO 152–153, SS 71–72. Louvain: Secretariat of the CSCO, 1955. English translation in Edward Mathews and Joseph Amar. *St. Ephrem the Syrian, Selected Prose Works: Commentary on Genesis, Commentary on Exodus, Homily on our Lord, Letter to Publius.* FC 91. Washington, D.C.: The Catholic University of American Press, 1994, 59–213.

———. *Contra Haereses.* Text and German translation in *Des Heiligen Ephraem des Syrers Hymnen contra Haereses.* 2. vols. Edited by Edmund Beck. CSCO 169–170, SS 76–77. Louvain: Imprimerie Orientaliste, 1957.

———. *Hymnen contra Julianum.* Text and German translation in *Des Heiligen Ephraem des Syrers Hymnen de Paradiso und Contra Julianum.* 2 vols. Edited by Edmund Beck. CSCO 174–175, SS 78–79. Louvain: Secretariat of the CSCO, 1957. English translation in Kathleen McVey. *Ephrem the Syrian: Hymns.* New York: Paulist Press, 1989, 227–57.

———. *Hymnen de azymis.* Text and German translation in *Des Heiligen Ephraem des Syrers Paschahymnen.* 2 vols. Edited by Edmund Beck. CSCO 248–249, SS 108–109. Louvain: Secretariat of the CSCO, 1964.

———. *Hymnen de crucifixione.* Text and German translation in *Des Heiligen Ephraem des SyrersPaschahymnen.* 2 vols. Edited by Edmund Beck. CSCO 248–249, SS 108–109. Louvain: Secretariat of the CSCO, 1964.

———. *Hymnen de ecclesia.* Text and German translation in *Des Heiligen Ephraem des Syrers Hymnen de Ecclesia.* 2 vols. Edited by Edmund Beck. CSCO 198–199, SS 84–85. Louvain: Secretariat of the CSCO, 1960.

———. *Hymnen de fide.* Text and German translation in *Des Heiligen Ephraem des Syrers Hymnen de Fide.* 2 vols. Edited by Edmund Beck. CSCO 154–155, SS 73–74. Louvain: Secretariat of the CSCO, 1955.

———. *Hymnen de ieiunio.* Text and German translation in *Des Heiligen Ephraem des Syrers Hymnen de Ieiunio.* 2 vols. Edited by Edmund Beck. CSCO 246–247, SS 106–107. Louvain: Secretariat of the CSCO, 1964.

———. *Hymnen de nativitate.* Text and German translation in *Des Heiligen Ephraem des Syrers Hymnen de Nativitate (Epiphania).* 2 vols. Edited by Edmund Beck. CSCO 186–187, SS 82–83. Louvain: Secretariat of the CSCO, 1959. English translation in Kathleen McVey. *Ephrem the Syrian: Hymns.* New York: Paulist Press, 1989, 63–217.

———. *Hymnen de paradiso.* Text and German translation in *Des Heiligen Ephraem des Syrers Hymnen de Paradiso und Contra Julianum.* 2 vols. Edited by Edmund Beck. CSCO 174–175, SS 78–79. Louvain: Secretariat of the CSCO, 1957. English translation in Sebastian Brock. *St. Ephrem the Syrian: Hymns on Paradise.* New York: St. Vladimir's Seminary Press, 1990.

———. *Hymnen de resurrectione.* Text and German translation in *Des Heiligen Ephraem des Syrers Paschahymnen.* 2 vols. Edited by Edmund Beck. CSCO 248–249, SS 108–109. Louvain: Secretariat of the CSCO, 1964.

———. *Hymnen de virginitate.* Text and German translation in *Des Heiligen Ephraem des Syrers Hymnen de Virginitate.* 2 vols. Edited by Edmund Beck. CSCO 223–224, SS 94–95. Louvain: Secretariat of the CSCO, 1962. English translation in Kathleen McVey. *Ephrem the Syrian: Hymns.* New York: Paulist Press, 1989, 259–468.

———. *Prose Refutations.* Text and English translation in *S. Ephraim's Prose Refutations, I.* Edited by C. W. Mitchell. London: Williams and Norgate, 1912. And

S. Ephraim's Prose Refutations, II. Edited by A. A. Bevan and F. C. Burkitt. London: Williams and Norgate, 1921.

———. *Sermo I (Nineveh).* Text and German translation in *Des Heiligen Ephraem des Syrers, Sermones II.* Edited by Edmund Beck. CSCO 311–312, SS 134–135. Louvain: Secretariat of the CSCO, 1970.

———. *Sermo de domino nostro.* Text and German translation in *Des Heiligen Ephraem des Syrers Sermo de Domino Nostro.* 2 vols. Edited by Edmund Beck. CSCO 270–271, SS 116–117. Louvain: Secretariat of the CSCO, 1966. English translation in Edward Mathews and Joseph Amar. *St. Ephrem the Syrian, Selected Prose Works: Commentary on Genesis, Commentary on Exodus, Homily on our Lord, Letter to Publius.* FC 91. Washington, D.C.: The Catholic University of America Press, 1994, 269–332.

———. *Sermones de fide.* Text and German translation in *Des Heiligen Ephraem des Syrers Sermones de Fide.* 2 vols. Edited by Edmund Beck. CSCO 212–213, SS 88–89. Louvain: Secretariat of the CSCO, 1961.

Epiphanius. *Panarion.* Text in *Epiphanius Werke,* 3 vols. Edited by Karl Holl. GCS 25, 31, 37. Leipzig: J. C. Hinrichs, 1915–33. English translation in Frank Williams. *The Panarion of Epiphanius of Salamis.* Nag Hammadi [and Manichaean] Studies 35–36. Leiden: Brill, 1987–1994.

Epistle of Barnabas. Text and French translation in *Epître de Barnabe: Greek Text.* Edited by R. A. Kraft. Translated by K. Prigent. SC 172. Paris: Éditions du Cerf, 1971.

Eunomius. *Apology.* Text and English translation in *Eunomius: The Extant Works.* Edited by Richard Paul Vaggione. Oxford: Clarendon Press, 1987.

———. *Apology for the Apology.* Text and English translation in *Eunomius: The Extant Works.* Edited by Richard Paul Vaggione. Oxford: Clarendon Press, 1987.

Eusebius of Caesarea. *Demonstratio evangelica.* Text in *Eusebius Werke,* vol. 2. Edited by Eduard Schwartz, T. Mommsen, and F. Winckelmann. GCS n.f. 6.1–3. Berlin: Academy Press, 1999.

———. *Historia ecclesiastica.* Text and French translation in *Eusèbe de Césarée.* Edited by Gustave Bardy. SC 55. Paris: Éditions du Cerf, 1958.

———. *Preparatio evangelica.* Text and French translation in *La préparation évangelique,* 9 vols. Edited by J. Sirineeli et al. SC 206, 228, 262, 266, 215, 292, 307, 338. Paris: Éditions du Cerf, 1974, 1976, 1979, 1980, 1975, 1982, 1983, 1987.

———. *Vita Constantini.* Text in *Eusebius Werke,* vol. 1.1. Edited by F. Winkelmann. GCS 7. Berlin: Academy Press, 1991.

Eusebius of Emesa. *Homilies.* Text in *Eusèbe d'Emèse. Discours conservés en latin.* 2 vols. Edited by E. M. Buytaert. Spicilegium Sacrum Lovaniense Études et Documents 26, 27. Louvain: Spicilegium Sacrum Lovaniense, 1953–1957.

Eusebius of Nicomedia. *Epistula ad Paulinum.* Text in *Athanasius Werke,* vol. 3. *Urkunden zur Geschichte des arianischen Streits: 318–328.* Doc. 8.7. Edited by Hans-Georg Opitz. Berlin: W. de Gruyter, 1936.

Gregory of Nazianzus. *Epistulae.* Text and French translation in *Grégoire de Nazianze: Lettres théologiques.* Edited by Paul Gallay and Maurice Jourjon. SC 208. Paris: Éditions du Cerf, 1974.

———. *Orationes 20–23.* Text and French translation in *Grégoire de Nazianze: Discours 20–23.* Edited by Justin Mossay and Guy Lafontaine. SC 270. Paris: Éditions du Cerf, 1980.

———. *Orationes 27–31.* Text and French translation in *Grégoire de Nazianze: Discours 27–31.* Edited by Paul Gallay and Maurice Jourjon. SC 250. Paris: Éditions du Cerf, 1978. English translation in Frederick W. Norris. *Faith Gives Fullness to Reasoning: The Five Theological Orations of Gregory Nazianzen.* Translated by Lionel Wickham and Frederick Williams. New York: Brill, 1991.

———. *Orationes 32–37.* Text and French translation in *Grégoire de Nazianze: Discours 32–37.* Edited by Claudio Moreschini. Translated by Paul Gallay. SC 318. Paris: Éditions du Cerf, 1985.

Gregory of Nyssa. *Contra Eunomium.* Text in *Gregorii Nysseni Opera,* vol. I–II: *Contra Eunomium Libri.* Edited by Vernerus Jaeger. Berlin: Weidman, 1921. English translation in *Select Writings and Letters of Gregory, Bishop of Nyssa.* Edited by William Moore and Henry Austin Wilson. NPNF, 2nd series, vol. 5. Grand Rapids: Eerdmans, 1954.

Ignatius of Antioch. *Epistulae.* Text in *Die apostolischen Väter.* Edited by Karl Bihlmeyer. Tübingen: J. C. B. Mohr, 1956. English translation in J. B. Lightfoot and J. R. Harmer. *The Apostolic Fathers,* 2nd ed. Grand Rapids: Baker Book House, 1989.

Jerome. *De viris illustribus.* Text in *Hieronymus: Liber De viris inlustribus. Gennadius: Liber de viris inlustribus.* Edited by E. C. Richardson. TU 14. Leipzig: J. C. Hinrichs, 1896. English translation in Thomas P. Halton. *Saint Jerome: On Illustrious Men.* FC 100. Washington, D.C.: The Catholic University of America Press, 1999.

John Chrysostom. *Adversus Judaeos.* PG 48: 843–942. English translation in Paul Harkins. *St. John Chrysostom: Discourses against Judaizing Christians.* FC 68. Washington, D.C.: The Catholic University of America Press, 1979.

———. *De incomprehensibili Dei natura.* PG 48: 701–812. English translation in Paul Harkins. *St. John Chrysostom: On the Incomprehensibile Nature of God.* FC 72. Washington, D.C.: The Catholic University of America Press, 1982.

Josephus. *Antiquitates Judaicae.* Text and translation in *Josephus,* 9 vols. Edited and translated by H. St. J. Thackeray and Ralph Marcus. LCL. Cambridge, Mass.: Harvard University Press, 1958.

———. *Bellicum Judaicum.* Text and translation in *Josephus,* 9 vols. Edited and translated by H. St. J. Thackeray and Ralph Marcus. LCL. Cambridge, Mass.: Harvard University Press, 1958.

Justin Martyr. *Apologiae.* Text and French translation in *Saint Justin, Apologies: Introduction, texte critique, traduction, commentaire et index.* Edited by André Wartelle. Paris: Études Augustiniennes, 1987.

———. *Dialogue with Trypho the Jew.* PG 6. English translation in *Apostolic Fathers.* Edited by A. Roberts and J. Donaldson. ANF, vol. 1. Edinburgh: T&T Clark, 1980.

Lactantius. *De mortibus persecutorum.* Text and translation in *Lactantius: De mortibus persecutorum.* Edited and translated by J. L. Creed. Oxford Early Christian Texts. Oxford: Oxford University Press, 1984.

Life of Rabbula. Text in *Acta Martyrum et Sanctorum,* vol. 4. Edited by P. Bedjan. Paris: Harrassowitz, 1894. Reprint, Hildesheim: Olms, 1968.

Melito of Sardis. *Peri Pascha.* Text and French translation in *Peri Pascha: Sur la Pâque, et fragments.* Edited by O. Perler. SC 123. Paris: Éditions du Cerf, 1966.

Odes of Solomon. Text in *The Odes of Solomon.* Edited by J. H. Charlesworth. Oxford: Clarendon Press, 1973.

Old Syriac Gospels. Text in *Comparative Edition of the Syriac Gospels: Aligning the Sinaiticus, Curetonianus, Peshîttâ and Harklean Versions,* vol. 1: *Matthew.* Edited by George Kiraz. New York: Brill, 1996.

Origen. *Commentarius in Epistolam ad Romanos.* Text in *Der Römerbrief Kommentar des Origenes: Kritische Ausgabe der Übersetzung Rufins, Buch 1–3.* Edited by Caroline Hammond Bammel. Vetus Latina: Aus der Geschichte der Lateinischen Bibel 16. Freiburg: Herder Press, 1990.

———. *Commentary on John.* Text and French translation in *Origène: Commentaire sur S. Jean.* Edited by Cécile Blanc. SC 385. Paris: Éditions du Cerf, 1992.

———. *Contra Celsum.* Text and French translation in *Contre Celse,* 5 vols. Edited by Marcel Borret. SC 132, 136, 147, 150, 227. Paris: Éditions du Cerf, 1967–1976.

———. *Peri Pascha.* Text in *Sur la Pâque.* Edited by O. Guérard and P. Nautin. Christianisme Antique 2. Paris: Beauchesne, 1979.

Palladius. *Historia Lausiaca.* Text and Italian translation in *Palladio: La storia Lausiaca.* Edited by G. J. M. Bartelink with introduction by Chrsitine Mohrmann. Translated by Marison Barchiesi. Vite dei Santi 2. Milan: Lorenzo Valla Foundation, 1974. English translation in R. T. Meyer. *Palladius: The Lausiac History.* Ancient Christian Writers 34. Westminster, Md.: Newman Press, 1964.

pseudo-Ephrem. *Sermo III (Hosanna).* Text and German in *Des Heiligen Ephraem des Syrers, Sermones II.* Edited by Edmund Beck. CSCO 311–12, SS 134–35. Louvain: Secretariat of the CSCO, 1970.

Rabbula. *Canons.* Text and English translation in *Syriac and Arabic Documents Regarding Legislation Relative to Syrian Asceticism.* Edited by Arthur Vööbus. Stockholm: ETSE, 1960.

Sozomen. *Historia ecclesiastica.* Text in *Kirchengeschichte Sozomenus.* Edited by Joseph Bidez. GCS 50. Berlin: Academy Press, 1957.

Talmud Bavli. Text in *Talmud Bavli,* 20 vols. Vilna: Almanah & Romm, 1880–1892. Reprint, Jerusalem, 1980. Translation in *The Babylonian Talmud,* 34 vols. Edited by I. Epstein et al. London: Soncino Press, 1935–1952.

Talmud Yerushalmi. Text in *Talmud Yerushalmi,* 7 vols. Vilna: Romm, 1922. Reprint, Jerusalem, 1970.

The Teaching of Addai. Text and English translation in *The Teaching of Addai.* Edited and translated by George Howard. Chico, Calif.: Scholars Press, 1981.

Theodore of Mopsuestia. *Catechetical Homilies.* Text in *Les homélies catéchétiques.* Edited and translated by R. Tonneau and R. Devréesse. Studi e Testi 145. Rome: Vatican, 1949. German translation in Peter Bruns, *Theodor von Mopsuestia: Katechetische Homilien,* 2 vols. New York: Herder, 1994.

Theodoret. *Historia ecclesiastica.* Text in *Theodoret: Kirchengeschichte.* Edited by F. Scheidweiler and L. Parmentier. GCS 44. Berlin: Academy Press, 1954. English translation in B. Jackson. *The Ecclesiastical History of Theodoret.* NPNF, 2nd series, vol. 3. New York: Christian Literature Company, 1892. Reprint, Edinburgh, 1987.

Secondary Sources

Aageson, James W. "Paul's Use of Scripture: A Comparative Study of Biblical Interpretation in Early Palestinian Judaism and the New Testament, with Special Reference to Romans 9–11." Ph.D. diss., University of Oxford, 1983.

Aberbach, Moses, and Leivy Smolar. "Aaron, Jereboam, and the Golden Calves." *JBL* 86 (1967): 129–40.

Alexander, P. S. "The Rabbinic Lists of Forbidden Targumim." *JJS* 27, no. 2 (1976): 177–91.

Althusser, Louis. "Ideology and Ideological State Apparatuses (Notes towards an Investigation)." In *Lenin and Philosophy and Other Essays.* Translated by Ben Brewster. New York: Monthly Review Press, 1971, 127–86.

Alvarez, J. "Apostolic Writings and the Roots of Anti-Semitism." *Studia Patristica* 13 (1975): 69–76.

Amar, Joseph. "The Syriac *Vita* Tradition of Ephrem the Syrian." Ph.D. diss., The Catholic University of America, 1988.

———. "A Metrical Homily on the Holy Mar Ephrem by Mar Jacob of Sarug: Critical Edition of the Syriac Text, Translation and Introduction." *PdO* 47, no. 1 (1995).

Ankersmit, F. R. *Historical Representation.* Stanford: Stanford University Press, 2001.

Arnold, Wade-Hampton. *The Early Episcopal Career of Athanasius of Alexandria.* Notre Dame: University of Notre Dame Press, 1991.

Ashton, J. "The Identity and Function of the 'Judaioi' in the Fourth Gospel." *NovT* 27, no. 1 (1985): 40–75.

Ayres, Lewis. *Nicaea and Its Legacy: An Approach to Fourth-Century Trinitarian Theology.* Oxford: Oxford University Press, 2004.

Ayres, Lewis, and G. Jones, eds. *Christian Origins: Theology, Rhetoric, and Community.* New York: Routledge, 1998.

Azkoul, Michael. *St. Gregory of Nyssa and the Tradition of the Fathers.* New York: Edwin Mellen Press, 1995.

Bacchiocchi, S. *Anti-Judaism and the Origin of Sunday.* Rome, 1975.

Barclay, John. *Jews in the Mediterranean Diaspora: From Alexander to Trajan (323 BCE–117 CE).* Edinburgh: T&T Clark, 1996.

Barnard, L. W. "Is the Epistle of Barnabas a Paschal Homily?" *VC* 15 (1961): 8–22.

———. "The Old Testament and Judaism in the Writings of Justin Martyr." *VT* 14 (1964): 395–406.

———. *Justin Martyr: His Life and Thought.* Cambridge: Cambridge University Press, 1966.

———. "The Origins and Emergence of the Church in Edessa during the First Two Centuries A.D." *VC* 22 (1968): 161–75.

———. *Athenagoras: A Study in Second Century Christian Apologetic.* Paris: Beauchesne, 1972.

Barnes, Timothy D. "Constantine and the Christians of Persian." *JRS* 75 (1985): 126–36.

———. "Trajan and the Jews." *JJS* 40 (1989): 145–62.

———. *Athanasius and Constantius: Theology and Politics in the Constantinian Empire.* Cambridge, Mass.: Harvard University Press, 1993.

Barnes, Timothy D., and Rowan Williams. *Arianism after Arius.* Edinburgh: T&T Clark, 1993.

Bauer, Walter. *Orthodoxy and Heresy in Earliest Christianity.* Translated by Philadelphia Seminar on Christian Origins. Mifflintown, Pa.: Sigler Press, 1996. Original German edition, *Rechtgläubigkeit und Ketzerei im ältesten Christentum.* Tübingen: Mohr, 1934.

Baur, F. C. *Kirchengeschichte der drei ersten Jahrhunderte.* Tübingen: Fues, 1861.

Beard, Mary, John North, and Simon Price. *Religions of Rome.* Vol. 1, *A History.* New York: Cambridge University Press, 1998.

Beck, Edmund. *Die Theologie des heilige Ephraem in seinen Hymnen über den Glauben.* Rome: Orbis Catholicus, 1949.

———. *Ephräms Reden über den Glauben.* Rome: Orbis Catholicus, 1953.

———. "Symbolum-Mysterium bei Aphrahat und Ephraem." *OC* 42 (1958): 19–40.

———. *Ephräms Polemik gegen Mani und die Manichäer im Rahmen der zeitgenössischen griechischen Polemik und der des Augustinus.* CSCO 391, Sub. 55. Louvain: Secretariat of the CSCO, 1978.

———. "Das Bild vom Sauerteig bei Ephräm." *OC* 63 (1979): 1–19.

———. *Ephräm des Syrers: Psychologie und Erkenntnislehre.* CSCO 419, Sub. 58. Louvain: Peeters, 1980.

———. *Ephräms Trinitätslehre im Bild von Sonne/Feuer, Licht und Wärme.* CSCO 425, Sub. 62. Louvain: Peeters, 1981.

———. "Zur Terminologie von Ephraems Bildtheologie." In *Typus, Symbol, Allegorie bei den östlichen Vätern und ihren Parallelen im Mittelalter.* Edited by M. Schmidt. Regensberg: Pustet, 1982, 239–77.

———. "Ephräm des Syrers Hymnik." In *Liturgie und Dichtung.* Edited by Hans-Jakob Becker and Reiner Kaczynski. St. Ottilien: EOS Press, 1983, 345–79.

Becker, Adam. "Anti-Judaism and Care for the Poor in Aphrahat's *Demonstration* 20." *JECS* 10, no. 3 (2002): 305–27.

———. *Fear of God and the Beginning of Wisdom: The School of Nisibis and the Development of Scholastic Culture in Late Antique Mesopotamia.* Philadelphia: University of Pennsylvania Press, 2006.

Becker, Adam, and Annette Yoshiko Reed, eds. *The Ways that Never Parted: Jews and Christians in Late Antiquity and the Early Middle Ages.* Tübingen: Mohr Siebeck, 2003.

Bell, G. *The Churches and Monasteries of the Tur ʿAbdin.* London: Pindar Press, 1982.

Benin, Stephen D. "Commandments, Covenants and the Jews in Aphrahat, Ephrem and Jacob of Sarug." In *Approaches to Judaism in Medieval Times.* Edited by David R. Blumenthal. Chico, Calif.: Scholars Press, 1984, 135–56.

Bernardi, Jean. *Saint Grégoire de Nazianze: Le théologien et son temps (330–390).* Paris: Éditions du Cerf, 1995.

Bickerman, Elias J. *The Jews in the Greek Age.* Cambridge, Mass.: Harvard University Press, 1988.

Biesen, Kees den. *Simple and Bold: Ephrem's Art of Symbolic Thought.* Piscataway, N. J.: Gorgias Press, 2006.

Blum, G. G. *Rabbula von Edessa: Der Christ, der Bischof, der Theologe.* CSCO, Sub. 34. Louvain: Secretariat of the CSCO, 1969.

Böhm, Thomas. "Basil of Caesarea, *Adversus Eunomium* I–III and Ps. Basil, *Adversus Eunomium* IV–V." In *Studia Patristica XXXVII.* Louvain: Peeters, 2001, 20–26.

Bokser, B. Z. "Justin Martyr and the Jews." *JQR* 64 (1973–1974): 97–122, 204–11.

Bori, Pier Cesare. *The Golden Calf and the Origins of the Anti-Jewish Controversy.* Translated by David Ward. Atlanta: Scholars Press, 1990.

Botha, H. "A Poetic Analysis of Ephrem the Syrian's Hymn de Azymis XIII," *Acta Patristica et Byzantina* 14 (2003): 21–38.

Botha, P. J. "The Poetic Face of Rhetoric: Ephrem's Polemics against the Jews and Heretics in *Contra Haereses* xxv." *Acta Patristica et Byzantina* 2 (1991): 16–36.

———. "The Significance of the Senses in St. Ephrem's Description of Paradise." *Acta Patristica et Byzantina* 5 (1994): 28–37.

Bou Mansour, T. "La défense éphrémienne de la liberté contre les doctrines marcionite, bardésanite et manichéenne." *OCP* 50 (1984): 331–46.

———. "Etude de la terminologie symbolique chez Saint Ephrem." *PdO* 14 (1987): 221–62.

———. *La pensée symbolique de saint Ephrem le Syrien*. Beirut: Bibliothèque de l'Université Saint Esprit, 1988.

Bowersock, G. W. *Studies on the Eastern Roman Empire: Social, Economic and Administrative History, Religion, Historiography*. Goldbach: Keip, 1994.

Bowerstock, G. W., Peter Brown, and Oleg Grabar, eds. *Interpreting Late Antiquity: Essays on the Post-Classical World*. Cambridge, Mass.: Belknap Press of Harvard University Press, 2001.

Boyarin, Daniel. *Carnal Israel: Reading Sex in Talmudic Culture*. Berkeley: University of California Press, 1993.

———. *Border Lines: The Partition of Judaeo-Christianity*. Philadelphia: University of Pennsylvania Press, 2004.

Brakke, David. *Athanasius and Asceticism*. Baltimore: Johns Hopkins University Press, 1995.

———. "Jewish Flesh and Christian Spirit in Athanasius of Alexandria." *JECS* 9, no. 4 (2001): 453–81.

Brichto, Herbert Chanan. "The Worship of the Golden Calf: A Literary Analysis of a Fable on Idolatry." *Hebrew Union College Annual* 54 (1983): 1–44.

Brock, Sebastian. "Jewish Traditions in Syriac Sources." *JJS* 30 (1979): 212–32.

———. "Christians in the Sasanian Empire: A Case of Divided Loyalties." In *Religion and National Identity*. Edited by Stuart Mews. Oxford: Basil Blackwell, 1982, 1–19.

———. "Clothing Metaphors as a Means of Theological Expression in Syriac Tradition." In *Typus, Symbol, Allegorie bei den östlichen Vätern und ihren Parallelen im Mittelalter*. Edited by M. Schmidt. Regensberg: Pustet, 1982, 11–40.

———. "From Antagonism to Assimilation: Syriac Attitudes to Greek Learning." In *East of Byzantium: Syria and Armenia in the Formative Period*. Edited by Nina Garsoïan, Thomas Mathews, and Robert Thomson. Washington, D.C.: Dumbarton Oaks, 1982, 17–33.

———. *The Bible in the Syriac Tradition*. Kerala, India: St. Ephrem Ecumenical Research Institute, 1989.

———. "Introduction." In *St. Ephrem the Syrian: Hymns on Paradise*. Crestwood, N.Y.: St. Vladimir's Seminary Press, 1990, 7–75.

———. "Eusebius and Syriac Christianity." In *Eusebius, Christianity, and Judaism*. Edited by Attridge and Hatra. Detroit: Wayne State University, 1991, 212–34.

———. *The Luminous Eye: The Spiritual World Vision of Saint Ephrem the Syrian*. Kalamazoo: Cistercian Publications, 1992.

———. "Greek and Syriac in Late Antique Syria." In *Literacy and Power in the Ancient World*. Edited by A. K. Bowman and G. Woolf. Cambridge: Cambridge University Press, 1994, 149–60.

———. "A Palestinian Targum Feature in Syriac." *JJS* 46 (1995): 182–271.

———. "The Transmission of Ephrem's Madrashe in the Syriac Liturgical Tradition." *Studia Patristica* 33 (1997): 490–505.

———. "The Peshitta Old Testament: Between Judaism and Christianity." *Cristianesimo nella Storia* 19 (1998): 483–502.

———. *From Ephrem to Romanos: Interactions between Syriac and Greek in Late Antiquity.* Brookfield, Vt.: Ashgate Press, 1999.

———. "St. Ephrem in the Eyes of Later Syriac Liturgical Tradition." *Hugoye: Journal of Syriac Studies* 2.1 (1999). Online journal. Available from http://syrcom.cua.edu/hugoye/Vol2No1/HV2N1Brock.html (accessed 1/18/05).

———. "The Changing Faces of St. Ephrem as Read in the West." In *Abba: The Tradition of Orthodoxy in the West.* Edited by John Behr, Andrew Louth, and Dimitri Conomos. Crestwood, N.Y.: St. Vladimir's Seminary Press, 2003, 65–80.

Brown, Raymond. *The Gospel According to John,* vol. 1. New York: Doubleday Press, 1966.

Brubaker, Leslie. *Vision and Meaning in Ninth-Century Byzantium: Image as Exegesis in the Homilies of Gregory of Nazianzus.* New York: Cambridge University Press, 1999.

Bruns, Peter. "Arius hellenizans?--Ephräm der Syrer und die neoarianischen Kontroversen seiner Zeit." *ZKG* 101 (1990): 21–57.

Bundy, David. "Ephrem's Critique of Mani: The Limits of Knowledge and the Nature of Language." In *Gnosticisme et Monde Hellénistique.* Edited by Julien Ries. Louvain la Neuve: The Catholic University of Louvain, 1982, 289–98.

———. "Language and the Knowledge of God in Ephrem Syrus." *Dialogue and Alliance* 1 (1988): 56–64.

———. "Marcion and the Marcionites in Early Syriac Apologetics." *Le Muséon: Revues d'Études Orientales* 101 (1998): 21–32.

———. "Bishop Vologese and the Persian Siege of Nisibis in 359 C.E.: A Study in Ephrem's *Memre on Nicomedia.*" *Encounter* 63, no. 1–2 (2002): 55–63.

Burkitt, F. C. *Early Eastern Christianity.* London: John Murray, 1904.

Burrus, Virginia. *"Begotten, Not Made": Conceiving Manhood in Late Antiquity.* Stanford: Stanford University Press, 2000.

Butcher, Kevin. *Roman Syria.* London: British Museum Press, 2003.

Cameron, Averil. *Christianity and the Rhetoric of Empire: The Development of Christian Discourse.* Berkeley: University of California Press, 1991.

———. *The Later Roman Empire, AD 284–430.* Cambridge, Mass.: Harvard University Press, 1993.

———. "Jews and Heretics--A Category Error?" In *The Ways that Never Parted: Jews and Christians in Late Antiquity and the Middle Ages.* Edited by Adam Becker and Annette Yoshiko Reed. Tübingen: Mohr Siebeck, 2003, 345–60.

Carleton Paget, James. "Anti-Judaism and Early Christian Identity." *Zeitschrift für Antikes Christentum* 1 (1997): 195–225.

———. "Jewish Christianity." In *The Cambridge History of Judaism,* vol. 3. Edited by William Horbury, W. D. Davies, and John Sturdy. Cambridge: Cambridge University Press, 1999, 721–75.

Cerbelaud, Dominique. "L'antijudaïsme dans les hymnes *de Pascha* d'Éphrem le Syrien." *PdO* 20 (1995): 201–7.

Certeau, Michel de. *The Writing of History.* Translated by Tom Conley. New York: Columbia University Press, 1988.

Chadwick, Henry. *Early Christian Thought and the Classical Tradition.* Oxford: Clarendon Press, 1966.

Chaumont, M.-L. *La christianisation de l'empire iranien des origines aux grandes persécutions du IVe siècle.* CSCO 499, Sub. 80. Louvain: Peeters, 1988.

Clark, Elizabeth A. "The Lady Vanishes: Dilemmas of a Feminist Historian after the 'Linguistic Turn.'" *CH* 67, no. 1 (1998): 1–31.

———. *Reading Renunciation: Asceticism and Scripture in Early Christianity.* Princeton: Princeton University Press, 1999.

———. *History-Theory-Text.* Cambridge, Mass.: Harvard University Press, 2004.

Classen, Constance, David Howes, and Anthony Synnott. *Aroma: The Cultural History of Smell.* New York: Routledge, 1994.

Coakley, Sarah, ed. "Re-thinking Gregory of Nyssa." *Modern Theology* 18, no. 4 (2002): 431–561.

Daly, Mary. *Beyond God the Father: Toward a Philosophy of Women's Liberation.* Boston: Beacon Press, 1973.

Daniélou, Jean. *Les manuscrits de la Mer Morte et les origines du christianisme.* Paris: Desclée, 1957.

———. *Théologie du judéo-christianisme.* Paris: Desclée, 1958.

Darling, Robin A. "The 'Church from the Nations,' in the Exegesis of Ephrem." In *IV Symposium Syriacum, 1984.* Edited by H. J. W. Drijvers et al. Rome: Pontifical Institute, 1987, 111–21.

Davies, Alan, ed. *Anti-Semitism and the Foundations of Christianity.* New York: Paulist Press, 1979.

Dawson, David. *Allegorical Readers and Cultural Revision in Ancient Alexandria.* Berkeley: University of California Press, 1992.

Dinter, Paul Edward. "The Remnant of Israel and the Stone of Stumbling in Zion According to Paul (Romans 9–11)." Ph.D. diss., Union Theological Seminary, 1980.

Donahue, P. J. "Jewish Christian Controversy in the Second Century: A Study in the Dialogue of Justin Martyr." Ph.D. diss., Yale University, 1977.

Doran, R. *Stewards of the Poor: The Man of God, Rabbula, and Hiba in Fifth-Century Edessa.* Cistercian Studies 208. Kalamazoo: Cistercian Publications, 2006.

Drake, Hal A. *Constantine and the Bishops: The Politics of Intolerance.* Baltimore: Johns Hopkins University Press, 2000.

Drecoll, V. H. *Die Entwicklun der Trinitätslehre des Basilius von Cäsarea: Sein Weg vom Homöusianer zum Neonizäner.* Göttingen: Vandenhoeck & Ruprecht, 1996.

Drijvers, H. J. W. "Edessa und das jüdische Christentum." *VC* 24 (1970): 3–33.

———. *Cults and Beliefs at Edessa.* Leiden: Brill, 1980.

———. "The Persistence of Pagan Cults and Practices in Christian Syria." In *East of Byzantium: Syria and Armenia in the Formative Period.* Edited by Nina Garsoïan, Thomas Mathews, and Robert Thompson. Washington, D.C.: Dumbarton Oaks, 1982, 35–43.

———. "Jews and Christians at Edessa." *JJS* 36, no. 1 (1985): 97–98.

———. "Syrian Christianity and Judaism." In *The Jews among Pagans and Christians in the Roman Empire.* Edited by Judith Lieu, John North, and Tessa Rajak. New York: Routledge, 1992, 124–46.

Dugmore, C. W. "A Note on the Quartodecimans." *Studia Patristica* 79.4.2 (1961): 411–21.

Duval, Rubens. *Histoire d'Édesse, politique, religieuse et littéraire*. Paris: Imprimerie Nationale, 1892.

Eagleton, Terry, *Ideology: An Introduction*. New York: Verso, 1991.

———, ed. *Ideology*. New York: Logman, 1994.

Ehrman, Bart D. *The Orthodox Corruption of Scripture: The Effect of Early Christological Controversies on the Text of the New Testament*. New York: Oxford University Press, 1993.

Ernest, James D. *The Bible in Athanasius of Alexandria*. Boston: Brill, 2004.

Fedwick, Paul Jonathan. *The Church and the Charisma of Leadership in Basil of Caesarea*. Toronto: Pontifical Institute of Mediaeval Studies, 1979.

———, ed. *Basil of Caesarea: Christian, Humanist, Ascetic*. 2 vols. Toronto: Pontifical Institute of Mediaeval Studies, 1981.

Feghali, Paul. "Influence des targums sur la pensée exégétique d'Ephrem?" In *IV Symposium Syriacum 1984*. Edited by H. J. W. Drijvers et al. Rome: Pontifical Institute, 1987, 71–82.

Fiey, Jean-Maurice. *Nisibe: Métropole syriaque orientale et ses suffragants des origines à nos jours*. CSCO 388, Sub. 54. Louvain: Secretariat of the CSCO, 1977.

———. "Les évêques de Nisibe au temps de saint Éphrem." *PdO* 4 (1973): 123–36.

Fonrobert, Charlotte. "The *Didascalia Apostolorum*: A Mishnah for the Disciples of Jesus." *JECS* 9, no. 4 (2001): 483–509.

Fortna, Robert. *The Gospel of Signs: A Reconstruction of the Narrative Source Underlying the Fourth Gospel*. London: Cambridge University Press, 1970.

Foucault, Michel. *The History of Sexuality*. Translated by Robert Hurley. New York: Pantheon Books, 1978.

———. *Discipline and Punish: The Birth of the Prison*. 2nd ed. Translated by Alan Sheridan. New York: Vintage Books, 1995.

———. *Power*. Edited by James D. Faubion. Translated by Robert Hurley. New York: New Press, 2000.

Frank, K. *Adversus Judaeos in der Alten Kirke: Die Juden als Minderheit in der Geschichte*. Munich, 1981.

Fredriksen, Paula. *Augustine and the Jews: The Story of Christianity's Great Theologian and His Defense of Judaism*. New York: Doubleday, 2008.

Freyne, Sean. "Vilifying the Other and Defining the Self: Matthew's and John's Anti-Jewish Polemic in Focus." In *"To See Ourselves as Others See Us": Christians, Jews, "Others" in Late Antiquity*. Edited by Jacob Neusner and Ernest S. Frerichs. Chico, Calif.: Scholars Press, 1985, 117–43.

Gager, John G. *The Origins of Anti-Semitism*. New York: Oxford University Press, 1983.

———. "Jews, Christians and the Dangerous Ones in between." In *Interpretation in Religion*. Edited by S. Biderman and B. A. Scharfstein. Leiden: Brill, 1992, 249–57.

———. *Reinventing Paul*. New York: Oxford University Press, 2000.

Gain, B. *L'église de Cappadoce au IVe siècle d'après la correspondance de Basile de Césarée*. OCA 225. Rome: Pontifical Institute, 1985.

Gallay, Paul. *Grégoire de Nazianze*. Paris: Éditions ouvrières, 1959.

Gamble, Harry. *Books and Readers in the Early Church: A History of Early Christian Texts*. New Haven: Yale University Press, 1995.

Gavin, F. "Aphraates and the Jews." *JSOR* 7 (1923): 95–166.

Geffcken, Johannes. *Zwei griechische Apologeten*. New York: Georg Olms Press, 1970.

Gibson, J. C. L. "From Qumran to Edessa or the Aramaic Speaking Church before and after 70 A.D." *Annual of Leeds Oriental Society* 5 (1966): 24–39.

Giddens, Anthony. "Four Theses on Ideology." *Canadian Journal of Political and Social Theory* 7, no. 1–2 (1983): 18–21.

Gill, Christopher, and T. P. Wiseman, eds. *Lies and Fiction in the Ancient World.* Austin: University of Texas Press, 1993.

Grant, Robert. Forms and Occasions of the Greek Apologists." *Studi e Materiali di Storia delle Religioni* 52 (1986): 213–26.

———. *Greek Apologists of the Second Century.* Philadelphia: Westminster, 1988.

Gregg, Robert C. *Arianism: Historical and Theological Reassessments.* Cambridge, Mass.: Philadelphia Patristic Foundation, 1985.

Gregg, Robert C., and Dennis E. Groh. *Early Arianism: A View of Salvation.* Philadelphia: Fortress Press, 1981.

Gribomont, J. "La tradition liturgique des Hymnes Pascales de Saint Ephrem." *PdO* 4 (1973): 191–246.

———. "Le triomphe de Pâques d'après S. Ephrem." *PdO* 4 (1973): 147–89.

Griffith, Sidney. "Ephraem, the Deacon of Edessa, and the Church of the Empire." In *Diakonia: Studies in Honor of Robert T. Meyer.* Edited by Thomas Halton and Joseph Williman. Washington, D.C.: The Catholic University of America Press, 1986, 22–52.

———. "Ephraem the Syrian's Hymns 'Against Julian': Meditations on History and Imperial Power." *VC* 41 (1987): 238–66.

———. *"Faith Adoring the Mystery": Reading the Bible with Ephrem the Syrian.* Milwaukee: Marquette University Press, 1997.

———. "The Marks of the 'True Church' according to Ephraem's *Hymns against Heresies.*" In *After Bardaisan: Studies on Continuity and Change in Syriac Christianity in Honour of Professor Han J. W. Drijvers.* Edited by G. J. Reinink and A. C. Klugkist. Louvain: Peeters, 1999, 125–40.

———. "Setting Right the Church of Syria: Saint Ephraem's *Hymns against Heresies.*" In *The Limits of Ancient Christianity: Essays on Late Antique Thought and Culture in Honor of R. A. Markus.* Edited by William Klingshirn and Mark Vessey. Ann Arbor: University of Michigan Press, 1999, 97–114.

Grissom, Fred Allen. "Chrysostom and the Jews: Studies in Jewish-Christian Relations in Fourth-Century Antioch." Ph.D. diss., Southern Baptist Theological Seminary, 1978.

Gwatkin, H. M. *The Arian Controversy.* New York: Longmans, Green, and Co., 1914.

———. *Studies of Arianism.* 2nd ed. Cambridge: Deighton, Bell and Co, 1900 (originally 1882). Reprint, New York: AMS Press, 1978.

Haar Romeny, R. B. ter. *A Syrian in Greek Dress: The Use of Greek, Hebrew, and Syriac Biblical Texts in Eusebius of Emesa's* Commentary on Genesis. Louvain: Peeters, 1997.

———. "Hypothesis on the Development of Judaism and Christianity in Syria in the Period after 70 C.E." In *Matthew and the Didache: Two Documents from the Same Jewish-Christian Milieu?* Edited by H. van de Sandt. Minneapolis: Fortress Press, 2005, 13–33.

Haas, Christopher. *Alexandria in Late Antiquity: Topography and Social Conflict.* Baltimore: Johns Hopkins University Press, 1997.

Hall, S. G. "Melito in Light of the Passover Haggadah." *JTS* 22 (1971): 29–46.

de Halleux, André. "Saint Ephrem le Syrien." *Revue théologique de Louvain* 14 (1983): 328–55.

Hanson, R. P. C. *The Search for the Doctrine of God: The Arian Controversy 318–381.* Edinburgh: T&T Clark, 1988.

Hare, Douglas. "The Rejection of the Jews in the Synoptic Gospels and Acts." In *Anti-Semitism and the Foundations of Christianity.* Edited by Alan Davies. New York: Paulist Press, 1979, 27–47.

Harkins, Paul W. "Introduction." In *Saint John Chrysostom: Discourses against Judaizing Christians.* Translated by Paul Harkins. FC 68. Washington, D.C.: The Catholic University of America Press, 1979.

Harrak, Amir. "Trade Routes and the Christianization of the Near East." *Journal of the Canadian Society for Syriac Studies* 2 (2002): 46–61.

Harvey, Graham. *The True Israel: Uses of the Names Jew, Hebrew and Israel in Ancient Jewish and Early Christian Literature.* New York: Brill, 1996.

Harvey, Susan Ashbrook. "St. Ephrem on the Scent of Salvation." *JTS* n.s. 49 (1998): 109–28.

———. "Olfactory Knowing: Signs of Smell in the vitae of Simeon Stylites." In *After Bardaisan: Studies on Continuity and Change in Syriac Christianity in Honour of Professor Han J. W. Drijvers.* Edited by G. J. Reinink and A. C. Klugkist. Louvain: Peeters, 1999, 23–34.

———. "Spoken Words, Voiced Silence: Biblical Women in Syriac Tradition." *JECS* 9, no. 1 (2001): 105–31.

———. "Revisiting the Daughters of the Covenant: Women's Choirs and Sacred Song in Ancient Syriac Christianity." *Hugoye: Journal of Syriac Studies* 8, no. 3 (2005).

———. *Scenting Salvation: Ancient Christianity and the Olfactory Imagination.* Berkeley: University of California Press, 2006.

Hayman, Andy P. "The Image of the Jew in the Syriac Anti-Jewish Polemical Literature." In *"To See Ourselves as Others See Us": Christians, Jews, "Others" in Late Antiquity.* Edited by Jacob Neusner and Ernest S. Frerichs. Chico, Calif.: Scholars Press, 1985, 423–41.

Heil, Uta. *Athanasius von Alexandrien: De Sententia Dionysii.* Patristische Texte und Studien 52. Berlin: de Gruyter, 1999.

Heinz, Andreas. "Antijudaismus in der christlichen Liturgie? Das Beispiel der Syrischen Kirchen in der 'Grossen Woche.'" In *Syriaca II: Beiträge zum 3. deutschen Syrologen- Symposium in Vierzehnheiligen 2002.* Studien zur Orientalischen Kirchengeschichte 33. Edited by M. Tamcke. Münster: LIT Press, 2004, 307–25.

Hengel, Martin. "The Septuagint as a Collection of Writings Claimed by Christians: Justin and the Church Fathers before Origen." In *Jews and Christians: The Parting of the Ways, A.D. 70 to 135.* Edited by James Dunn. Grand Rapids: Eerdmans, 1992, 39–83.

Hennings, Ralph. "Eusebius von Emesa und die Juden." *Journal of Ancient Christianity* 5, no. 2 (2001): 240–60.

Hidal, Sten. *Interpretatio Syriaca: Die Kommentare des Heiligen Ephräm des Syrers zu Genesis und Exodus mit besonderer Berücksichtigung ihrer auslegungsgeschichtlichen Stellung.* Coniectanea Biblica, Old Tesament Series, 6. Sweden: Lund, 1974.

Hilgenfeld, Adolf. *Judentum und Judenchristentum. Eine Nachlese zu der Ketzergeschichte des Urchristentums.* Hildesheim: Olms, 1966.

Hirshman, Marc. *A Rivalry of Genius: Jewish and Christian Biblical Interpretation in Late Antiquity* Translated by Batya Stein. Albany: SUNY Press, 1996.

———. "The Exegetical Debate: Justin Martyr and the *Dialogue with Trypho the Jew.*" In *A Rivalry of Genius: Jewish and Christian Biblical Interpretation in Late Antiquity.* Translated by Batya Stein. Albany: SUNY Press, 1996, 31–41.

Honigmann, E. "Liste originale des Pères de Nicée." *Byzantion* 14 (1939): 17–76.

Horbury, William. "The Benediction of the Minim and Early Jewish-Christian Controversy." *JTS* 33 (1982): 19–61.

———. "Jewish-Christian Relations in Barnabas and Justin Martyr." In *Jews and Christians: The Parting of the Ways, A.D. 70 to 135.* Edited by James Dunn. Grand Rapids, Mich.: Eerdmans, 1992, 315–45.

———. *Jews and Christians in Contact and Controversy.* Edinburgh: T&T Clark, 1998.

Huber, Wolfgang. *Passa und Ostern: Untersuchungen zur Osterfeier der alten Kirche.* Berlin: Töpelmann, 1969.

Hübner, Hans. *Gottes Ich und Israel: Zum Schriftgebrauch des Paulus in Römer 9–11.* Göttingen: Vandenhoeck & Ruprecht, 1984.

Isaac, Benjamin. "Orientals and Jews in the Historia Augusta: Fourth-Century Prejudice and Stereotypes." In *The Near East Under Roman Rule.* Edited by Benjamin Isaac. New York: Brill, 1998, 268–82.

———. *The Invention of Racism in Classical Antiquity.* Princeton: Princeton University Press, 2004.

Jacobs, Andrew S. "The Imperial Construction of the Jew in the Early Christian Holy Land." Ph.D. diss., Duke University, 2001.

———. *The Remains of the Jews: The Holy Land and Christian Empire in Late Antiquity.* Stanford: Stanford University Press, 2004.

Just, Patricia. *Imperator et episcopus: Zum Verhältnis von Staatsgewalt und christlicher Kirche zwischen dem 1. Konzil von Nicaea (325) und dem 1. Konzil von Konstantinopel (381).* Stuttgart: Steiner, 2003.

Juster, Jean. *Les juifs dans l'empire romain: Leur condition juridique, économique, et sociale,* vol. 1. Paris: Paul Geuthner Library, 1914.

Kannengiesser, Charles. "Athanasius of Alexandria and the Foundation of Traditional Christology." *JTS* 34 (1973): 103–13.

———. *Holy Scripture and Hellenistic Hermeneutics in Alexandrian Christology: The Arian Crisis.* Colloquy 41. Berkeley: Center for Hermeneutical Studies in Hellenistic and Modern Culture, 1982.

———. "Arius and the Arians." *JTS* 44 (1983): 456–75.

———. *Athanase d'Alexandrie évêque et écrivain: Une lecture des traités "Contre les Ariens."* Paris: Beauchesne, 1983.

———. "Athanasius of Alexandria vs. Arius: The Alexandrian Crisis." In *The Roots of Egyptian Christianity.* Edited by Birger Pearson and James Goehring. Philadelphia: Fortress Press, 1986, 204–15.

Kavanagh, James H. "Ideology." In *Critical Terms for Literary Study.* Edited by Frank Lentricchia and Thomas M. Laughlin. Chicago: University of Chicago Press, 1990, 306–20.

Kazan, Stanley. "Isaac of Antioch's Homily against the Jews." *OrChr* 45 (1961): 30–53;
    46 (1962): 87–98; 47 (1963): 88–97; 49 (1965): 57–78.
Kelly, J. N. D. *Golden Mouth: The Story of John Chrysostom--Ascetic, Preacher, Bishop.*
    London: Duckworth, 1995.
Kennedy, George. *Classical Rhetoric and Its Christian and Secular Tradition.* Chapel
    Hill: University of North Carolina Press, 1980.
el-Khoury, N. "The Use of Language by Ephraim the Syrian." *Studia Patristica* 16
    (1985): 93–99.
———. "Hermeneutics in the Works of Ephraim the Syrian." *OCA* 229 (1987): 93–100.
Kim, Angela. "Signs of Ephrem's Exegetical Techniques in his *Homily on Our Lord.*"
    Hugoye: Journal of Syriac Studies 3.1 (2000). Online journal. Available from http://
    syrcom.cua.edu/hugoye/Vol3No1/HV3N1Kim.html (accessed 1/15/05).
Kim, Johann D. *God, Israel, and the Gentiles: Rhetoric and Situation in Romans 9–11.* At-
    lanta: SBL, 2000.
Kimelman, Reuven. "*Birkat Ha-Minim* and the Lack of Evidence for an Anti-
    Christian Jewish Prayer in Late Antiquity." In *Jewish and Christian Self-Definition,*
    vol. 2. Edited by E. P. Sanders, A. I. Baumgarten, and Alan Mendelson. Philadel-
    phia: Fortress Press, 1981, 226–44.
———. "Identifying Jews and Christians in Roman Syria-Palestine." In *Galilee through
    the Centuries: Confluences of Cultures.* Edited by Eric Meyers. Winona Lake, Ind.:
    Eisenbrauns, 1999, 301–33.
Kinzig, Wolfram. "'Non-Separation': Closeness and Cooperation between Jews and
    Christians in the Fourth Century." *VC* 45 (1991): 27–53.
Kiraz, George. *Comparative Edition of the Syriac Gospels: Aligning the Sinaiticus, Cureto-
    nianus, Peshîttâ and Harklean Versions.* Piscataway, N. J.: Gorgias Press, 2004.
Klijn, F. J. "The Study of Jewish Christianity." *NTS* 20 (1973/4): 419–31.
Klijn, F. J., and G. J. Reinink. *Patristic Evidence for Jewish-Christian Sects.* Leiden: Brill,
    1973.
Knoppers, G. N. "Aaron's Calf and Jereboam's Calves." In *Fortunate the Eyes that See:
    Essays in Honor of David Noel Freedman in Celebration of his Seventieth Birthday.* Ed-
    ited by A. B. Beck et al. Grand Rapids: Eerdmans, 1995, 92–104.
Kofsky, Aryeh. *Eusebius of Caesarea against Paganism.* Boston: Brill, 2000.
Koltun-Fromm, Naomi. "Jewish-Christian Polemics in Fourth-Century Persian Mes-
    opotamia: A Reconstructed Conversation." Ph.D. diss., Stanford University, 1993.
———. "A Jewish-Christian Conversation in Fourth-Century Persian Mesopotamia."
    JJS 47 (1996): 45–63.
Koonammakkal, Thomas. "St. Ephrem and Greek Wisdom." In *VI Symposium Syri-
    acum, 1992.* Edited by René Lavenant. Rome: Pontificio Istituto Orientale, 1994,
    168–76.
———. "Ephrem's Imagery of Chasm." In *Symposium Syriacum VII, 1996.* OCA 256.
    Rome, 1998, 175–83.
Kopecek, Thomas. *A History of Neo-Arianism.* 2 vols. Cambridge, Mass.: Philadelphia
    Patristic Foundation, 1970.
Kraft, Robert. Review of *Théologie de judéo-christianisme,* by Jean Daniélou. *JBL* 79
    (1960): 91–94.
———. "In Search of 'Jewish Christianity' and Its 'Theology': Problems of Defini-
    tion and Methodology." *RSR* 60 (1972): 81–96.

Krauss, S. "The Jews in the Works of the Church Fathers." *JQR* 5 (1893–1894): 122–57.

Kronholm, Tryggve. *Motifs from Genesis 1–11 in the Genuine Hymns of Ephrem the Syrian, with particular reference to the influence of Jewish exegetical tradition.* Coniectanea Biblica, Old Testament Series, 11. Lund: Gleerup, 1978.

———. "Abraham, the Physician: The Image of Abraham the Patriarch in the Genuine Hymns of Ephraem Syrus." In *Solving Riddles and Untying Knots.* Edited by Ziony Zevit et al. Winona Lake, Ind.: Eisenbrauns, 1995, 107–15.

Krueger, Derek. *Writing and Holiness: The Practice of Authorship in the Early Christian East.* Philadelphia: University of Pennsylvania Press, 2004.

Kugel, James L., and Rowan A. Greer. *Early Biblical Interpretation.* Philadelphia: Westminster Press, 1986.

Kysar, Robert. "Anti-Semitism and the Gospel of John." In *Anti-Semitism and Early Christianity: Issues of Polemic and Faith.* Edited by Craig Evans and Donald Hanger. Minneapolis: Fortress Press, 1993.

Laird, Martin S. *Gregory of Nyssa and the Grasp of Faith: Union, Knowledge, and Divine Presence.* New York: Oxford University Press, 2004.

Lange, Christian. "A View on the Integrity of the Syriac Commentary on the Diatessaron." *Journal of Eastern Christian Studies* 56 (2004): 129–44.

———. *The Portrayal of Christ in the Syriac Commentary on the Diatessaron.* CSCO 616, Subsidia 118 (Louvain: Peeters, 2005).

Larrain, Jorge. *The Concept of Ideology.* London: Hutchinson, 1979.

———. *Ideology and Cultural Identity: Modernity and the Third World Presence.* Cambridge, Mass.: Polity Press, 1994.

Lash, Ephrem. "The Greek Writings attributed to Saint Ephrem the Syrian." In *Abba: The Tradition of Orthodoxy in the West.* Edited by John Behr, Andrew Louth, and Dimitri Conomos. Crestwood, N.Y.: St. Vladimir's Seminary Press, 2003, 81–98.

Lattke, Michael. "Sind Ephraems Madrâshê Hymnen?" *OC* 73 (1989): 38–43.

Lienhard, Joseph T. "The 'Arian' Controversy: Some Categories Reconsidered." *TS* 48 (1987): 415–37.

Lieu, Judith M. "'The Parting of the Ways': Theological Construct or Historical Reality?" *JSNT* 56 (1994): 101–19.

———. *Image and Reality: The Jews in the World of the Christians in the Second Century.* Edinburgh: T&T Clark, 1996.

———. *Neither Jew nor Greek? Constructing Early Christianity.* New York: T&T Clark, 2002.

Lim, Richard. *Public Disputation, Power, and Social Order in Late Antiquity.* Berkeley: University of California Press, 1995.

Limor, Ora, and Guy G. Stroumsa, eds. *Contra Iudaeos: Ancient and Medieval Polemics between Christians and Jews.* Texts and Studies in Medieval and Early Modern Judaism, 10. Tübingen: Mohr, Paul Siebeck, 1996.

Linders, Barnabas. *The Theology of the Letter to the Hebrews.* Cambridge: Cambridge University Press, 1991.

Lorenz, Rudolf. *Arius judaizans? Untersuchungen zur dogmengeschichtlichen Einordnung des Arius.* Göttingen: Vandenhoeck & Ruprecht, 1979.

Lowy, S. "The Confrontation of Judaism in the Epistle of Barnabas." *JJS* 11 (1960): 1–33.

Lübking, Hans-Martin. *Paulus und Israel im Römerbrief: Eine Untersuchung zu Römer 9–11.* New York: Peter Lang, 1986.

Lyman, Rebecca. "A Topography of Heresy: Mapping the Rhetorical Creation of Arianism." In *Arianism after Arius.* Edited by Michel R. Barnes and Daniel H. Williams. Edinburgh: T&T Clark, 1993, 45–62.

MacLennan, Robert. "Four Christian Writers on Jews and Judaism in the Second Century." In *From Ancient Israel to Modern Judaism,* vol. 1. Edited by Jacob Neusner. Atlanta: Scholars Press, 1989, 187–202.

———. *Early Christian Texts on Jews and Judaism.* Atlanta: Scholars Press, 1990.

Malina, Bruce. "Jewish Christianity or Christian Judaism: Toward a Hypothetical Definition." *JSJ* 7 (1976): 46–57.

Mandelbaum, I. J. "Tannaitic Exegesis of the Golden Calf Episode." In *A Tribute to Geza Vermes: Essays on Jewish and Christian Literature and History.* Edited by P. R. Davies and R. T. White. Sheffield: Sheffield Academic Press, 1990, 207–33.

de Margerie, Bertrand. "La poésie biblique de Saint Ephrem exégète Syrien (306–373)." In *Introduction à l'histoire de l'exégèse: I. Les pères grecs et orientaux.* Edited by Bertrand de Margerie. Paris: Éditions de Cerf, 1980, 165–87.

Maróth, M. "Le siege de Nisibe en 350 ap. J.-Ch. d'apres des sources syriennes." *Acta Antiqua Academiae Scientiarum Hungaricae* 27 (1979): 239–43.

Martikainen, J. *Das Böse und der Teufel in der Theologie Ephraems des Syrers: Ein systematisch-theologishe Untersuchungen.* Abo: Abo Academy Research Institute, 1978.

Martyn, Louis. "Glimpses into the History of the Johannine Community." In *The Gospel of John in Christian History.* New York: Paulist Press, 1978, 90–121.

Mathews, Edward. "The *Vita* Tradition of Ephrem the Syrian, the Deacon of Edessa." *Diakonia* 22 (1988–1989): 15–42.

Mathews, Edward, and Joseph Amar. "General Introduction." In *St. Ephrem the Syrian: Selected Prose Works: Commentary on Genesis, Commentary on Exodus, Homily on Our Lord, Letter to Publius.* Edited by Kathleen McVey. FC 91. Washington, D.C.: The Catholic University of America Press, 1994.

McCarthy, Carmel. "Allusions and Illusions: St. Ephrem's Verbal Magic in the Diatessaron Commentary." In *Targumic and Cognate Studies: Essays in Honour of Martin McNamara.* Edited by K. J. Cathcart and M. Maher. Sheffield: Sheffield Academic Press, 1996, 187–207.

McGuckin, John A. *St. Gregory of Nazianzus: An Intellectual Biography.* Crestwood, N.Y.: St. Vladimir's Seminary Press, 2001.

McVey, Kathleen. "Introduction." In *Ephrem the Syrian: Hymns.* Edited and translated by Kathleen McVey. New York: Paulist Press, 1989, 3–48.

———. "The Anti-Judaic Polemic of Ephrem Syrus' Hymns on the Nativity." In *Of Scribes and Scrolls: Studies on the Hebrew Bible, Intertestamental Judaism, and Christian Origins.* Edited by Harold W. Attridge, John J. Collins, and Thomas H. Tobin. New York: University Press of America, 1990, 229–40.

Meagher, John. "As the Twig Was Bent: Antisemitism in Greco-Roman and Earliest Christian Times." In *Antisemitism and the Foundations of Christianity.* Edited by Alan Davies. New York: Paulist Press, 1979, 1–26.

Meeks, Wayne. "'Am I a Jew?': Johannine Christianity and Judaism." In *Christianity, Judaism and Other Greco-Roman Cults,* vol. I. Edited by Jacob Neusner. Leiden: Brill, 1975, 163–86.

———. "Breaking Away: Three New Testament Pictures of Christianity's Separation from the Jewish Communities." In *"To See Ourselves as Others See Us": Christians,*

Jews, "Others" in Late Antiquity. Edited by Jacob Neusner and Ernest S. Frerichs. Chico, Calif.: Scholars Press, 1985, 93–115.

Meeks, Wayne, and Robert Wilken. *Jews and Christians in Antioch in the First Four Centuries of the Common Era.* Missoula: Scholars Press, 1978.

Meijering, E. P. *Athanasius: Die dritte Rede gegen die Arianer, t. 1, 1–25.* Amsterdam: J. C. Gieben, 1996.

Meredith, Anthony. *The Cappadocians.* Crestwood, N.Y.: St. Vladimir's Seminary Press, 1995.

———. *Gregory of Nyssa.* London: Routledge, 1999

Millar, Fergus. *The Roman Near East, 31 B.C.–A.D. 337.* Cambridge, Mass.: Harvard University Press, 1993.

Mimouni, Simon. "Le judéo-christianisme syriaque: Mythe littéraire ou réalité historique?" In *VI Symposium Syriacum, 1992.* Edited by René Levenant. Rome: Pontifical Institute, 1994, 269–79.

Morris, J. B. *Select Works of St. Ephrem the Syrian.* Oxford, 1847.

Müller, Christian. *Gottes Gerechtigkeit und Gottes Volk: Eine Untersuchung zu Römer 9–11.* Göttingen: Vandenhoeck & Ruprecht, 1964.

Munck, Johannes. *Christus und Israel: Eine auslegung von Röm. 9–11.* Aarhus: University Press, 1956.

Murray, Robert. "Ephrem Syrus." *Catholic Dictionary of Theology*, vol. 2. New York: Nelson, 1967, 220–23.

———. "The Theory of Symbolism in St. Ephrem's Theology." *PdO* 6/7 (1975/1976): 1–20.

———. "The Characteristics of the Earliest Syriac Chrsitianity." In *East of Byzantium: Syria and Armenia in the Formative Period.* Edited by Nina Garsoïan, Thomas Mathews, and Robert Thomson. Washington, D.C.: Dumbarton Oaks, 1982, 3–16.

———. *Symbols of Church and Kingdom: A Study in Early Syriac Tradition.* Cambridge: Cambridge University Press, 1975. Revised and republished. Piscataway, N. J.: Gorgias Press, 2004.

Neusner, Jacob. *A History of the Jews in Babylonia,* vols. 1–5. Leiden: Brill, 1965–1970.

———. *Aphrahat and Judaism: The Christian-Jewish Argument in Fourth-Century Iran.* Leiden: Brill, 1971.

Newman, John Henry. *The Arians of the Fourth Century.* New York: Longmans, Green and Co., 1919.

Noakes, K. "Melito of Sardis and the Jews." *Studia Patristica* 13, no. 2 (1975): 244–49.

Norris, Frederick W. "Introduction." In *Faith Gives Fullness to Reasoning: The Five Theological Orations of Gregory Nazianzen.* New York: Brill, 1991, 1–82.

Outtier, B. "Saint Éphrem d'après ses biographies et ses oeuvres." *PdO* 4 (1973): 11–33.

Pancaro, Severino. *The Law in the Fourth Gospel.* Leiden: Brill, 1975.

Pereira, A. S. Rodrigues. *Studies in Aramaic Poetry (c. 100 B.C.E.–c. 600 C.E.).* Assen, Netherlands: Van Gorcum, 1997.

Pettersen, Alvyn. "The Arian Context of Athanasius of Alexandria's *Tomus ad Antiochenos VII." JEH* 41, no. 2 (1990) 183–98.

———. *Athanasius and the Human Body.* Bristol: Bristol Press, 1990.

Pognon, H. *Inscriptions sémitiques de la Syrie, de la Mésopotamie et de la région de Mossoul.* Paris: Imprimerie Nationale, 1907.

Possekel, Ute. *Evidence of Greek Philosophical Concepts in the Writings of Ephrem the Syrian*. Louvain: Peeters, 1999.

Quispel, Gilles. "The Discussion of Judaic Christianity." *VC* 22 (1968): 81–93.

Rajak, Tessa. "Talking at Trypho: Christian Apologetic as Anti-Judaism in Justin's *Dialogue with Trypho the Jew*." In *Apologetics in the Roman Empire: Pagans, Jews, and Christians*. Edited by Mark Edwards, Martin Goodman, and Simon Price. Oxford: Oxford University Press, 2000, 59–80.

Remus, H. "Justin Martyr's Argument with Judaism." In *Anti-Judaism in Early Christianity*, vol. 2. Edited by Stephen Wilson. Waterloo: Wilfrid Laurier University, 1986, 59–80.

Reynard, Jean. "L'Antijudaïsme de Grégoire de Nysse et du pseudo-Grégoire de Nysse." In *Studia Patristica XXXVII*. Louvain: Peeters, 2001, 257–76.

Richard, Anne. *Cosmologie et théologie chez Grégoire de Nazianze*. Paris: Institut d'études augustiniennes, 2003.

Richardson, Peter, David Granskou, and Stephen Wilson, eds. *Anti-Judaism in Early Christianity*, vols. 1–2. Waterloo: Wilfrid Laurier University, 1986.

Richter, G. "Über die älteste Auseinandersetzung der syrischen Christen mit den Juden." *ZNW* 35 (1936): 101–14.

Riegel, S. K. "Jewish Christianity: Definition and Terminology." *NTS* 24 (1977–1978): 410–15.

Ritter, Adolf Martin. "John Chrysostom and the Jews: A Reconsideration." In *Ancient Christianity in the Caucasus*. Edited by Tamila Mgaloblishvili. Surrey, England: Curzon, 1998, 141–52, 231–32.

Rohrbacher, D. "Iudaei Fetentes at Amm. Marc. 22.5.5." *Mnemosyne* 58 (2005): 441–42.

Ross, Steven. *Roman Edessa: Politics and Culture on the Eastern Fringes of the Roman Empire, 114–242 C.E.* New York: Routledge, 2001.

Rousseau, O. "La rencontre de S. Ephrem et de S. Basile." *L'Orient Syrien* 2 (1957): 261–84, and 3 (1958): 73–90.

Rousseau, Philip. *Basil of Caesarea*. Berkeley: University of California Press, 1994.

Rouwhorst, G. *Les hymnes pascales d'Ephrem de Nisibe: Analyse théologique et recherche sur l'évolution de la fête pascale chrétienne à Nisibe et à Edesse et dans quelques églises voisines au quatrième siècle*. Supplements to *VC* 7, no. 1/2. New York: Brill, 1989.

———. "Jewish Liturgical Traditions in Early Syriac Christianity." *VC* 51 (1997): 74–82.

Ruether, Rosemary Radford. *Gregory of Nazianzus: Rhetor and Philosoper*. Oxford: Oxford University Press, 1969.

———. *Faith and Fratricide: The Theological Roots of Anti-Semitism*. New York: Seabury, 1974.

Runia, David T. "'Where, Tell Me, Is the Jew . . . ?': Basil, Philo, and Isidore of Pelusium." *VC* 46 (1992): 172–89.

Russell, Paul S. *St. Ephraem the Syrian and St. Gregory the Theologian Confront the Arians*. Kerala, India: St. Ephrem Ecumenical Research Institute, 1994.

———. "An Anti-neo-Arian Interpolation in Ephraem of Nisibis' Hymn 46 *On Faith*." In *Studia Patristica XXXIII*. Louvain: Peeters, 1997, 568–72.

———. "Ephraem the Syrian on the Utility of Language and the Place of Silence." *JECS* 8, no. 1 (2000): 21–37.

Rutgers, Leonard V. "The Importance of Scripture in the Conflict between Jews and

Christians: The Example of Antioch." In *The Use of Sacred Books in the Ancient World*. Edited by L. V. Rutgers et al. Louvain: Peeters, 1998, 287–303.

Saber, Georges. *La théologie baptismale de Saint Ephrem*. Kaslik: Université de Saint Esprit de Kaslik, 1974.

Said, Edward. *Orientalism*. New York: Pantheon Books, 1978.

Sanders, E. P., ed. *Jewish and Christian Self-Definition*. 3 vols. Philadelphia: Fortress Press, 1980–1982.

Schäfer, Peter. *Judeophobia: Attitudes toward the Jews in the Ancient World*. Cambridge, Mass.: Harvard University Press, 1997.

Schmidt, Karl Ludwig. *Die Judenfrage im Lichte der Kapitel 9–11 des Römerbriefes*. Zürich: Evangelical Press, 1947.

Schmidt, Margot. "Alttestamentliche Typologien in den Paradieseshymnen von Ephräm dem Syrer." In *Paradeigmata: Literarische Typologie des Alten Testaments*. Edited by Franz Link. Berlin: Duncker & Humblot, 1989, 55–81.

Schoeps, Hans-Joachim. *Jewish Christianity: Factional Disputes in the Early Church*. Translated by Douglas R. A. Hare. Philadelphia: Fortress Press, 1969.

Schreckenberg, H. *Die christlichen Adversus-Judaeos-Texte und ihr literarisches und historisches Umfeld (1.–11. Jh.)*. Frankfurt am Main: Peter Lang, 1982.

Séd, N. "Les hymnes sur le paradis de saint Ephrem et les traditions juives." *Le Muséon* 81 (1968): 455–501.

Segal, Alan F. "Jewish Christianity." In *Eusebius, Christianity, and Judaism*. Edited by Harold Attridge and Gohei Hata. Detroit: Wayne State University Press, 1992, 326–51.

Segal, J. B. "The Jews of North Mesopotamia." In *Sepher Segal*. Edited by J. M. Grintz and J. Liver. Jerusalem: Kiryat Sepher, 1964, 32–63.

———. *Edessa, "The Blessed City."* New York: Oxford University Press, 1970.

Sevenster, J. *The Roots of Pagan Anti-Semitism in the Ancient World*. Leiden: Brill, 1975.

Shemunkasho, Aho. "The Healing of Interior and Exterior Blindness in Ephrem." In *Studia Patristica XXXV*. Louvain: Peeters, 2001, 494–501.

Shepardson, Christine. "Anti-Jewish Rhetoric and Intra-Christian Conflict in the Sermons of Ephrem Syrus." In *Studia Patristica*, vol. 35. XIII International Conference on Patristic Studies. Louvain: Peeters, 2001, 502–7.

———. "'Exchanging Reed for Reed': Mapping Contemporary Heretics onto Biblical Jews in Ephrem's *Hymns on Faith*." *Hugoye: Journal of Syriac Studies* 5, no. 1 (2002). Online journal. Available from http://syrcom.cua.edu/hugoye/Vol5No1/HV5N1Shepardson.html.

———. "In the Service of Orthodoxy: Anti-Jewish Language and Intra-Jewish Conflict in the Writings of Ephrem the Syrian." Ph.D. diss., Duke University, 2003.

———. "Controlling Contested Places: John Chrysostom's *Adversus Iudaeos* Homilies and the Spatial Politics of Religious Controversy." *JECS* 15, no. 4 (2007): 483–516.

———. "Defining the Boundaries of Orthodoxy: Eunomius in the Anti-Jewish Polemic of His Cappadocian Opponents." *CH* 76, no. 4 (2007): 699–723.

———. "Paschal Politics: The Temple's Destruction Deployed by Fourth-Century Christians." *VC* 62, no. 3 (2008): 233–60.

———. "Syria, Syriac, Syrian: Negotiating East and West in Late Antiquity." In *Blackwell Companion to Late Antiquity*. Edited by Philip Rousseau. Oxford: Blackwell, 2008, forthcoming.

Sher, Addai. "Mar Barhadbehabba ʿArbaya: Cause de la fondation des écoles." *PdO* 4, no. 4 (1908): 327–97.

Shoemaker, Stephen. "'Let Us Go and Burn Her Body': The Image of the Jews in the Early Dormition Traditions." *CH* 68 (1999): 775–823.

Simon, Marcel. *Verus Israel: Etude sur les relations entre Chrétiens et Juifs dans l'Empire Romain (135–425)*. Paris: Editions de Boccard, 1948.

———. "Problèmes du judéo-christianisme." In *Aspects du judéo-christianisme: Colloque de Strasbourg, 23–25 avril, 1964*. Paris: University of France Press, 1965, 1–17.

———. "Reflexions sur le judéo-christianisme." In *Christianity, Judaism and Other Graeco-Roman Cults* 2. Edited by Jacob Neusner. Leiden: Brill, 1975, 53–76.

Slusser, Michael. "Traditional Views of Late Arianism." In *Arianism after Arius*. Edited by Michel R. Barnes and Daniel H. Williams. Edinburgh: T&T Clark, 1993, 3–30.

Smallwood, Mary. *The Jews under Roman Rule: From Pompey to Diocletian*. Leiden: Brill, 1976.

Smelik, Klaas A. D. "John Chrysostom's Homilies against the Jews: Some Comments." *Nederlands Theologish Tijdschrift* 39 (1985): 194–200.

Smith, Jonathan Z. "What a Difference a Difference Makes." In *"To See Ourselves as Others See Us": Christians, Jews, "Others" in Late Antiquity*. Edited by Jacob Neusner and Ernest S. Frerichs. Chico, Calif.: Scholars Press, 1985, 3–48.

Smith, Moody. "Judaism and the Gospel of John." In *Jews and Christians: Exploring the Past, Present, and Future*. Edited by J. Charlesworth. New York: Crossroad Press, 1990, 76–96.

Smolar, Leivy, and Moshe Aberbach. "The Golden Calf Episode in Postbiblical Literature." *Hebrew Union College Annual* 39 (1968): 91–116.

Snaith, J. G. "Aphrahat and the Jews." In *Interpreting the Hebrew Bible: Essays in the Honor of E. I. J. Rosenthal*. Edited by J. A. Emerton and S. E. Reif. Cambridge: Cambridge University Press, 1982, 236–50.

Spiegel, Gabrielle, ed. *Practicing History: New Directions in Historical Writing after the Linguistic Turn*. New York: Routledge, 2005.

Stanton, G. "Aspects of Early Christian-Jewish Polemic and Apologetic." *NTS* 31 (1985): 377–92.

Sterk, Andrea. *Renouncing the World, Yet Leading the Church: The Monk-Bishop in Late Antiquity*. Cambridge, Mass.: Harvard University Press, 2004.

Stern, Menahem, ed. *Greek and Latin Authors on Jews and Judaism*. 3 vols. Jerusalem: Israel Academy of Sciences, 1974–1984.

Strecker, Georg. "Appendix 1: On the Problem of Jewish Chrsitianity." In *Orthodoxy and Heresy in Earliest Christianity (Rechtgläubigkeit und Ketzerei im ältesten Christentum*. Walter Bauer. Tübingen: Mohr, 1964; Philadelphia: Fortress Press, 1971, 241–85.

Taylor, David. "St. Ephraim's Influence on the Greeks." *Hugoye: Journal of Syriac Studies* 1, no. 2 (1998). Online journal. Available from http://syrcom.cua.edu/hugoye/Vol1No2/HV1N2Taylor.html (accessed 5/2/05).

Taylor, Joan E. "The Phenomenon of Early Jewish-Christianity: Reality or Scholarly Invention?" *VC* 44 (1990): 313–34.

Taylor, Miriam S. *Anti-Judaism and Early Christian Identity: A Critique of the Scholarly Consensus*. Leiden: Brill, 1995.

Thomas, John Christopher. "The Fourth Gospel and Rabbinic Judaism." *ZNW* 82 (1991): 159–82.

Thompson, John B. *Studies in the Theory of Ideology.* Cambridge: Polity Press, 1984.
———. *Ideology and Modern Culture: Critical Social Theory and the Era of Mass Communication.* Stanford: Stanford University Press, 1990.
Tonneau, R.-M. "Moïse dans la tradition syrienne." In *Moïse, l'homme de l'Alliance.* New York: Desclée, 1955.
Townsend, J. "The Gospel of John and the Jews: The Story of a Religious Divorce." In *Anti-Semitism and the Foundations of Christianity.* Edited by Alan Davies. New York: Paulist Press, 1979, 72–97.
Vaggione, Richard Paul. "Some Neglected Fragments of Theodore of Mopsuestia's *Contra Eunomium.*" *JTS* n.s. 31 (1980): 403–70.
———. *Eunomius of Cyzicus and the Nicene Revolution.* Oxford: Oxford University Press, 2000.
Valavanolickal, Kuriakose A. *The Use of the Gospel Parables in the Writings of Aphrahat and Ephrem.* Studies in the Religion and History of Early Christianity 2. New York: Peter Lang, 1996.
Van Dam, Raymond. *Families and Friends in Late Roman Cappadocia.* Philadelphia: University of Pennsylvania Press, 2003.
van der Horst, Pieter. "Jews and Christians in Antioch at the End of the Fourth Century." In *Christian-Jewish Relations through the Centuries.* Edited by Stanley Porter and Brook Pearson. Sheffield: Sheffield Academic Press, 2000, 228–38.
Van Rompay, Lucas. "A Letter of the Jews to the Emperor Marcian Concerning the Council of Chalcedon." *Orientalia Lovaniensia Periodica* 12 (1981): 215–24.
———. "Antiochene Biblical Interpretation: Greek and Syriac." In *The Book of Genesis in Jewish and Oriental Christian Interpretation.* Edited by Judith Frishman and Lucas Van Rompay. Louvain: Peeters, 1997, 103–23.
von Harnack, Adolf. *Die Altercatio Simonis Judaei et Theophili Christiani nebst Untersuchungen über die antijüdische Polemik in der alten Kirche.* Texte und Untersuchungen 1.3. Leipzig: J. C. Hinrichs, 1883.
———. "Judentum und Judenchristentum in Justin Dialog mit Trypho." *TU* 39 (1913): 47–98.
von Wahlde, Urban. "The Terms for Religious Authorities in the Fourth Gospel: A Key to Literary Strata?" *JBL* 98, no. 2 (1979): 231–53.
———. "The Gospel of John and the Presentation of Jews and Judaism." In *Within Context: Essays on Jews and Judaism in the New Testament.* Edited by David Efroymson et al. Collegeville, Minn.: Liturgical Press, 1993, 67–84.
Vööbus, Arthur. *Celibacy: A Requirement for Admission to Baptism in the Early Syrian Church.* Stockholm: ETSE, 1951.
———. *Literary Critical and Historical Studies in Ephrem the Syrian.* Stockholm: ETSE, 1958.
Weitzman, Michael P. "From Judaism to Christianity: The Syriac Version of the Hebrew Bible." In *The Jews among Pagans and Christians in the Roman Empire.* Edited by Judith Lieu, John North, and Tessa Rajak. New York: Routledge, 1992, 147–73.
———. *The Syriac Version of the Old Testament: An Introduction.* New York: Cambridge University, 1999.
Werner, E. "Melito of Sardes: The First Poet of Deicide." *HUCA* 37 (1966): 191–210.
White, Hayden. *Metahistory: The Historical Imagination in Nineteenth-Century Europe.* Baltimore: Johns Hopkins University Press, 1973.

————. *Tropics of Discourse: Essays in Cultural Criticism.* Baltimore: Johns Hopkins University Press, 1978.

————. *The Content of the Form: Narrative Discourse and Historical Representation.* Baltimore: Johns Hopkins University Press, 1987.

————. *Figural Realism: Studies in the Mimesis Effect.* Baltimore: Johns Hopkins University Press, 1999.

Wilde, Robert. *Treatment of the Jews in the Greek Christian Writers of the First Three Centuries.* Washington, D.C.: The Catholic University of America Press, 1949.

Wiles, Maurice. *Archetypal Heresy: Arianism through the Centuries.* Oxford: Clarendon Press, 1996.

Wilken, Robert L. *John Chrysostom and the Jews.* Berkeley: University of California Press, 1983.

Williams, Lukyn. *Adversus Judaeos: A Bird's-eye View of Christian Apologiae until the Renaissance.* Cambridge: Cambridge University Press, 1935.

Williams, Rowan, ed. *The Making of Orthodoxy: Essays in Honour of Henry Chadwick.* New York: Cambridge University Press, 1989.

————. *Arius: Heresy and Tradition.* 2nd ed. London: SCM Press, 2001.

Wilson, Stephen. "Passover, Easter, and Anti-Judaism: Melito of Sardis and Others." In *"To See Ourselves as Others See Us": Christians, Jews, "Others" in Late Antiquity.* Edited by Jacob Neusner and Ernest Frerichs. Chico, Calif.: Scholars Press, 1985, 337–55.

————. "Melito and Israel." In *Anti-Judaism in Early Christianity,* vol. 2. Edited by Stephen Wilson. Waterloo: Wilfrid Laurier University, 1986, 81–102.

————. "Dialogue and Dispute: Justin." In *Related Strangers: Jews and Christians, 70–170 C.E.* Minneapolis: Fortress Press, 1995, 258–84.

————. "Supersession: Hebrews and *Barnabas.*" In *Related Strangers: Jews and Christians, 70–170 C.E.* Minneapolis: Fortress Press, 1995, 110–42.

Wiseman, T. P. *Historiography and Imagination: Eight Essays on Roman Culture.* Exeter: University of Exeter Press, 1994.

————. *The Myths of Rome.* Exeter: University of Exeter Press, 2004.

Woods, David. "Strategius and the Manichaeans." *Classical Quarterly* 51 (2001): 255–64.

————. "Ammianus Marcellinus and Bishop Eusebius of Emesa." *JTS* 54 (2003): 585–91.

Yousif, Pierre. "Les controverses de S. Ephrem sur l'Eucharistie." *Euntes Docete* 33 (1980): 405–26.

————. "Histoire et temps dans la pensée de Saint Ephrem de Nisibe." *PdO* 10 (1981/1982): 3–33.

————. *L'eucharistie chez Saint Ephrem de Nisibe.* Rome: Pontifical Institute, 1984.

————. "Foi et raison dans l'apologétique de Saint Ephrem de Nisibe." *PdO* 12 (1984/1985): 133–51.

————. "Exégèse et typologie bibliques chez S. Ephrem de Nisibe et chez S. Thomas d'Aquin." *PdO* 13 (1986): 31–50.

————. "Le sacrifice et l'offrande chez Saint Ephrem de Nisibe." *PdO* 15 (1988–1989): 21–40.

————. "Exegetical Principles of St. Ephraem of Nisibis." *Studia Patristica* 18, no. 4 (1990): 296–302.

General Index

Index of Ephrem's Writings

Anti-Judaism and Christian Orthodoxy: Ephrem's Hymns in Fourth-Century Syria was designed and typeset in Dante by Kachergis Book Design of Pittsboro, North Carolina. It was printed on 60-pound Natures Book Natural and bound by Thomson-Shore of Dexter, Michigan.